CAME THE REVOLUTION

*HARCOURT
BRACE
JOVANOVICH*

San Diego   New York   London

DANIEL PATRICK MOYNIHAN

—

CAME THE REVOLUTION

ARGUMENT
IN THE
REAGAN ERA

Requests for permission to make copies of
any part of the work should be mailed to:
Permissions, Harcourt Brace Jovanovich, Publishers,
Orlando, Florida 32887.

Library of Congress Cataloging-in-Publication Data

Moynihan, Daniel P. (Daniel Patrick), 1927–
Came the revolution.
Includes bibliographical references and index.
1. United States—Politics and government—1981–
2. United States—Economic policy—1981–
3. New York (State)—Politics and government—1951–
4. New York (State)—Economic policy. I. Title.
JK261.M68   1988   973.927   87-19676
ISBN 0-15-115375-2

Designed by Michael Farmer
Printed in the United States of America
First edition
A B C D E

For Kit and Joe Reed

Acknowledgments

Timothy P. Moynihan, sometime assistant managing editor at the *Public Interest*, made the first selection of these items. I, in turn, edited them with a view to keeping repetition to a minimum without concealing the grim necessity in political argument of repetition. Of repetition. Of repetition. Of . . .

Contents

FOREWORD XV

1981

The Gridiron Address 3

Letter to New York: The Assassination
Attempt on President Reagan 8

Old New Problems 12

Beyond 96–0 18

The Democratic Response to President
Reagan's Televised Address 22

Address to the Business Council of New York State 29

Please Do Not Crucify 93.01 Percent of Mankind
on a Cross of Gold, and Other Thoughts 36

Federal Aid to Education: A Zero-Sum Game? 42

Letter to New York: A Season of Solidarity 51

CONTENTS

1982

The Early Confessions of David Stockman 61

The Utility of a Senate: Reflections
from *The Federalist Papers* 65

A Two-Trillion-Dollar Debt? 73

A Path to Peace 78

"We Confront, at This Very Moment, the Greatest
Constitutional Crisis Since the Civil War" 87

One-Third of a Nation 94

Looking for a Kid? 105

Address to the Sheet Metal Workers'
International Association 110

World Trade and World Peace 115

1983

Social Security Secured 129

Address to the American Newspaper
Publishers' Association 134

Commencement Address,
Rensselaer Polytechnic Institute 140

MX Plan Commits U.S. to First-Strike Policy 145

Reagan's Bankrupt Budget 151

CONTENTS

1984

Letter to New York: *1984*   163

U.S. Has Abandoned International Law   169

"It Gets Down to One, Little, Simple
Phrase: I Am Pissed Off!"   175

Commencement Address, New York University   186

Preserving a Pillar of Crisis Stability   192

The Deficit—The Real Crisis   196

Richard Rovere   201

Tax Changes That Would Devastate New York   211

1985

President Reagan and Chairman Morill:
A Constitutional Reflection   217

Letter to New York: The Dollar and
Eastman Kodak Company   225

Letter to New York: The $35,000
Telephone, a Spy Story   233

The Potemkin Palace   242

A Tale of Two Cities   260

1986

Letter to New York:
The $28-Billion Heist, a Mystery   269

CONTENTS

Political AIDS: On the Immune
System of the American Parties   275

A Return to Social Policy   289

Government and Social Research: Reflections
on an Uneasy Relationship   295

The "New Science of Politics" and
the Old Art of Governing   301

EPILOGUE   325

INDEX   329

Foreword

Joe Reed, that is to say Professor Joseph W. Reed, sometime chairman of the Department of English at Wesleyan University, editor, with W. S. Lewis, of *Horace Walpole's Family Correspondence*, with F. A. Pottle, of the eleventh volume of the Yale edition of the Boswell papers, and author of *Faulkner's Narrative*, suggested this book, and he may have been right.

The thought came to him some years ago when he happened on remarks I made at a dedication ceremony of "Isis," a massive work by the sculptor Mark di Suvero.

As chairman of the board of the Hirshhorn Museum and Sculpture Garden it falls to me to accept this splendid gift from the Institute of Scrap Iron and Steel, and I recall that on the occasion that Margaret Fuller declared, 'I accept the universe,' Carlyle remarked that she had better.

"Isis" achieves an aesthetic transubstantiation of that which is at once elusive yet ineluctable in the modern sensibility.

Transcending socialist realism with an unequalled abstractionist range, Mr. di Suvero brings to the theme of recycling both the hard-edge reality of the modern world and the transcendent fecundity of the universe itself; a lasting assertion both of the fleetingness of the living, and the permanence of life; a consummation before which we stand in consistorial witness.

It will be with us a long time.

This seemed to Reed to make about as much sense as most of what passes for oratory down here (or up here, or over here: Forgive my regionalism!), and it occurred to him that there is not now at hand, or not that we know, a volume that brings together the range and form of political debate as currently conducted in American politics. It is more various than would be supposed from the occasional campaign biography or collection of speeches. *The Public Papers of the Presidents* are invaluable compilations, but the writing is, now, almost entirely that of other persons.

Senators have the same problem. We are all of us overextended. This is not necessarily the same thing as being overworked, but it comes to an equal pressure on time. No one of us could by ourselves write all of the testimony, all of the speeches, all of the letters, all of the messages that have to get written. Others do most of it for us, even to editing the occasional impromptu address on the Senate floor such that it appears in the *Congressional Record* in a reasonably coherent form.

This bothers Reed. Who are *we*, he wants to know. What is *our* voice? How do *our* letters read; *our* occasional rumination? Hence this volume. These are the words of a United States senator serving in the ninth decade of the twentieth century, specifically in the Ninety-seventh, Ninety-eighth, and Ninety-ninth Congresses. I have left out anything that has appeared in the *Record* as being already available, and have further omitted any materials from the necessarily considerable volume of correspondence and suchlike materials which I may sign but which others write. (No small matter. A New York senator has a constituency equivalent to that of a third of the members of the British House of Commons.) All that follows is mine, written in a one-room schoolhouse near Pindars Corners in upstate New York or, as in the case of this foreword, at my typewriter in the Russell

Senate Office Building with the Capitol dome looming outside
the window over my right shoulder. Equally admonitory envi-
ronments and, come to think, more or less contemporaneous.
District School No. 18 in Prosser Hollow was built in 1854 at a
cost of $156.* The dome commenced in 1859. No one seems to
know just what it cost, but it was worth it to me.

I have taken special care to include a number of Letters to
New York, which is to say the newsletter that I (and do other
senators and representatives) send to constituents. This is a ven-
erable form of American political literature, not to my knowledge
found elsewhere, and I attest a serious one. People read carefully
and they respond.**

This, then, in all its confusion, is a sampling of what goes
on from day to day. With the thought that it might create a more
general interest, I have also kept to a more or less single theme.

During these years, I was a member of the Democratic Minority in the Senate, and the normal day was in large part taken
up in argument against the policies of the Republican Majority.
In turn, these policies were mostly those of the newly elected
Republican president Ronald Reagan. I do not wish to suggest
constant strife. The Senate is a collegial body, with few fixed
lines. Even so, the function of the opposition is to oppose, and,
besides, much of the time I *was* opposed.

It happens I gave the Democratic speech at the first Gridiron
dinner of the Reagan administration, in March of 1981. I was
asked, in effect, to set a theme for our opposition. (Not too weight-
ily, or for that matter, not too well. The ritual truth-telling of
this singular Washington event is pretty much the preserve of
the press, whose guests and victims we are. Still you are allowed
to make some points, and I did my best.) It happens also that it

---

* Mary S. Briggs, *Bits and Pieces About the Schools of Davenport, NY, 1817–1986*,
Davenport Historical Society, 1986.
** Readers with a historical bent will enjoy browsing through Nobel E. Cunningham,
Jr.'s three-volume *Circular Letters of Congressmen to Their Constituents, 1789 through
1829*. They were printed and franked and passed along to neighbors, much as ours
are today.

fell to me to give the Democratic Response to the President's weekly radio broadcast on November 29, 1986, almost six years later, when I found myself saying: "Your presidency, Sir, is tottering. . . ." And so indeed it was. The presidency was saved, but for most purposes the administration was over. The 1988 election season commenced. And so there is a certain completeness to this chronicle.

May I say again, however, that my primary purpose is to present a sampling of political discourse of a particular time. I present arguments. Some had some success. Most failed in the sense that policies didn't change, or public opinion didn't change. That was the political history of these years.* If on examination it appears that some of the arguments were sound, the question arises, why did they fail?

I have a tentative answer. It is what animal psychologists call cognitive dissonance. The problem with debating the Reagan administration was that the White House kept doing exactly what it was understood it would never do. To point to what actually was happening only induced confusion.

An example. One week before the tax bill of 1981 was passed, in a televised response to an address by the president, I argued that over on the House side, his tax bill was being turned into an "auction of the Treasury." Having voted for a tax cut the previous year, I finally voted for this tax bill, which of course the president promptly signed. A summer break followed, and I had time to ponder what we had done. I am not good at numbers, but it finally became clear that the revenue loss was much greater than anyone had realized. And so it came to pass in early September that I went before the New York State Business Council and proposed a mid-course correction. Did we really want, I asked, to spend a decade arguing about deficits? Were we prepared to see the defense budget, now, finally rising, inevitably turn down?

I recounted all this to the Business Council with a feeling

---

* The reader will also come upon a number of arguments in support of Reagan policies. These were more successful.

that it would be easy for that audience to follow. They are *good* at numbers. But I don't think they believed a word I said. I was asking them to believe that *this* president had set in motion a decade of deficits, something they knew he would never do.

And so it went. Fairly early, I cottoned on to David A. Stockman's deficit strategy. This is to say his plan to use the deficit to force the political system to dismantle "big government." No one believed me. Conservative Republicans do not deliberately create staggeringly large and continuous deficits. Mind, Mr. Stockman has now written that that was exactly his strategy, and so far as I can see no one believes him either.

All of which I accept with good cheer, not least because the president, against whose policies I contended, was and remains a public figure of rare civility and, well, good cheer. He commanded courtesy in argument because he deserved it, and in the main, returned it. Courtesy, that is; *not* argument.

For years, I have been going on about the leakage of reality in American life: our seeming weakness at grasping the probable consequences of what we do or fail to do. As I write, 1986 is coming to a close. It is now just a quarter century since I first came to Washington as a young member of the Kennedy administration. I served in the cabinet or subcabinet of Kennedy, Johnson, Nixon, and Ford. Calamity followed calamity. Then, in the Senate, I watched yet further calamity overwhelm Carter. Now Reagan. A quarter century of failed or broken presidencies. Something beyond personality is involved. The institution has evidently entered a period of protracted crisis: which, on the margin at least, makes a case for attention to argument. Gentle reader, be the judge.

Daniel Patrick Moynihan
Washington, D.C.
December 29, 1986

1981

—————

The Gridiron Address

Fred Barnes described the scene in the New Republic:

> One Saturday . . . [in] March, more than 1,000 reporters, congressmen, and Administration luminaries (including the President) gathered in a Washington hotel for the annual dinner of the Gridiron Club. By long custom, the event features two speakers, a Democrat and a Republican. This year the Democrat was Senator Daniel Patrick Moynihan. . . . As expected, he was . . . irreverent. . . . President Reagan, he said, was really a "mole" planted by liberals "to destroy the Republican Party from within" by pursuing outlandishly right-wing policies. . . . After the jokes, Moynihan spoke in defense of an institution that had been the target of virtually every politician's wrath in the 1980 election: government. . . . When the time came for Stockman to give the Republican speech, his response to Moynihan was lame. Moynihan, triumphant, seemed to be on the verge of political acclaim as a real spokesman for his party. But two days later Reagan was shot. The Moynihan performance was forgotten. . . .

Even so, six years later, the argument is worth recalling. Government is the most precious of human institutions, and no care can be too great to preserve its integrity.

Well, there *they* go again, Mr. President. The Washington press corps never seem to get the real story, do they?

You surely know about—as a matter of fact, Mr. President, you probably remember—the occasion at the Congress of Vienna when Metternich was told the Russian ambassador had just dropped dead. He paused a moment and then asked: "What can have been his motive?"*

But just think. Back in 1962 when you resigned from Americans for Democratic Action, renounced the New Deal, and turned Republican, all the press could figure out was that you wanted to make a living.

Little did they suspect that the old mole was at work. Winter was coming. Some of us had to burrow.

Remember the chant?

Infiltrate
Be like the founders of the welfare state
Pretend to be
Aristocracy
Dupe the wealthy
Be cunning and stealthy
And steadily infiltrate

But who would have dreamed you'd make it all the way to the White House? And institute the basic plan to destroy the Republican party *from within.*

I see where the other day the publisher of *Forbes* magazine

---

* Contrary to a widespread but unwarranted impression, nothing is wasted in Washington. Some years later, the president, addressing the General Assembly of the United Nations, "this great hall of hope where, in the name of peace, we practice diplomacy," went on to explain: "Now, diplomacy, of course, is a subtle and nuanced craft—so much so that it's said that when one of the most wily diplomats of the 19th century passed away, other diplomats asked, on reports of his death, "What do you suppose the old fox meant by that?"

paid a bundle for a cancelled $50 check you once made out to ADA. Poor capitalist tool. It would never occur to him that for years now *ADA* might as well have been paying *you*.

How Franklin D. Roosevelt would have loved it!

You know, his entire first *budget* only came to seven billion dollars. Your first *deficit* will be *seventy* billion! We left-wing intellectuals are really proud of our president. To be fair, others did their part. I certainly tried. I worked up that neoconservative routine and made it as far as the Nixon White House.

But my greatest work was still ahead of me.

Back at Harvard, Liz and I were assigned David Stockman. Fresh from Michigan State and the Students for a Democratic Society and Vietnam Summer.

Dave was *everything* you could dream of in a mole. Corn-fed and cowlicked, he was the best boob bait for conservatives ever to come out of the Middle West.

The only trouble was he couldn't stop talking about the Viet Cong and American imperialism and the immorality of the Vietnam War.

So we installed him on the top floor of our house and got him into the Harvard Divinity School. There he was taught, of course, that there *is* no such thing as morality. Now, if there is no morality, it follows there is no immorality. *Tertium non datur.* (That's Latin, Mr. President.) Dave caught on right away and started to think about *numero uno*. (That's Gaelic, Mr. President.) We let him in on the plan, and assigned him his objective.

I remember drilling him over sherry.

Now, Dave, repeat after me:

The SDS will soon desist
Being so obstructionist
Made the City Fathers nervous
Ended up in the Civil Service.

(Mind, I never thought he'd end up running the Civil Service.)

But Stockman is peerless. I have never known a man capable of such sustained self-hypnotic ideological fervor. One day he arrives at Harvard preaching the infallibility of Ho Chi Minh. Next thing you know, he turns up in Washington proclaiming the immutability of the Laffer curve.

Mr. President, you've been perfect, and by the time *you're through*, we Democrats will be all set for yet another half century.

There are some people in this town just now who remind me of that character in one of Disraeli's novels who is described as a man "distinguished for ignorance as he had but one idea and that was wrong." Such are those who think they've seen the beginning of the end of the Democratic party.

Democrats lost an election last year but we did not lose a tradition. For ours is the oldest political party on earth. We have known good times and bad. Sometimes we have merely endured. But more often, we have prevailed because at heart we have embodied a great idea, which is that an elected government can be the instrument of the common purpose of a free people; that government can embrace great causes; and do great things.

There are limits, to be sure. Alfred Marshall once wrote:

> Government is the most precious of human institutions; and no care can be too great to be spent on enabling it to do its work in the best way. A chief condition to that end is that it should not be set to work for which it is not specially qualified, under the conditions of time and place.

It may be that Democrats have sometimes paid too little heed to Marshall's qualification. But we have never failed to respect his premise. A free government is indeed the most precious of human institutions.

We *believe* in American government and we fully expect that those who now denigrate it, and even despise it, will sooner or later find themselves turning to it in necessity, even desperation. When they do, they will find the Democratic party on hand to help.

And when at length they learn how much is demanded of those who *would* govern—we *will* be back.

In the meantime, Mr. President—seriously—good luck.

Washington, D.C.
March 28, 1981

Letter to New York: The Assassination Attempt on President Reagan

An April newsletter included this tribute to the president: meant as such, meant to be understood as such. And yet there I am at the end, arguing about handguns. Something in the new administration had sent me into opposition in a way I had not ever been before, not felt before. I know this is true; columnists noted it. Some welcomed me back from neoconservatism: no, thank you very much. As noted, I had for some time been talking about a "leakage of reality" in American life. Something like a hemorrhage seemed about to take place. Here was the near-ultimate example—the president gunned down by a crazed youth who possessed a handgun no law should have allowed to be sold, or sold to this nut. But any such law we might pass in the Congress would be instantly vetoed by this president.

Dear New Yorker:

I was in the White House at the moment word reached us that President Kennedy was dead. Or, rather, at the moment the realization came. It was, by an objective assessment, a moment of the greatest peril. Only a very few persons in the government were in Washington. The president and vice president were, of course, in Dallas.

It is not generally remembered that much of the Cabinet was

in a plane half way across the Pacific, headed for Japan. As if to symbolize the event, the General Services Administration was using the occasion of the president's absence to take up the rug in the Oval Office. His furniture was piled up in the hallway outside, with his rocking chair on top. Was there ever a setting in which the possibility of conspiracy would more readily come to mind?

And yet I think the thought never occurred to us. We were sitting in a circle, hardly talking, in the large southwest corner office that Ralph Dungan occupied. The only thing that could actually be said to have happened was the arrival of Hubert H. Humphrey, who surged into the room in shock. "What have they done to us!" he exclaimed as he hugged Dungan. But there *was* no "they." None of us thought that. McGeorge Bundy rose quietly and went into Mrs. Lincoln's office, picked up the telephone, and said to the White House operator, "This is Mr. Bundy. Would you please get me Mr. McNamara." Government never missed a beat.

Our only mistake was not getting custody of Oswald. It was all too clear that he would not survive the Dallas police station, and that conspiracy theories would follow ever after. (President Johnson, hearing of my arguments that a conspiracy would be alleged, concluded that I was alleging one. Thereafter, my days in Washington were less happy.) Our judgment about Oswald was flawed perhaps, but the government never faltered. Far from shaken, it seemed almost to take strength from this demonstration of its stability.

It was not different this time. The shooting of President Reagan occurred before our eyes as we sat in the cloakroom watching the television replay of the actual event, watching the struggle with the assassin, watching Jim Brady struggle to recover. The Secret Service agents were magnificent. So too were the doctors and the emergency room staff, skilled beyond any understanding by the rest of us. The White House staff was almost practiced, summoning the Cabinet to the Situation Room in the basement of the West Wing should it be judged that the president was for the moment "unable to discharge the powers and duties of his office" (Amendment XXV). The vice president was superbly responsive to his responsibilities and to any line where he might have overstepped them.

Above all, President Reagan. In the history of the office has any man ever so triumphed over danger and pain and near death? It is awful to quote oneself, but I was on the floor at the time when Majority Leader Howard Baker—no less masterful in crisis—gave an early report of the president's condition. There being no one else present (he was really informing the Press Gallery) at just that moment, I responded.

> I was glad to hear how well the president is recovering, but there is something larger at stake. Ernest Hemingway once described courage as grace under pressure. I do not know that in our time we have seen so great a display. It makes us proud of our president. It is perhaps no time to talk about the Nation, but it is the Nation that nurtured that quality in him, and we are all enhanced by it.

And once again the Republic did not falter. There was not the least tremor. We should appreciate this more about ourselves, and others might usefully do so as well. There are today 154 members of the United Nations. Of these, there are exactly 7 that both existed in 1914 and have not had their form of government changed by force since then. The stability of the American Republic is without equivalent in the experience of mankind, and only the continuity of the British monarchy . . . compares with it.

That is not to say that President Reagan's administration has not been hurt. (That of President Kennedy was extinguished.) The president cannot for some time now have the strength he had before, and the president is the center of our system. This argues a certain holding back in the pounding we tend to give one another. (It fell to me to give the "Democratic" speech this year at the Gridiron Dinner, the great ritual truth-telling that the

10

Washington press corps put on each spring, in this case the Saturday evening before the president was shot. I pounded pretty well, and he pounded back even better. If you think of him as a great performer, let me say he is an even greater audience, looking up, beaming and glinting, as you try to say things that are both wicked *and* true.

We are surely proud of him.

Washington, D.C.
April 1981

Old New Problems

This text holds up fairly well as an early effort to suggest that the fiscal policies emerging from the new administration were wondrously strange and just possibly lunatic. Five years later, Stockman would write that for "ignorance and grossest irresponsibility" in "the entire twentieth-century fiscal history of the nation there has been nothing to rival it." The address was given to the Economic Club of New York. They haven't asked me back.

In the fall of 1965, the first issue of the *Public Interest*, edited by Irving Kristol and Daniel Bell, made its appearance. It happens I wrote the first article in that issue, entitled "The Professionalization of Reform," describing a tendency, which I think was soon to be still more evident, for social policy to be taken over by persons whose nominal profession was that of social change. This had become possible, I argued, in the first instance because economics was attaining to the condition of an "applied science," the result of theoretical advances which we associated with the *General Theory* and the empirical tradition represented by C. Wesley Mills of Columbia University and the National Bureau of Economic Research. "Men are learning how to make an industrial economy work," I declared with the confidence of youth.

The industrial democracies had undertaken systematic programs for industrial growth, and had achieved it.

> The ability to predict events, as against controlling them, has developed even more impressively—the Council of Economic Advisers' forecast of GNP for 1964 was off by only $400 million in a total of $632 billion; the unemployment forecast was on the nose.

I had not wholly lost my senses. I noted that we had not, in fact, achieved full employment. I worried:

> We have accepted the use of federal taxing and spending powers as a means of social adjustment, but so far only in pleasant formulations. Our willingness to raise taxes, for example, is yet to be tested. In general, the political economy remains very much uncertain.

And yet I saw a future in which an economy, if managed well enough, could be used to undertake, for example, the abolition of poverty.

In short order, our willingness to raise taxes was to be tested, and of course we failed. Inflation began. But there were other signs of disorder. Unemployment persisted.

In the spring of 1970 at the annual dinner of the Fellows of the London School of Economics, Dr. Otmar Emminger, chairman of the Deutsche Bundesbank, spoke of the simultaneous appearance of unemployment *and* inflation: something that wasn't supposed to be possible. I dimly perceived that he had said something important. Not too long thereafter, Arthur F. Burns told a congressional committee that the economic laws weren't operating as they were supposed to. This, too, made an impression. And, most of all, events argued against earlier beliefs. The inflation of the early 1970s, followed by the imposition of peacetime wage and price controls, persuaded me that our theoretical grasp was weak indeed, whilst our political capacity to carry out what theory did decree was weaker yet. Earlier than some, perhaps, I grew alarmed.

At that time, Nelson Rockefeller left the governorship of New York to establish the Commission on Critical Choices for Americans, an enterprise that he thought would be his last great public service. I was asked to prepare a long paper on the quality of American life, which appeared in 1976. I prefaced it with a two-sentence summary.

> There are two critical choices affecting the quality of American life. The first is how much growth we want; the second is how much government we want.

This was not a political statement. It was simply what seemed to me the observable condition of the time. For much of the third quarter of the twentieth century, Americans, in choices actually made, had more or less consistently opted for more government and less growth. Extrapolated, as mathematicians say, these curves could only lead to a condition of no growth and total government. Before that, or so it seemed to me, there would be a reaction.

The most striking aspect of this condition is the degree to which government growth is seemingly out of anyone's control. What more striking instance could there be than for President Reagan in his State of the Union address to propose $41.4 billion in budget "cuts," and only seven days later to announce that there had been a severe underestimate of the growth of outlays, such that some $3 to $6 billion in additional cuts would have to be found on top of the $41.4 billion?

The task is to control a budget which, in the course of one presidential term, rose from $402 billion in fiscal year 1977, when President Carter took over from President Ford, to $673 billion when President Reagan took office. This is an increase of $271 billion in four fiscal years. I speak as one who, in the company of other assistant secretaries, sat in what is now the Roosevelt

14

Room of the White House and was informed by President Johnson that in no circumstances would the fiscal year 1965 budget exceed $99.99 billion. It took us 176 fiscal years to get to our first $100-billion budget. Recently (fiscal year 1980 to 1981), we have seen almost as much an increase ($83 billion) in a single year.

The administration proposes a response not less extraordinary than the circumstances to which it is responding. This is a necessary, even an urgent, undertaking. It should be clear that it will be tremendously difficult. James R. Schlesinger having said so just yesterday (*"In brief, it is not going to happen"*), we are all perhaps freer to acknowledge the improbability of some of the proposed budget cuts, the undesirability of others, the somewhat breathtaking economic forecasts on which the revenue estimates are based, and other such specifics. The deficit in fiscal year 1982, for example, will surely be in the neighborhood of $60 billion, and it could be higher. Even so, we could be at a turning point; we could be about to assert a significantly greater measure of control over our affairs than we have had, and that would be altogether good.

Let me emphasize that I make the point about the 1982 deficit not to criticize, much less to discredit. A situation that developed in the course of a dozen or more budgets will not be resolved in one budget. If the administration's specific forecasts have not been met in twelve- or eighteen-months' time, this will *not* mean the effort has failed.

I do, however, have a large concern.

It is that the administration may be making just the mistakes of those of its predecessors it least approves.

There is an obvious parallel. In the face of an economic emergency, or "Dunkirk"* if you prefer, what more Keynesian response could there be than a huge deficit, a whopping tax cut, and a sharp increase in spending? But that is *not* the parallel I

---

* Stockman's term: "I went Kemp's Inchon one better and titled [my paper]: 'On the Danger of a GOP Economic Dunkirk.' Its tone was admittedly alarmist."

wish to make. I have in mind another Keynesian reference. It is to his observation that every hardheaded businessman is the slave of some defunct economist.

An aspect of the professionalization of reform about which I wrote in the *Public Interest* in those now distant years is the extraordinary and growing influence on practical events of those frequently exceptionally impractical people known collectively as academics, and among these, most conspicuously the economists.

Only a fool will dismiss what academics know. But the greater fool is he who exaggerates what academics know. I refer especially to those who exaggerate what economists know.

It seems to me that conservatives were not merely philistine in the 1930s when they expressed alarm about the influence, as they saw it, of the New Deal "Brain Trust." My reading of that period is that Jesse Jones, a plain Texas millionaire, had a lot more to do with getting us through (I do not say "out of") the Depression than did any Fellows, as you might say, at Kings College, Cambridge, or Cambridge, Massachusetts. (And I would note that Jones was head of the Reconstruction Finance Corporation, a creation of Herbert Hoover, another eminently practical man.)

It was about liberal academics and liberal administrations that I was writing sixteen years ago. But . . . it has since become very much the disposition of conservatives also. *This* is the parallel I wish to make.

It is not the use of academics that I deplore. I previously was a member of President Ford's cabinet at a time when it included no fewer than five professors (Kissinger, Schlesinger, Shultz, Butz, Moynihan). We did no great harm, or no greater harm than the others.

But what I do find curious is the degree to which conservatives seem to have displaced liberals as starry-eyed advocates of exotic and newfangled economic doctrines. Some while ago, I observed that in the course of the 1970s, without anyone quite noticing, the Republicans became a party of ideas. This is something to be desired. But it is also something that takes practice. And where academic economics is involved, it takes more than experience: It requires a measure of knowledge as well.

It is necessary to know the *limits* of economic knowledge. Economists know them; or most do. There are some well-understood economic functions; some less well understood; some not understood at all. It is not a failed profession, as John Kenneth Galbraith has suggested, but neither is it a mature science, or likely ever to be. Not every economist is perhaps as candid on this point as he or she ought to be, but then let the buyer beware. Or keep in mind Melbourne's dictum that he wished he were as sure of anything as Macaulay was of everything.

New York, New York
March 5, 1981

Beyond 96–0

Social Security was our best issue with the new president, not least because he did not understand it. The system is not "funded" in the manner of a pension system. It can't be, or if it were, the federal government would have to own just about everything around. Social Security, in its pension aspect, is in fact an intergenerational transfer in which working-age people collectively take care of old people, as one-on-one as they used to do down on the farm. If you don't grasp this, it is easy to see the system as fraudulent and bankrupt, and that is how the new president saw it. In the early months of his administration, he would terrify Republican congressional leaders by reading them a speech he'd written himself proposing that the system be made voluntary. Dissuaded on this score, he absentmindedly, or rather his staff absentmindedly, sent to Congress a proposal drafted by political sorts in the Department of Health and Human Services calling for fierce and sudden benefit reductions. As ranking member of the subcommittee on Social Security, this was my responsibility and our moment. With help from the Democratic Policy staff, on the morning of May 20, I moved to disapprove. At the end of the day, the Senate unanimously agreed. Two days later, I proclaimed victory in an op ed article in the New York Times.

This was the administration's first defeat: an augury, not read, that the time would soon come when further domestic

budget cuts would no longer be acceptable even to Republicans
in the Congress.

How did it come to pass that a Republican administration
that came to office in January promising at most some modest
cuts and efficiencies in government spending ended up in May
proposing such devastating cuts in the Social Security system
that a Republican-dominated Senate voted 96 to 0 to reject the
entire proposal?

It is not all that complex. In its formative political stages,
the administration committed itself to a theory of taxation that
held that it was possible to make huge reductions in marginal
tax rates without suffering any significant loss in tax revenues.
This was the economist Arthur Laffer's famous curve.

If the notion invites a measure of derision, it ought not. The
respected conservative economist Herbert Stein wrote: "The
temptation for conservatives to stretch the limits of responsible
discussion of economic questions has been strong in the past
twenty or thirty years for several reasons. The background noise
of liberal talk was loud, and the popular media were not receptive
to conservative discourse. To penetrate the media curtain . . . it
seemed necessary to express conservative views in extreme, black-
and-white letters."

Thus, if the subject at hand is a balanced budget, don't simply
propose one; propose, rather, to amend the Constitution to require one. Similarly, if the subject is a tax cut, don't just offer
one; instead, offer to cut taxes "by about one-third" and assert
it would *cost nothing.*

President Reagan genuinely believed that this was feasible.
He would say, as he did in Flint, Michigan, on May 17, 1980:
"We would use the increased revenues from the tax decrease to
rebuild our defense capabilities." There would also, of course, be
a balanced budget.

Remember that the victorious party was not pledged to any
radical disruptions of social programs of the kind now being pro-

posed. In his major economic address of the campaign, given September 9, Ronald Reagan spoke only of eliminating some "waste and inefficiency" from government spending. No more. He said at that time: "I am confident that we can squeeze and trim two percent out of the budget in fiscal year 1981 and we will be able to increase this gradually to seven percent of what would otherwise have been spent in fiscal year 1985."

Then came office—and reality. One economist after another and, in the end, decisively, Wall Street, offered the view that there was no way that a one-third tax cut could pay for itself. This brought a crisis in policy. If the tax-cut proposal was to be retained, the balanced budget would have to be put off *and* major cuts in spending would have to be made. So, starting with budget director David A. Stockman's "black book" of early February, an almost daily succession of ever-deeper budget cuts was proposed.

Cut elementary and secondary education a quarter, preventive health a third, abolish mass-transit operating assistance. On May 5, the Senate Finance Committee was requested to repeal, and did repeal, the provision of the Social Security Act, forty-five years in place, that entitled orphans in foster care to federal assistance. Seven days later, a general proposal to slash Social Security retirement benefits was sent up even as the Republican National Committee was mailing out its publication, *Senior Republican*, with the headline: "President Reagan Keeps Promise, Retirement Benefits Go Untouched."

That did it. Perhaps predictably, the orphans had not been much heard from. But the 35 million people receiving Social Security benefits were. So also were those economists who, wishing the administration well, had been talking truth to power. It worked. On May 14, Martin Feldstein, president of the National Bureau of Economic Research, told the Finance Committee: "A year ago, the President's campaign rhetoric was still full of wishful thinking about major tax cuts without any reductions in government spending. Despite all of this early supply-side hyperbole, the President's actual program represents a total repudiation of the naive Laffer-curve theory that across-the-board tax cuts are self-financing."

And so there will now be a compromise tax bill. *But,* must the administration also abandon the idea of economic policy directed toward greater productivity and production?

We need—urgently need—a set of supply-side tax cuts that reward actual savings, successful investment, increased labor, enhanced capital. We cannot go on with the lowest rate of savings and investment of any industrial nation in the Western world.

Last August [1980], the Senate Finance Committee, 19 to 1, approved a tax proposal that, while cutting personal income taxes 1 percent to 3 percent in the middle brackets, concentrated on reducing capital-gains taxes, increasing depreciation allowances, and getting rid of at least half the "marriage penalty" (a true supply-side tax cut). We are now saving 5 percent of income. Saving 6 percent won't change a thing. It is time that we set our minds on 20 percent. Let the Reagan administration give us *that* goal; let campaign promises rest in peace; let the future begin.

The New York Times
May 22, 1981

Note the nervousness about taxes. Carter, mindlessly, had bullied the Senate not to accept a tax bill we passed out of the finance committee in 1980. The "bracket creep" brought on by inflation demanded that there be some tax "cut." But not a crippling one.

The Democratic Response
to President Reagan's
Televised Address

The president had not accepted defeat on Social Security, and decided to take the issue to the people, as the saying is, over the heads of Congress. Prime television time was requested and secured for July 27. I was chosen to respond and would do so later the same evening. At the last minute, the White House staff persuaded Mr. Reagan that cutting Social Security would be his undoing. His subject all of a sudden was changed to tax cuts.

I was left to do the best I could with both subjects, not wanting to give up on Social Security. Note the reference to a specific member of the public. I had learned something from the president's style. Not enough, however. My response was pronounced scholarly by the networks, and I think was thought a failure by my colleagues. Partly, perhaps, because they, as I, would soon be voting for that tax bill.

Good evening. I'm Senator Moynihan of New York. Tonight the president spoke to the nation on the subject of taxes. NBC, which carried his address, offered the Democratic party an opportunity to respond. As a member of the Finance Committee, which is the tax-writing body in the Senate, I have been asked to do so. I will also talk about Social Security.

I hope not to criticize, but to comment, and if I can, just the least bit to clarify. I have served in the cabinet or subcabinet of four presidents. Two were Democrats. Two were Republicans. I have some sense, as we all do, of what a president is up against where tax legislation is concerned. For it is Congress that makes the laws, and none are more complicated than the tax laws. They combine the most general theories of the public good with particulars that deal with the most concrete grasping, and indeed special, interests.

This mixture, if you like, of the sacred and the profane is nothing new. The first law passed by the United States Congress established the form of the oath of office to be taken by men and women who would serve our democracy. The second law passed by Congress imposed a duty on rum—a tax, that is, which would provide protection for our native distillers.

The Revenue Act of 1981, which Congress is going to pass any day now, has its share and more of special interest protection. In the last few days, something like an auction of the Treasury has been going on. The administration is seemingly willing to pay any price to win votes for its version of a tax cut, simply to gain a victory on its own terms. On Friday last, along with munificent benefits to those with the foresight to own oil wells, the administration threw in the kitchen stove as well—a tax credit, that is, for wood-burning kitchen stoves—whereupon the *Washington Star* reported that the total cost of the administration's bill would reach $730 billion over the next five years, larger than this year's entire federal budget.

What this is doing is taking a tax bill we could afford and transforming it into a great barbecue that we can't afford. I would say to the president that some victories come too dear. Whatever bill passes will go to him for signature, and when he signs it, he can take all the credit he wants.

If the administration would stop making concessions to special interests and get on with the business of government, we would be a lot better off, because there is a lot more business to be done.

An individual income tax cut is long overdue. In truth, in an era of inflation, the last time individual tax rates were significantly cut was in 1964, a measure President Kennedy proposed.

Clearly it is time to cut individual rates again and indeed, in the view of many of us, to index them so there is not this constant bracket creep, as it is called. I agree with the president on this.

The Senate Finance Committee voted out a major tax reduction on June 25 by a margin of 19 to 1. It is now on the floor. We will pass it on Wednesday. If the House does the same, we can have a bill on the president's desk in a matter of days.

And we should. Inflation has been called the cruelest tax of all, and it is. It has to be offset. But we shouldn't fool ourselves that we are doing much more than keeping even. In 1980, federal taxes were 20.3 percent of gross national product. This year they will be 21.1 percent. In 1982, they will be 20.4 percent, which is simply back to last year.

Let us pass a tax bill and get on with the business of government. Our business—the administration's business—is to promote the general welfare by getting the American economy moving again. It hasn't been and it isn't now. Inflation is up. Unemployment is high—two times the level we thought was acceptable in President Kennedy's time. Most of all, production is down. In the most recent quarter, real GNP was down 1.9 percent.

Sometimes these numbers seem small. A decimal point here or there. But keep up these small rates of growth, these recurrent declines, and our national life changes. Just such small lags transformed Great Britain in one generation from the wealthiest nation in Western Europe to one of the poorest. It could happen to us. Just a while ago, the World Bank reported that the United States, far from having the highest per capita income in the world, now ranks sixth.

And why? Because we are consuming too much and saving too little. We have a lower rate of investment than any of our competitors, save Great Britain. The average age of machinery in our factories is twice that of Japan.

Here the administration must be taken to task. It has deliberately brought about the highest real interest rates since the disastrous postwar inflation.*

Look at the federal funds rate, which is the interest rate the Federal Reserve charges its member banks. A year ago, it was 8.68 percent. Last week, it was 19.99 percent.

This is a disaster. How can we afford long-term investment at such cost: a steel plant, a power station? Who can afford a house even? When my wife, Liz, and I bought our first house with a GI-bill mortgage, we paid, if memory serves, an interest rate of 6 percent. That meant that in thirty years we would pay together just a little less than twice the price of our house. At current mortgage rates, a newly married couple with a thirty-year mortgage will have to pay nearly five times the purchase price.

Think about a merchant trying to keep an inventory of furniture or automobiles in his showroom. Think about a student borrowing money to put himself through college. It is no wonder the bond market has all but collapsed and the stock market sags.

This is calamitous but it is also administration policy. If it is kept up, the tax cut of 1981 will be the least instead of the most important economic event of this administration. Indeed, a sometime supporter of the administration's economic policies wrote yesterday that the administration seemed intent on whipping inflation "with a worldwide going-out-of-business sale."

Surprisingly, there is a rather simple explanation for all this. In its formative period, the present administration embraced an economic doctrine which held that there could be a huge reduction in taxes without any reduction in tax revenue.

Does that strike you as odd? It is odd. But they *did* believe it.

Let's walk through that once more. The president's men really did believe that if you had a big tax cut, you would get a

---

* It hadn't. The Federal Reserve had, but the administration had not resisted.

big increase in revenues. All their plans were based on this idea. Then in office they realized it just wasn't so. And now the administration has added so many special-interest provisions to the tax bill that the loss of revenue will be enormous. This means yet more deficits.

There were only two ways the administration could respond. First, by high interest rates. Second, slashing government.

Nothing like this was even hinted at in the last election. The president spoke of reducing government by some 2 percent this year and a little more in the years to come. That was all. But then came one cut after another until by May they went after Social Security itself.

Then Americans began remembering the campaign promises—and they began writing. I have received thousands of letters from constituents asking me to preserve their Social Security benefits.

Just today the Long Island newspaper *Newsday* tells the story of Bob Brown of West Islip, a supervisor for the New York Telephone Company. Mr. Brown had planned for years to retire in 1985. Now he fears this will not be possible.

In May, he wrote President Reagan, "I have been warned never to believe a politician. But I replied, 'This president is different.' " But Brown went on, "The distress and dismay that I feel cannot be expressed. You destroyed my dreams and broke your trust."

Let it be clear: We do not charge bad faith. It's just that the administration had this magic theory of taxation which it thought would solve all of its problems, which I suppose is a way of saying they were new to national government. The illusion held on. Older Americans who happen to be on the mailing list of the Republican National Committee received a newsletter last May. It said, "President Reagan Keeps Promise, Retirement Benefits Go Untouched."

But on May 12, even as that newsletter was being mailed out, the administration proposed devastating reductions in those Social Security programs. It was that or face a huge deficit in

1984, the next presidential election year. You see, any money not paid out as Social Security benefits remains in the Treasury. The proposed benefit cuts of about $80 billion over five years would have nearly balanced the budget.

Was this playing politics with Social Security? It surely was. *Newsweek* magazine said just that in a recent issue, and I quote:

> The Administration was indeed playing politics with social security last week, as one high official privately conceded. . . .

What they were doing, now that they realized their tax magic wasn't going to work, was try another magic. They would convince everyone that the Social Security system was going bankrupt. The budget director, David Stockman, put it:

> The stark, ominous, and unavoidable fact . . . is that the most devastating bankruptcy in history will occur.

If they could panic people about bankruptcy, they reasoned, no one would object to slashing Social Security benefits. This in turn would build up a surplus in Social Security, thereby offsetting the budget deficit.

It didn't work.

The Congress, which doesn't shock easily, was truly shocked. So were the American people. Social Security is a trust. It is a compact the American people have with their government and themselves. Apart from our own family relations, it is the single most important system we have for looking after one another. Thirty-six million people, including five million children, depend on Social Security for their income and their health care. It goes to the heart of the general welfare. . . .

Congress rebelled. But the administration persisted. Last week, the president wrote to congressional leaders, stating that he insists on his Social Security reductions and stating that he would go on television to take the issue to you, the American people. That was what his address tonight was supposed to be about. Evidently he changed his mind. So the *Washington Post* reported yesterday:

Reagan Backs Off
Televised Speech
on Social Security

Well, if the president won't talk about Social Security, someone should.

First off, the Social Security system is *not* bankrupt. It is not going bankrupt. Those of you now receiving benefits *will* continue to do so. At least, and I suppose I am forced to put it this way, at least while the Democratic party has anything to say about the way we keep our promises in this nation. Those of you expecting to receive benefits will do so as well, and in full. It is your right, and so far, at least, this is a nation in which the people's rights are respected and upheld.

Washington, D.C.
July 27, 1981

Address to the Business Council
of New York State

This was my best effort yet, and a total failure. I had got it. The new administration was filled with radicals. They were "to conservatives as anarchists are to liberals." I mention Stockman, who would one day attest to the matter with the greatest specificity and remorse. I had got it that they had "fashioned" a "crisis." I had got it that deficits were coming in inexorable rank. I had even got the five-year debt accumulation about right. I had got it that this would give us a decade of debate about the deficit. The audience thought I was crazed.

In 1977, I spoke to the then Associated Industries of New York State on the subject of the imbalance of the fiscal relation between the national government and the state of New York. I gave to my address the somewhat academic title "On the Time It Takes to Explain Something," but my purpose was to suggest that the problem was all the more urgent because it was not one that was easily set forth or readily comprehended. This evening, I return to the same theme, but to a much larger subject.

The United States is facing an economic and in consequence a political crisis—I hope I do not use the word "crisis" casually—which is all the more ominous because it, too, is somehow difficult to explain, difficult to comprehend.

The signs of crisis are not hard to find. Rates of interest are

higher than any, I believe, known to our history. They recall the
rates the Fuggers charged the Hapsburgs, but have no equivalent
in the economic history of the United States, and with respect
to the rates of government securities, none, at least to my knowledge, in the history of the Republic. At a time when General
Burgoyne was still in the field, the Continental Congress could
sell its securities for less.

Our president, whom we admire and wish success, told his
economic policy advisory board just last Thursday that there
must be yet greater reductions in the budget as the only way to
prevent "eventual collapse" of the economy. On that day, his
senior White House spokesman told the press, and I quote an
account:

> Mr. Reagan's statements did not reflect a sense of panic
> in the White House over the declining financial markets or
> over a Congressional Budget Office estimate that the 1982
> deficit will exceed Mr. Reagan's estimate by over $22 billion.

The only meaning of—the only reason for—such a statement is
that, of course, there *is* panic.

The extent of the panic is to be found in the statements of
the leaders of the president's party in Congress. They are talking
of punishing the markets for not behaving. Quite specifically,
the majority whip of the Senate has suggested a windfall profits
tax might be in order for those who benefit from high interest
rates. The majority leader of the Senate sent word north, to you
know where, saying he wanted things to shape up not in a matter
of weeks, but "days." "It's time indeed," he said, "that the financial markets realize that they are playing a dangerous game."
They are, in a word, getting government mad.

I need not tell you that we are not far from proposals for
wage and price controls, although the power of the executive to
impose these unilaterally has, to my knowledge, expired.

How can this have happened to an administration so exuberantly committed to the free market as an economic and moral ideal?

It is *not* easy to explain, but it is, I think, explicable.

Two basic elements are involved: first, a political tradition; second, an economic idea.

There is no handy term for the political tradition, although it recurs in American history at all points in the political spectrum. It involves a profound distrust of institutions, be they governmental, financial, or corporate. It occurs on the right and on the left. The Carter administration, for example, had more than its share of the latter variety. But the present administration, on the other end of the spectrum, is the most advanced case we have yet encountered. I served in the cabinet of the two preceding *Republican* presidents. This new group—one of whose more prominent members was once a student of mine—are like nothing we have seen.

They are to conservatives as anarchists are to liberals.

This would all be innocent enough were it not for the economic idea they brought to office with the idea that the revenue system of the federal government was not an institution of any great importance, that the most extraordinary things could be done to it with relative impunity. Specifically, this doctrine held that any given level of revenue can be obtained by two levels of taxation: one high, one low. This was not a mere extension of the principle of price elasticity. It was a fundamental rejection of the notion of restraint, of limit as the necessary environment of government.

The proposition took as its most popular form the proposal that taxes could be cut by one-third at no cost to revenues.

A first restraint which has had to yield is the balanced budget, which one would have thought was at the core of the doctrine of economic conservatism.

Some knew this all along. For others, it comes as a surprise. My colleague and friend Jack Kemp, an author of the Kemp–Roth tax bill, declared last spring in the House: "We don't worship any longer at the shrine of the balanced budget."

And more recently, when the tax bill was signed, the congressman told the president:

> I want your support for my next tax bill—a 30-percent rate reduction in your second term. 'Gee, Jack,' the President responded, 'I thought we'd go for a 40-percent reduction next time.'

At first, it seemed to me that if everyone made allowances for the understandable—and wholly attractive—enthusiasm which new ideas generate, we could get through it all well enough, "voodoo" economics or not.

On March 5, I spoke to the Economic Club of New York. The deficit for fiscal year 1982 was being projected at some $42 billion. This, I said, was not going to happen. There would be some loss of revenue. "The deficit in fiscal year 1982," I continued, "will surely be in the neighborhood of $60 billion, and it could go higher." (On September 10, the Congressional Budget Office forecast $65 billion.) I made this point "not to criticize, much less to discredit." We had to get hold of spending, we had to cut taxes, but we also had to be realistic about what would happen when we did.

The economic debate went on all spring and into summer. It culminated, for me at all events, on the evening of July 27.

That was the evening the president spoke to the nation about the tax bill. I was asked by my party to respond.

The president wanted to cut taxes; so did we all. My concern was with the battle then reaching its climax in the House of Representatives between the administration and the Democratic Majority. Most everyone had lost sight of the fact that there was basic agreement on the need for a "clean" tax bill, while all attention had turned to the question of just *whose* bill it would be. A bidding process had begun: Votes were being won by offering yet further special-interest tax cuts.

My concern was that we would wake up to an empty Treasury, with the grimmest consequences. To begin with, it would be discovered that the new economic doctrine did not have many adherents. One of its essential, almost chiliastic elements is that people must *believe* it. If it turned out they didn't, well. . . .

Well what? The absolute predictable conclusion was that the lost revenues would not be replaced, and that in consequence an unending sequence of deficits loomed. . . .

I repeat, I repeat, I repeat. The single most important economic problem facing our nation is capital formation. We have gone on for a generation now with the lowest or second lowest rate of capital formation in the Western world. We are eating our seed corn. Last year, for example, American personal income, in real terms, dropped 5 percent, the largest decline since this statistical series began in 1947.

Sustained deficits destroy capital formation.

They divert capital otherwise available for the private sector to the uses of government, most of which goes to consumption. Worse yet, in the present situation the demands of government are so great that interest rates soar beyond bearing. The cost of capital formation becomes prohibitive, unless a permanent inflation is foreseen.

Hence the demands for further budget cuts. Our defense budget, which finally was getting on a steady course, will now be torn apart once more; our domestic budget is being shredded; and with it the social compact of a half century concerning the role of government in abetting the health, education, and welfare of our people.

Is there any hope? Some.

There are signs in Washington that the shallowness of some of that early economic doctrine is beginning to sink in. Commenting on the wreckage of the defense program, a department spokesman, the distinguished public servant Henry Catto, quoted Emerson:

A foolish consistency is the hobgoblin of little minds.

That, I fear, is the mark of experience in government, and it is no accident that Mr. Catto is an experienced official. Nor any accident that so many of those who fashioned the present crisis have no real experience or responsibility at the national executive level of government.

But why not be friends? Be forgiving? Be amnesiac if it comes to that?

The tax bill was too large. Let me give you its measure.

In round terms a revenue loss of $750 billion. What we need is a midcourse correction, keeping many of the fine features of the new bill (which is why I voted for it), reducing this cost by, let us say, $250 billion. Take away one-quarter trillion dollars, and a one-half-trillion-dollar tax cut remains. Surely next month, when we raise the debt ceiling above the $1 trillion mark, we could lower that tax loss over the next five years by a quarter trillion. The benefits to the economy would surely be enormous, and even more to the tone of public debate.

Do we really want a decade in which *the* issue of public discourse, over and over and over, will be how big must the budget cuts be in order to prevent the deficit from being even bigger? Surely larger, more noble purposes ought to engage us.

The tax cut was too large. That need not be the end of the world. Cut it back a bit.

I plead now as I pleaded six weeks ago for continuity and for rationale. For six months, in Washington we have been subjected to ever more radical proposals for change in fundamental national commitments which don't originate in any new thinking about those commitments, but simply in the dawning recognition that the new economics isn't credible.

Just after the tax cut, our distinguished majority leader, Howard Baker, called the whole thing "a riverboat gamble." That seemed to me admirably candid. But why, if the flush doesn't fill out, start breaking up the place?

Kiamesha Lake, New York
September 13, 1981

Please Do Not Crucify 93.01 Percent
of Mankind on a Cross of Gold,
and Other Thoughts

*I think this speech did succeed. It was given to a conference
of United Press International editors. It was a new way of pre-
senting the argument against a return to gold, i.e., that the Saudis
and the Soviets and the South Africans would be the benefi-
ciaries. In any event, the "gold bugs" were beginning to lose
their suddenly revived influence in Washington.*

Here in New York, we are enjoying one of our recurrent
Shavian revivals, and it may not be inappropriate to open these
remarks by recalling the father-and-son scene from *Major Bar-
bara* in which Undershaft, the munitions manufacturer, presses
his idle and useless son on how the youth planned to make a
living. One option after another is discarded, as the boy knows
nothing of the subject. Finally, in exasperation, the father asks:
Is there *anything* you know? To which the young man replies
that he knows the difference between right and wrong. Well, the
father declares, if you know nothing more than the difference
between right and wrong, you shall have to be a journalist.

I am asked to speak of the administration's economic program, and do not wonder that the journalists should be intrigued,
for not in a generation has there been such a stir in the United
States over economic *doctrine*, nor yet so much assertion that
new theories are right and old theories are wrong.

Our new doctrine was labeled, and most effectively so, "supply-side economics." It comes, as new beliefs so often do, at a time of evident crisis in old beliefs, more specifically of the evident inability of older doctrines to account for new realities.

This change has come suddenly, and without warning. The period roughly approximating the third quarter of the twentieth century was for mankind generally, and especially for the nations of "the West," the most prosperous period in the history of the race. Never, for such a sustained period, has there been so much wealth, so much liberty, so much, yes, peace. Then the prosperity—specifically, the growth in economic product—leveled off. We are now in the latest of a succession of recessions which have kept American GNP about flat since 1978. As our population grows, last year—for the first time in the history of the economic series in question—the real incomes of Americans declined.

This crisis has produced a number of explanations of the variety which economists call "structural," which is a way of saying things are truly out-of-joint, and our way of going about them must change. Supply-side economics calls for removing the restraints on production—the supply as against the traditional Keynesian demand side of the equation—through reducing the inhibitions of production which government imposes by taxes, regulations, and other measures.

Obviously, there is much to say for such a proposition, although as yet, little to report. The Carter administration—and during those years, the Congress—committed itself to a general program of "deregulation," and given a little time, there will be some results on this front. But in the meantime, all attention has turned to what I am going to call a "heresy" of supply-side economics, the peculiar proposition that tax cuts, no matter how great, more or less automatically replenish themselves, with no cost to revenue. This is the famous Laffer curve. It holds, to be specific, that any given level of revenue can be obtained at two levels of taxation, one high, one low.

I have no inside knowledge, but I hypothesize that several years ago a poll was taken of prominent business executives:

What level of taxes would they prefer, always remembering that it did not matter, high or low? Evidently, a substantial majority picked low. In any event, at a critical point in the formation of the present administration, this peculiar subset of beliefs was adopted. It was stated most succinctly by the president, then a candidate, in Flint, Michigan, on May 17, 1980.

> We would use the increased revenues the federal government would get from this tax decrease to build our defense capabilities.

A kind of role reversal took place: All of a sudden, Republicans were going about expounding the theories of professors of economics, whilst Democrats grumbled that in the real world of running a government theory wouldn't get you far.

No doubt. But it got this particular faction of the GOP to the White House. Scarcely a half year later, we had the largest tax cut in history: pursued no doubt in part out of sheer joy of battle, but with a measure of the true believer's conviction that no harm can come to the faithful.

The tax cut was and remains simply too large to make sense as genuine supply-side economics. Let me give you two examples, one familiar by now, one perhaps less so.

First, because the revenues are not going to be replenished at anything like the levels expected, we face a decade of huge and possibly growing deficits.

> The numbers for fiscal year 1984 are stunning. A former member of the Council of Economic Advisors has suggested to me privately that the fiscal 1984 deficit will be in the range of $150 billion to $200 billion.*

Now all this has not escaped the advocates of supply-side economics within administration circles. Huge deficits, in the

---

* It turned out to be $185 billion.

absence of high savings rates, must displace private capital and thereby lower the investment rate. But that is behind us. Ahead is the gold standard.*

Specifically, the special group of "supply siders" that has most influenced the administration's economics is now putting it out that the small print, you might say, of their manifesto decrees that the Laffer curve only works if the nation is on the gold standard. In fairness, this was always a feature of their literature, but its salience comes only in the aftermath of the revenue debacle. Hence, the *Economist* writes, there is

> the suspicion that the sudden enthusiasm for gold provides a convenient escape route for those whose huge tax cuts are more likely to bust the budget than to usher in a new era of economic growth.

At this point, or so it seems to me, a certain intellectual duty rests with the opposition, which is to say the Democratic party. *Everyone*—the administration, the Congress, the public— is trying to think through the puzzlement of recent economic developments. None of us has any final answers, and none of us, as far as I am concerned, has any right to be mad at anybody else. The administration is still new, still learning. A measure of tolerance is to be expected of all.

There is a difference, however, between tolerance of new ideas and indifference to them.

I happen to think that some of us, myself included, were derelict in a duty we should have known we had in the late 1970s to challenge the more bizarre nostrums—the heresies, if you will allow my term—of the supply-side school. We could have done so. But they had gained such plausibility—note the evasion: I mean such popularity—that we did not. We assured ourselves

---

* In June 1981, Congress directed the secretary of the Treasury [then Donald T. Regan] to head the Commission on the Role of Gold in the Domestic and International Monetary Systems and to prepare a report for the legislature.

that in any event, such propositions would never get anywhere.

I suggest that we can make amends—if at all—only by giving a good thump this very moment to the idea of a return to the gold standard.

First of all, what is the idea? It has little to do with gold. It has much to do with the curious aversion to government of the new radicals. George Will, a genuine conservative, has noted a disposition of many such radicals to fear their own government more than the government of the Soviet Union! The idea behind the gold standard is to restore financial stability by taking the creation of money out of the hands of government. For many of its advocates that in itself is enough.

What are the problems this would present? (Here I would wish to acknowledge my debt to Professor Robert Gilpin, without in any way implicating him in my views.)

The problems are twofold.

First is the problem of negotiating a "reentry rate." What will be the dollar price of an ounce of gold? With literally hundreds of billions of dollars in various forms floating about in the world, what price will be high enough to persuade the holders of such dollars not to exchange them for bullion? What price will be high enough, for example, to persuade Saudi Arabia that it would prefer to have its wealth in time deposits in Manhattan rather than in real treasure right there in Riyadh? If the price *is* high enough, does that not, by the automatic responses which are said to be the virtue of the gold standard, mean a sharp contraction of the money supply, and deflation, and depression?

It is not much in fashion any longer to invoke Maynard Keynes, but that is just what happened in Britain when it returned to the gold standard after World War I, as the great economist explained at the time in his short volume *The Economic Consequences of Mr. Churchill.*

I note in passing that any reentry price, indeed any return to the gold standard, would have to be negotiated with Europe, Japan, and OPEC.

If that does not put an end to the matter, let me present the

second set of problems. Seventy-seven percent of the gold produced in the world comes from the Soviet Union and South Africa. To return to the gold standard means to put our money
supply in the hands of two of the most hateful regimes on earth.
Period.

If yet further argument is needed, economic historians could
be of help. There is a myth of the gold standard and nineteenth-
century Europe, most of it wrong. The standard really only existed
from 1870 to 1915. It was put in place by the Bank of England
at a time when the British could do such things. And, if I may
add, its regime corresponds precisely to the period when Britain
lost its industrial supremacy in the world. This was the period
when William Jennings Bryan flourished, and some sport has been
made of him in recent years. But there was a profound truth to
his concerns. No economy can grow unless the supply of money
grows. If the supply of money is defined as a supply of narrowly
held, closely controlled metal, the rest of us suffer.

Together, the Soviet Union, South Africa, and Saudi Arabia
make up some 6.99 percent of the world's population. Let us
forthwith resolve not to crucify the remaining 93.01 percent of
mankind on a cross of gold!

New York, New York
October 5, 1981

Federal Aid to Education:
A Zero-Sum Game?

———

Bill Buckley asked me to give this talk on the occasion of the Fiftieth Anniversary of Millbrook School, from which he graduated. I accepted because I fear to refuse Buckley anything, and because I had heard such fine things about the school's founder, Edward Pulling. Further, it was an occasion to remind the founder of National Review *and one of the president's close counselors that he was educated in a high Tory atmosphere whose ranks would be appalled at much of the talk and most of the things then going on in Washington.*

The speech was a complete success. It was to be given outdoors after dinner in the Taconic hills in mid-October. There was a tent, but it only seemed to keep the cold in. I arose, and announced I would put my address in the Congressional Record *and report to the headmaster the names of those students who failed to write for a free copy. I sat down to great applause.*

Well, not entirely true. I did take three or four minutes to say that while wealthy young men were being educated very nicely at Millbrook School in the countryside, an administration in Washington seemed not at all interested in poor children in cities the nation over who were being educated very badly indeed. The students applauded and the alumni applauded and, had he been there, I expect Buckley would have applauded.

As many of us learned in the *New York Times Magazine*,* William F. Buckley, Jr., graduated from Millbrook School, in Dutchess County, in the Class of 1943. That is the year I graduated from Benjamin Franklin High School in East Harlem. Although these places were apart in a number of senses, I was struck, on reading Mr. Buckley's sensitive and insightful memoir, by the similarity of our experiences.

Each of us received a fine education. Each at an institution which was the creation (at about the same time, 1931 and 1934) of an extraordinary man. In the case of Millbrook, Edward Pulling, a first-generation American who had come from England. In the case of Benjamin Franklin, Leonard Covello, a first-generation American of Italian extraction. (I call attention to this: The experience of migration has much to do with the peculiar American approach to education as a process of preserving older traditions while acquiring newer ones.)

It will be remarked that these schools were surely different, in that one was public and the other private. I would reply that there is no more unifying tradition in American education than this diversity.

It is to these several concerns, then, that I would address myself on this grand occasion of Millbrook's Fiftieth Anniversary.

A certain serendipity, which one gathers has ever attended your affairs, brings your anniversary in a year when a great new debate on education is beginning in our nation—or, as I shall argue, ought to be beginning.

In Washington, Secretary of Education Terrel H. Bell has proposed to the White House that his department be downgraded to a subcabinet-level foundation. Furthermore, he proposes that there be a fundamental realignment of the federal role in American education. Specifically, Secretary Bell's report, as obtained

---

* In an article on Millbrook School.

by *Education Week*, asserts that "the Federal Government does not have responsibility for education."

It is proposed not merely to reduce funding, but in many areas to abolish it; to strip the federal government of virtually all activities save such as the collection of statistics and an odd bit of research support. It is said that the Tenth Amendment forbids, or at very least frowns upon, the developments in which

> we have seen special-interest groups successfully shifting power, in the decade of the 1970s, away from teacher, parent, and school board, and toward organized lobby, civil servant, committed elected officials, and convinced judges. . . .

Lest anyone suppose that this is little more than good conservative fun—*épater les fonctionnaires*—the *Washington Post* reports that Title I outlays, the basic program of "federal aid to education," will be cut by a quarter if the administration has its way.

To repeat, a large debate is about to begin, or at least ought to begin. Allow me at the outset two remarks sure to distress, impartially, both sides of the impending dispute.

First, having read the long extract from the document sent by the education secretary to the White House, I must report that the passages purporting to reflect American history and constitutional doctrine are mostly nonsense.

How else to account for the proposition that "the federal government does not have responsibility for education"? The statement implies a universal, plenipotentiary obligation. Not "some responsibility," or "any responsibility," or "primary responsibility." But "responsibility," period. Which is to say "all responsibility." In that, to my knowledge, no serious person has ever suggested anything of the sort, it signifies nothing that the proposition is set up and then knocked down. I gather Mr. Pulling taught English when young Buckley was at Millbrook. I doubt he would have accepted any such meretricious argument. I know that Mr. Gotlieb who taught English at Benjamin Franklin would not have.

Nor would Mr. Bernstein, who taught us history. Perhaps the most important act of the Continental Congress was the Northwest Ordinance which provided a direct federal subsidy for education. Almost the first act of the Congress established by the present Constitution was to reaffirm this grant. A plaque on the Sub-Treasury on Wall Street commemorates both actions. This does not invalidate the view that the federal government *ought* not to exercise any responsibility, but it does make nonsense of the view that the Constitution—presumedly because it does not mention the subject—somehow bars such an exercise.

As for those who hold that the federal government should exercise large responsibility for education, and has yet fully to meet that responsibility, it appears to me that a measure of imprudence on their part has endangered the purposes they so ardently and genuinely seek to advance. They have of late been seeking too much of the federal government. Elementary and secondary education in America, as well as being diverse, have always, in our nation, been first of all local. This is very different, for example, from much European experience. But it was rather to the European model that American educators turned when they acquired their enthusiasm for the creation of a department of education.

It is tedious to go over the argument yet again, but more important than ever to do so. For this time around, there might be a greater willingness—no, let me not say that—a greater *capacity* to listen than there was several years ago. (Experience also teaches!)

The Department of Education was created in 1979, the fulfillment of a promise made by President Carter during the 1976 campaign. It was thus an openly political act. Its explicit purpose was to give greater saliency to education in the federal government, and to use that leverage to bring about a greater allocation of resources to education. It was the most direct possible challenge to the views of those now responsible for education in the federal government.

I voted against the bill.

I felt that the outcome would just as likely be the opposite of what its sponsors intended; that by gathering all, or almost all, of education together in one place, it would become possible for the opponents of a federal role in education to do away with it at one blow.

David Riesman, who for a generation now has been our nation's foremost student of education, was much of this view. As the debate progressed, he sent me a long and thoughtful letter on the subject, portions of which I read to the Senate. I read them now to you as an example of the capacity of a trained intelligence not only to understand events, but also to foresee them:

> Education, contrary to people who speak of it as an "establishment," is a weak power, subject to whims and fashions in the country at large, and these show up in the attitudes of individual members of Congress and their aides, assistants, and others. Therefore, education is best served by being part of a much more powerful coalition in which it is joined with the rest of HEW with its labor union and medical and other affiliations. Furthermore, education is, because of its weakness, vulnerable to attack because something done in one of the 3,000 accredited post-secondary institutions by somebody may offend somebody or get in the papers.
>
> It therefore needs to have many diverse sources of support, combined with a certain precious obscurity. Once it is separate, its target quality and actual weakness will be visible and this a weakness not only vis-a-vis potential critics, but potential lobbyists—captors—in the country. Education is best served by decentralization, not only in this huge and diverse country, but also within the federal government and its many agencies.

Riesman argued that diffuseness is valuable for defense, but also that diversity is desirable in its own right. Monoculture, be it in agriculture, education, or whatever, is inherently instable. Obviously, this argues for *many* levels of government—including the federal—to *share* responsibility for education, and also for modes of education that are not government-sponsored at all.

Here, interestingly, the present administration tends rather to share Riesman's outlook. Specifically, the president has committed himself to providing tax credits to the parents of children in nonpublic schools. It is not new for persons aspiring to the presidency to propose such aid. George S. McGovern did; Hubert H. Humphrey did. But President Reagan is the first such person to do so in office, a very different thing. Moreover, this advocacy comes at a time when a major study of nonpublic secondary schools by a group headed by James S. Coleman has concluded that they are quite good schools indeed, and that

> the factual premises of underlying policies that would facilitate use of private schools are much better supported on the whole than those underlying policies that would constrain their use.

To be sure, Coleman's findings have been disputed; but I would caution the disputants. The findings of his 1966 report *Equality of Educational Opportunity* were just as hotly contested. In 1966 and 1967, Professor Thomas F. Pettigrew and I conducted a faculty seminar at Harvard University to reexamine the data. Subsequently, Professor Frederick Mosteller and I published a great thick volume of results. Coleman had got it right. I expect he has got it right this time, too. Indeed, the findings are complementary. After a point, it is not the number of books in a library that counts in student achievement as much as the number of hours students spend reading them. Critical variables in school achievement turn out to be such things as the level of attendance in classes and the amount of homework done. It is amazing what modern social science can teach us!

The *problem* with the administration's advocacy of aid to nonpublic schools is that, of late, it is proposed to provide it *at the expense of public schools*. This is implicit in proposals to eliminate, or drastically reduce, present elementary and secondary education programs.

I believe the *Education Times* accurately summarized this view in a headline: "Administration Says Tuition Tax Credits Would Cut Other Education Funding."

What an ironic, even bitter development in the troubled history of relations between public and private schooling in America.

In this, as in much now, I go back some distance. The proposal for federal aid arose in the years following World War II as the "baby boom" of that period nearly overwhelmed the capacity of local and state governments to carry on their traditional roles. There was in any event a growing movement, which political scientists have not failed to record, to take social issues upwards on the federal scale, in the expectation that the reception at the national level would be more "liberal." But the movement was stalemated. Specifically, it was divided between those who wanted federal aid only for public schools, and those who wanted nonpublic schools included as well. As long as these forces were divided, those who wished no federal aid of any kind prevailed. It was not until the assassination of John F. Kennedy that the two groups which favored federal aid came together. And together *they* prevailed. I know this history. I was present. I wrote the plank in the 1964 Democratic National Platform which constituted the agreement, which led some eight months later to the Elementary and Secondary Education Act of 1965. It was as simple as that. Once the two groups joined in common purpose, legislation stalemated for a generation was enacted in a matter of months.

Things did not work out as they ought to have. Nonpublic schools did not receive anything like the proportionate share of federal assistance they had a right to expect under the compact of 1964. There arose, in consequence, a movement to provide aid through tax credits. This is at best a substitute approach, but it would serve its purpose. And at a time when federal aid to public education was ample, it seemed both practical and equitable.

Now, however, tax credits are proposed in an atmosphere in which federal aid to public education is declining. A zero-sum game is proposed. What one set of schools wins, another loses.

It appears to me that there can be no successful outcome to any such confrontation. In a sense, we are reproducing the stalemate that preceded the compromise of 1964.

It is entirely possible that we will shortly see a significant cutback in federal aid to education. This need not, *per se*, be a calamity. A number of innovative governors, such as Bruce Babbitt of Arizona and Lamar Alexander of Tennessee, have proposed that the federal government take over all income maintenance programs in exchange for the states assuming full responsibility for elementary and secondary education. Such a case can be made. I expect, however, that the real choice is between a sharp cut in all forms of federal aid and the preservation of existing levels of aid with the addition of some form of aid to nonpublic schools and a public–private coalition able to defend the resulting program.

If this is to happen, ought not proponents of aid to nonpublic schools state right away that equal means equal; that they will not accept aid for nonpublic schools at the expense of the public systems; and further, that if there is to be no federal aid to public schools, then there should be none to nonpublic schools?

Similarly, ought school boards and other groups involved in public schools devoutly ask themselves whether they ought not now to join forces—once again—with their opposites in the private sector? At the risk of giving offense—a risk worth taking, for something like social peace is at stake—ought not the champions of the public schools, which must and do come first in *all* our concerns, ask themselves whether they have tried to reach out to their private counterparts, to regroup the coalition of 1964?

And *both* groups surely should rise as one on this occasion to assert that *whatever else happens*, the federal government must not back away from its responsibilities to ensure that civil-rights standards are observed and, if need be, enforced throughout our many and varied school systems. That *is* a federal responsibility. Period.

One would hope, finally, for discourse. Debate if you like. Large issues are at stake here. They ought not be disposed of as secondary consequences of a budget squeeze or a campaign promise.

I say to my fellow teachers that a kind of denial is taking place down in Washington. Those who represent public education are for the most part hoping that somehow the Congress will come to their rescue or the administration will come to its senses. Those who advocate aid to nonpublic education cannot sit by silently as a confrontation develops between their schools and the public schools—a confrontation they are fated to lose. If the respective groups will not cooperate, can they not at least talk with one another?

Millbrook, New York
October 17, 1981

Not the worst advice. Not taken.

Letter to New York:
A Season of Solidarity

The year had begun with the inauguration of a presidential candidate who had called for an end to the Soviet grain embargo imposed by his predecessor following the invasion of Afghanistan. It ended with the new administration selling crucial machinery to Moscow, whilst urging embargoes on the part of the Allies. A pattern!

Dear New Yorker:

The holidays are a time to reflect on the year past and to hope for peace and happiness in the year ahead. Christmas, as an official holiday, came late to the United States. The English Puritans detested it as a papist rite, and there were laws against its observance in the Commonwealth of Massachusetts. The Scots celebrated on New Year's. The Germans kept Christmas, as they say, but in those days also kept somewhat to themselves.

The first Christmas tree in the White House was the inspiration of one of those presidents of the 1880s whose sequence I can never keep straight. This was imported behavior, Prince Albert having introduced the custom to Buckingham Palace a generation earlier. But it was not until 1894 that Grover Cleveland, perhaps responding to his political experiences among the German folk of Buffalo, gave the civil service the day off. The occasion has been, in that sense, sacred ever since. The Capitol shuts down and becomes rather a private place. For once, all is calm. It is possible to think.

This year, all it has been possible to think about is Poland, and it has been heartbreaking.

Three years ago, I published a book about my experience as ambassador to India and the United Nations. I began with a bit of biography: I had first gone to Washington, I wrote, with John F. Kennedy and then stayed on with Lyndon Johnson. "There I learned as an adult what I had known as a child, which is that the world is a dangerous place—and learned also that not everyone knows this." My editor picked up the phrase—the theme, if you like—and the book was given the title *A Dangerous Place*.

Nothing has happened since to change this view. Looking back, that is, from the vantage of the day after Christmas 1981. But in between, something did happen. Solidarity. "Solidarnosc," the Polish word with which we are all becoming familiar.

This is to say that, in the midst of a communist state, on the very border of the Soviet Union and, thanks to the Warsaw Pact, not only surrounded by Soviet armed forces but half occupied by them (there are two Soviet tank divisions stationed permanently on Polish soil, and "maneuvers" recurrently bring larger forces across the border), a free-trade-union movement was organized a d seemingly moved from strength to strength. It grew incredibly in numbers. Two weeks ago, Solidarity had some ten million members, perhaps half the adult population of Poland. Its leaders developed uncanny organizational skills, and its membership learned discipline. One-hour strikes would begin exactly at noon and end precisely at one o'clock and close down a whole city.

Solidarity's demands were elemental and just. It sought the right to free association. To free speech. To a somewhat better life for the working people of Poland. It brought down one set of Communist party leaders. It forced that group's successors to the bargaining table. It obtained formal contractual agreements. It produced an extraordinary leader, Lech Walesa. A man of the people, he was a shipyard electrician.

For years, persons in government and universities (myself included) have made their living teaching that this was not possible. The twentieth-century Marxist-Leninist state—first we learned, then we taught—was something wholly new in the history of man. It was all-powerful and implacable. It would never share power; it would permit no opposition. It was *total*. No institutions were permitted to exist independent of the state. And it endured. No such state was ever transformed from within.

That none should, that the course of history would make such an event impossible, is fundamental to Soviet belief. This is why the events in Chile in the mid-1970s assumed such importance for them, and retain that importance. It would be hard to find a country as far away from the Soviet Union, or of less consequence to it, than this South American country. Yet to this day, at any United Nations meeting, Chile will be found at the top of the agenda, along with Israel and South Africa, several hours devoted to ritual condemnation. Why? The current regime in Santiago is awful, but is it so much more awful than those of its neighbors? Or of the common lot of UN members? Not really. Yet it has seemed to defy historical determinism. It was, at one point, about to become a Marxist-Leninist state—or so, evidently, it seemed to the Soviets—and then did not. It may, for all I can testify, have become an even nastier state from our own point of view. But that is not what troubles the Soviets. What troubles the Soviets is that history, as they assumed it was working, didn't.

Moreover, by the 1970s, United States foreign policy had gone beyond accepting this conclusion; it had commenced to accommodate to it. There had been a period when American policy at least intimated that it favored the "liberation" of the "satellite" nations. But that was talk of the 1950s, and never more than talk.

The Helsinki Accords of 1975 accepted the military map of 1945 as legitimate, promising only that certain human rights would be accorded people in Eastern European countries. This was sincere American and Western European policy, but equally sincere was the desire not to have trouble there. An epiphany of sorts came in December 1975, at an otherwise routine meeting of American ambassadors in London. Helmut Sonnenfeldt, then counselor to the Department of State, spoke to the group. Someone took notes and they soon made their way into the press. Sonnenfeldt had remarked how much it was to be regretted that the Soviets were still so inept in their role as an emergent "superpower on a global scale." He explained: "They have not brought [to it] the ideological, legal, cultural, architectural, organizational, and other values and skills that characterized the British, French, and German adventures." Alas, also, "the Soviets' inability to acquire loyalty in Eastern Europe is an unfortunate historical failure. . . ." Accordingly, the United States must help. "We seek to influence the emergence of the Soviet imperial power by making the base in Eastern Europe more natural and organic, so that it will not remain founded in sheer power alone. . . ."

This view permeated official thinking. I suppose it is the case that President Ford made an honest mistake ten months later when, in a debate with Jimmy Carter, he declared that the Polish people were not under Soviet domination and were as free as we are. But that is the kind of error that comes from reading too many State Department briefing books.

President Carter was similarly affected, or so I would judge. On December 17, during the first week of Poland's martial law regime, he gave his first foreign policy address since leaving the White House, speaking before a meeting of the Council on Foreign Relations in New York City. His prepared text did not even mention Poland. Such is the power of doctrine! Specifically of the Sonnenfeldt Doctrine, as it came somewhat cynically to be known (which was not entirely fair to the decent career officer who was setting forth, as best he understood it, the position of his government in a setting that seemed to permit more than normal candor). For that was the object behind the American and, generally speaking, Western credits and trade agreements, grain sales and whatever, that began to shower on the Soviets and the Eastern bloc nations at this time. A doctrine of "entanglement" grew up which held that as the communist nations came more and more to depend on the Western economies, they would necessarily grow more cooperative and less adventurous.

Alas for the hard life of the theoretician. For it was just at this moment that Soviet policy commenced its most adventurous period since the end of the war. Cuban and Soviet troops were sent to Angola; Soviet forces under the command of a Soviet general appeared in Ethiopia; Afghanistan was invaded; events took a disheartening turn in Nicaragua; and so it has gone.

Almost any successful diplomacy involves the ability to see the world from the point of view of other parties. Unless you know how another nation will interpret your actions, you are not likely to have much success influencing its behavior. Southerners have a saying that even a blind hog finds an acorn sometimes; but random luck is not a good basis for a mature foreign policy, and mature diplomats work hard at seeing the world from the vantage point of those with whom they deal. This is an exercise not without risks: Many an ambassador succumbs to an overseas ailment known as "clientitis." The British call it "going native." But it is a necessary risk, and considerably lessened if there are texts to go by.

This is peculiarly the case both with our country and the Soviet Union. Read *The Federalist Papers*, the work of Madison, Hamilton, and Jay, and you will know a lot about America. Read Lenin and you will know a lot about Russia. If you do both, you will note how very much more the Soviet system is based on prophecies about future events in *this world*. Theirs, as they say, is *scientific* socialism which explains historically determined events.

The first such event was to have been the collapse of capitalism. In the middle of the nineteenth century, Karl Marx made this prophecy. The industrial revolution was in full swing at the time, but he saw this amazing transformation of man's condition coming to an early end. Briefly—if you are still with me—the wonderful new machines would overproduce. Capital would try to maintain its margin of profit by squeezing more out of labor. Labor, impoverished, would buy even less. And so it would go until the final crash. His book, remember, was called *Das Kapital—Capital*.

But the old century ended and the new one began and still no crash. Worse yet, the standard of living of workers was still going up, not down. Lenin came to the rescue with a revision of the prophecy: Imperialism had extended the life of capitalism. By taking over Africa and Asia, capitalism would create new markets for Western goods, thus postponing the collapse. Note that in Lenin's view the imperialists did not exploit the colonies. Rather, they enriched them by sending out their surplus production. I know that sounds wrong, but that *is* what he wrote. And it is crucial to understanding Soviet behavior today, because once in power, Lenin further prophesied that the West would commence dumping its surplus product on the Soviet Union as well.

There are many accounts of this prophecy. In its most simple and widely held version, Lenin tells a comrade, Karl Radek, "The imperialists are so hungry for profits that they will sell us the rope with which to hang them." There does not appear to be any solid textual evidence that Lenin ever actually said this. However, there is reason to believe he wrote something similar. Shortly after Lenin's death, the Russian artist I. U. Annenkov copied the following passage from Lenin's papers (which years later appeared in the New York Russian-language publication *Novyi Zhurnal*):

> The capitalists of the whole world and their governments in their rush to conquer the Soviet market will close their eyes to the activity referred to above [various diplomatic subterfuges of the Soviet government] and will thereby be turned into blind deaf mutes. They will furnish credits which will serve us for the support of the Communist Party in their countries and, by supplying us materials and technical equipment which we lack, will restore our military industry necessary for our future attacks against our suppliers. To put it

in other words, they will work on the preparation of their own suicide.

Is it not a problem that our recent behavior appears to *confirm* Lenin's prophecy? Following the invasion of Afghanistan, President Carter put an end to our sale of (surplus) wheat to the Soviets. Argentina and Australia quickly made up the difference. Came the 1980 presidential election, and candidates competed with one another in proclaiming their anticommunism and the speed with which, if elected, they would end the grain embargo. As it happened, Ronald Reagan was elected and it fell to him to do so, but most of his rivals would have done so as well.

Consider the famous Yamal pipeline that will bring Siberian natural gas to Western Europe. At a summit meeting of Western leaders held in Ottawa last July 19 through 21, the president proposed that the West not provide the credits and technology to build the pipeline. A week later, however, on July 29, it was announced that the administration had approved an export license for the Caterpillar Company to sell the Soviets pipe-laying equipment such as they would need to build the pipeline.

Now it happens the president's decision was made impulsively, at a meeting in the Cabinet room with the Republican congressional leadership. The Caterpillar Company of Peoria, Illinois, is in trouble, the Republican leader of the House of Representatives is from Peoria, and so forth and so forth. Even as the president was making his decision, the State Department was working up an "options paper." But this is precisely the point. No one is to "blame," at least from the Soviet point of view. Everyone acted as they "had" to act. Having glutted the American market with tractors and earth-moving equipment, the Caterpillar Company *had* to "rush to conquer the Soviet market . . . supplying us materials and technical equipment which we lack. . . ."

The problem for us in Lenin's prophecy is that he wasn't all that wrong. All the more important then to keep in mind that when we behave as we do, we shore up an otherwise collapsing set of Soviet doctrines.

At a Christmas lunch last week, a friend from the Department of State was predicting (correctly) that our allies would resist any real economic sanctions against the Soviets and even political sanctions, such as taking the issue to the United Nations. He gave a good imitation of a career diplomat explaining away the need for Western action by assuring everyone that by crushing Solidarity the Soviets will only show the world that "communism does not work." "To the contrary," said another friend present, "they show the world that communism *does* work." The all-powerful, pitiless, totalitarian state.

When news of the military repression of Poland arrived in Washington,* the United States ought instantly to have gone to the United Nations Security Council and declared that so massive a violation of human rights, so patent an intervention by one nation in the internal affairs of another, was a threat to international peace and security and must be condemned. As I write, the administration has decided not to do this, having first decided it would. The fear is that we would stand alone. Am I wrong in thinking that Madison, Hamilton, Jay stood alone? This is what our books are supposed to tell the world about *us*.

A dear friend, a lady born in Central Europe, who was put in jail by the Nazis during World War II and by the Communists afterwards, remarked the other day: "Are we losing our capacity for moral behavior?" Let us hope not. Let us hope for a better year. While we pray for Poland. Pray for the men and women described by the Soviet news agency, TASS, as "counterrevolutionary scum," but who we know to be patriots for whom no praise can be too great.

Washington, D.C.
December 26, 1981

---

* On Sunday, December 13, 1981, Solidarity leaders were arrested and Soviet-sponsored repression in Poland commenced.

1982

———

The Early Confessions
of David Stockman

As 1982 opened, the first round of the argument closed. In the December 1981 issue of the **Atlantic,** William Greider published what were, in effect, David Stockman's confessions. As he, Stockman, would later write in **The Triumph of Politics: Why the Reagan Revolution Failed,**

> The Reagan Revolution, as I had defined it, required a frontal assault on the American welfare state. That was the only way to pay for the massive . . . tax cut.

But he soon learned that "our Madisonian government of checks and balances . . . is conservative, not radical." And so by the end of the first year, he realized again, as he later wrote, that "the true Reagan Revolution never had a chance" and, so to speak, switched sides and became himself a conservative.

To this day, I don't think we understand that a conspiracy had seized the White House. The president had not been elected to mount a "frontal assault on the American welfare state." In the early Reagan years, George Will would begin speeches to bankers' conventions by offering a door prize of one toaster to anyone in the audience who could name a single federal program Mr. Reagan had proposed to abolish in the course of his 1980 campaign. The audiences would pause, individuals looking around expecting to see others raising their hands, none, whereupon Will *would remark that his toaster was safe for the simple reason that the president hadn't made any such proposal. Not one.*

Even so, the proposition still required indirection. In January 1982, I was asked to address the Washington Press Club's annual "Salute to Congress." The occasion is much like the Gridiron. The club president posed the following question: "Senator Moynihan, if you had it all to do over again, would you have told David Stockman [at Harvard] that confession is good for the soul?" I rose.

Madame President:

It is now, what? The year 2001. Odd, as I grow older, I have trouble recalling day-to-day events, but my recollections grow ever more keen of those distant, turbulent times.

The truth is I *did* try.

Admittedly, not directly. As was then well known to the draft board, and possibly to some of you even now, at the time of which we speak, young Stockman was a student at the Harvard School of Divinity.

Any conception of the soul had long been banished from that institution as a prescientific, objectively capitalist, and pertinaciously papist superstition.

Accordingly, strictly as literature, I assigned as extra reading *The Confessions of St. Augustine*. These seemed to be having a salutary effect until Stockman reached Book VIII, Chapter VII, in which Augustine describes his youthful desire to put aside, in his words, "the treasures and kingdoms of this world." But he could not bring himself directly to that vocation. He recalls addressing the Lord, ". . . I, miserable young man, . . . had entreated chastity of Thee and said, 'Grant me chastity and continency, but not yet.' "

Looking back, I can see how very much that arrangement commended itself to the young Stockman. Lord Byron observed that, and I quote, "Augustine in his fine *Confessions* makes the reader envy his transgressions." And who would not envy a man who, again to use Augustine's terms, passed a youth given over to "concupiscence," "perverse ways," and "sacrilegious superstition," and who yet dies a saint?

It was to be much the same with Stockman. He had learned that virtue delayed was the very opposite of opportunity denied. Thus began his Republican period.

Opinions vary as to the origins of his subsequent conversion to radical syndicalism. There are those who reason that a somewhat obscure sadomasochistic episode in a woodshed in the early 1980s was the origin.* Such notions are much too speculative for me. I hold that human nature is constant, and that the decisive event was Stockman's early and formative discovery that virtue could be turned to advantage in the right circumstances.

And as we all know, the right circumstances came. Following the Crash of 1983, with Jack Kemp's defection to the Democrats and election to the presidency as a champion of "the little guy," the nation went on to a "commodity-based currency." Stockman was banished, of course, but too late it was discovered that he had sold off all the government's gold to keep the 1984 deficit from going over a half trillion dollars. There was then no choice but to use hog bellies as a currency base, a promise in any event adumbrated during the preceding Iowa primary. This outraged the Arabs, with the consequence that the dollar disappeared as an international currency, the depression deepened, and a yet more radical regime won the White House. It was then, of course, that Stockman confessed to having all along retained his membership in the Students for a Democratic Society, and so returned to power.

I could go on to speculate as to the traces of Augustinian

---

* Following the appearance of William Greider's article, "The Education of David Stockman," in the December 1981 *Atlantic Monthly,* Stockman met with the president for lunch. He described the occasion as "more in the nature of a visit in the woodshed after supper."

influence on his subsequent decision to nationalize the banks and burn the bankers, but that would be beyond our subject this evening.

In sum, I conclude that Stockman never did actually *believe* that confession is good for the soul, but he did discover that it was good for Stockman.

Washington, D.C.
January 27, 1982

The Utility of a Senate:
Reflections from The Federalist Papers

It was time to suggest not all was well in foreign policy. I overstate the strains of the Atlantic Alliance, but am not far wrong in asking why the new administration did not see the invasion of the Falklands by the Argentine generals as a violation of international law. It took us a long time to side with Britain—as much as we ever did. The junta, presumedly intent on the restoration of Somoza, was even then training forces in Honduras that would become the original contras.

The occasion was the Patriots' Day Dinner at the Waldorf-Astoria; a safe setting in which to invoke republican virtue.

Patriots' Day is not much observed in New York but is remembered, still, in our neighbor Massachusetts as the anniversary of the Battle of Lexington, and the onset of the American Revolution.

We did not merely join in that convulsion, we were at the center of it. A majority of the battles of the Revolution were fought on New York soil, and following the peace, the new government was established in this city. When it was proposed to change the Articles of Confederation to the present Constitution, the principal and enduring exposition of the case for doing this was published in our press in the series we know as *The Federalist*

Papers, written by Alexander Hamilton and John Jay, of New York, and James Madison visiting here from Virginia.

Distant days, they are alive for us still by virtue of the great qualities of character and intellect of the men responsible for mankind's first effort to establish popular government in a nation, and indeed a vast nation, as against the city-state of antiquity.

I had occasion once, while at the United Nations, to reflect on this. It was a long afternoon in the General Assembly and to stay awake I set to figuring just how many of the then 144 member states both existed in 1914 and had not had their form of government changed by force since. The answer was seven.

To live in one of these seven, and in the one that is now by far the most considerable of them, is no small benefaction. It argues an occasional moment of reflection as to just how it all came about, in order that we might not simply inherit this fortune, but preserve it also.

If we do this, the first fact we encounter is the degree to which the founders of this nation thought about *government*. There was little they did not know of politics, seen as the struggle for office and reward, and much that they feared from politics as they understood it. Accordingly, it was to the institutions of government that they looked to confine and to moderate the struggle.

They cared so much because they knew so much. The night before he was to row over to Weehawken where he would surely die in a duel (for Burr was notoriously the better shot), Hamilton put his affairs in order, assigning this bit of property and that, but addressing himself with the greatest concern to recording just which of *The Federalist Papers* he had written. As it happens, he was curiously wrong in claiming that some were Madison's, a matter about which Madison said never a word while he lived, but took pains to correct in his own papers, published following his death many years later. But how right both were in their perception that perhaps the greatest of their legacies were the ideas concerning government which they left the nation they helped to found.

Of these, none is more appropriate to this particular theme than Number 62, concerning the role of the Senate under the proposed new Constitution. The Senate was to stand for continuity and for experience. By its attachment to stability, the Senate would be proof against what they termed "the mischievous effects of a mutable government. . . ."

But the Senate was to be more than a source of stable government; it was to be a repository of wisdom concerning *good* government.

> A good government implies two things: first, fidelity to the object of government, which is the happiness of the people; secondly, a knowledge of the means by which that object can be best attained. Some governments are deficient in both these qualities; most governments are deficient in the first. . . . The federal Constitution avoids this error; and what merits particular notice, it provides for the last in a mode which increases the security for the first.

And there you have it. That good government implies a knowledge of the means by which it is best attained.

As a people, we have been faithful to this understanding. We study our government, and seem ever to be tinkering with it, sometimes overreaching in attempting to have it do more than in the circumstances of time and place it can do. But of late, or so it seems to me, we risk losing our grasp on the overreaching concept of the founders, which is that government must be predictable in what it will do. Which is to say that government must be consistent in its adherence to the principles on which it was founded.

This is the great insight implicit in the very idea of a written constitution. It was the primal impulse behind the Declaration of Independence of 1776. It was the master concept of the New

York State Constitution of 1777, which was the work of John Jay, and the prime source of ideas for the Convention at Philadelphia ten years later.

Constitutions of the kind we were drafting in those days, and the one on which we finally settled for the nation, set forth basic principles cherished by the society and the procedures by which the government would, in the first instance, respect them and, thereafter, defend and advance them.

In just this way, citizenship in America was defined not as a matter of blood, or soil, or religious faith, but as adherence to certain political beliefs. Patriotism was defense of those beliefs.

What is not as evident today as it was two centuries ago is the understanding that the other nations also must understand our principles, the more so where they do not share them. It serves no purpose to overstate this concern on the part of the founders. It was enough for them that the United States should survive; but they were well enough aware that survival entailed an acceptance by others of the legitimacy of our purposes, and even a gradual, partial identification with them.

This understanding faded as generations passed, and the union strengthened. The time came, as Lord Bryce wrote, when America "sailed a summer sea." And sooner or later, or so it seemed, the peoples of the world would choose to govern themselves much as we had chosen. This era culminated with the presidency of Woodrow Wilson, who attained a degree of world respect and leadership never before and never since accorded to any man. His singular contribution to the American national experience was a definition of patriotism appropriate to the age America was entering at the time of his presidency. This is to say patriotism defined first of all as the duty to defend and, where feasible, to advance democratic principles in the world at large. It was the general belief that this advance was occurring in the natural evolution of things.

How distant that time seems. Following the First World War, we saw the rise of the totalitarian state, the antithesis of everything Wilson stood for. The Second World War brought an end to the great European empires, at first seeming to promise an extension of democracy. But decades later, what in the main do we see in the world but an assortment of despotisms, concentrated in a spectrum between "the unacceptable and the unspeakable"?

It is elemental that the United States cannot expect in any sense to be the natural leader of a world so comprised. What we can do, however, and increasingly must do is to recognize that in such a world our principles are grievously imperiled and must be asserted and defended.

This latter point might seem obvious. Strangely and worrisomely, it is not. Rather, more and more, there has been a leakage of reality from our view of the world.

I must talk now of the present administration not because it is singular in this regard, but, to the contrary, because it is representative of now persisting tendencies. I speak not to criticize, but to explicate. It is the task of the Senate to do that, and to do so out of love for our institutions and respect for the individuals in whose brief authority they are for the moment entrusted.

We do this with special affection for our president, who all but gave his life in the performance of his duties. But the Senate has duties also.

We have begun to mistake words for deeds. How brave were our words when the Soviets gave orders to crush the democratic forces of Poland's Solidarity, and thus the most astonishing rebirth of freedom in the history of totalitarianism. But what were our deeds? President Gerald Ford has asked the same question.

We begin to mistake deeds for words. The Atlantic Alliance is on the point of collapse.* Increasingly, allied opinion depicts Western Europe as trapped between two superpowers, each pursuing policies equally inimical to the interests of peace or security in the region, indeed the world. Whilst administration officials go on about "demonstration" nuclear explosions and the "40

---

* A somewhat exaggerated report!

percent" probability of nuclear war at some future date, the leaders of the political parties of Western Europe grow hostile, even contemptuous.

Our government appears to see little but posturing in what could in fact be a fateful and historic realignment.

We commence to equate friends with those who are in no sense friends. In stark defiance of the United Nations Charter, the neofascist, anti-Semitic regime of Argentina invades the Falkland Islands. At the outset, the official Pentagon spokesman declared, "We have no idea of doing anything but walking right down the middle." The straight and narrow path, you might say, between right and wrong.

The president has said, "We are trying to be a fair broker" in the dispute. Now it is understandable that an American president should wish to be friends with both parties in a dispute in this hemisphere, and helpful to both. Yet if we had a clear grasp of the principles for which our nation stands, it would also be understood that in this instance this is simply not possible.

The day before the president made his remark, I spoke at some length on the Senate floor about the Falkland Islands. I asked first of all that the dispute be seen in its NATO context. "The invasion by the Argentine military of the Falkland Islands," I said,

> is the first occasion since the establishment of NATO in 1948 that nationals of a NATO member have been subjected to military occupation by another power.

This would accordingly be a test of the Atlantic Alliance. Above all, it would be a test of the position set forth by General de Gaulle, who withdrew French military forces from NATO on the ground that, in a crisis, the United States would not stand by other members of the Alliance.

The Argentine aggression was a direct violation of the United Nations Charter. It was altogether proper, I suggested, for the matter to be taken to the International Court of Justice. Meantime, I concluded,

> Our secretary of state should make absolutely clear that there is nothing to mediate between a country using force without provocation and a country resisting the use of force.

There is nothing confounding in this dispute. A simple, direct reference to our professional principles—in support of peaceful settlement of disputes, self-determination of peoples—would have guided our policy in the most direct way. Why then do we find ourselves so confounded?

Part of our difficulties, I suggest, arise from a mistaken understanding among policy makers that cleverness is the mark of sophistication in foreign policy. Worse, they take complexity as the measure of sophistication, and judge as most sophisticated that which is so complex as to be doomed by the mathematics of probability. We are reminded of Edmund Burke's speech "On American Taxation," in which he described the origins of Lord North's tax on tea. "To please universally was the object of his life," said Burke of the then chancellor of the exchequer, "but to tax and to please, no more than to love and to be wise, is not given to men. However, he attempted it." And what a contrivance he attempted: a half dozen or so moving parts, each designed to offset the adverse impact of the other, each in the end incompatible and unworkable. "What need I say more?" asked Burke. "This fine-spun scheme had the usual fate of all-exquisite policy."

Now this is the ultimate leakage of reality: the idea that there can be any longer such a thing as superiority in the nuclear relations between the United States and the Soviet Union.

The fantasy of superiority leads naturally to the illusion of inferiority and willingness to proclaim inferiority with seemingly no notion of what the effect might be in the real world. To declare that the Soviet Union has a "definite margin of superiority" in strategic weapons and then propose to negotiate surrender. What other option is there in a military situation in which a nuclear war would be decided in thirty minutes?

Here the Senate enters. Number 62 of *The Federalist Papers*, on the problem of erratic policy, is followed by Number 63, on "the utility of a senate" in conveying "a due sense of national character" to foreign nations.

> Without a select and stable member of the government, the esteem of foreign powers will not only be forfeited by an unenlightened and variable policy . . . but the national councils will not possess that sensibility to the opinion of the world which is not less necessary in order to merit than it is to obtain its respect and confidence.

New York, New York
April 19, 1982

A Two-Trillion-Dollar Debt?

*It was time to tell a business audience, the Securities In-
dustry Association, that the size of the federal government was
growing under Ronald Reagan.*

First of all, let me assert that presidential candidates of late
have been saying some pretty outrageous things about our government. It is time we face up to the problem. What are we to
think of a man who puts out a position paper stating:

> Our government in Washington now is a horrible bu-
> reaucratic mess. It is disorganized, wasteful, has no purpose,
> and its policies—when they exist—are incomprehensible or
> devised by special-interest groups with little or no regard for
> the welfare of the average American citizen.

Or to say as this one did in Dallas in the course of the campaign:

> We've developed in recent years a welfare government.
> The American people believe in tough, competent manage-
> ment. We've seen evolved a bloated, confused, bureaucratic
> mess. The American people believe that we ought to control
> our government. On the other hand, we've seen government
> more and more controlling us.

73

I really do think those are excessive statements. And I thought so at the time, in 1976, when Jimmy Carter made them.

Yet this has become an all but standardized rhetoric in contemporary American *elections*. And it is dysfunctional. For it utterly misleads candidates about the problems they will face if they are successful.

Let me cite a passage from a *Washington Post* article by Mark Shields last April 9 complaining that everyone seemed to be turning against our present president.

> The essential 1980 Reagan campaign platform was straightforward. It called for cutting the size, scope, and spending of the federal government; cutting taxes by a third; and for the immediate and dramatic strengthening of our national defenses.

Now is that not a contradictory statement?

Or consider the recent institutional advertisement of the Mobil Corporation. Entitled "Back to Basics," the advertisement calls for the support of the president in the current budget debate:

> But the current debate is also a good thing. It allows the American people to again focus on the President's three objectives:
>
> • lower taxes
> • less government
> • a stronger military

Again, is the contradiction not obvious?

In each instance, there is a distinction made between decreasing the size of government and increasing the size of the military—as if the military were not part of the government. The 1980 Republican platform was quite bold about military matters.

It called for achieving:

> overall military and technological superiority over the Soviet Union.

No one making that assertion ought to have supposed that "less government" would be the result.

The simple problem is that the people who wrote that platform didn't think of the Defense Department—the army, the navy, the air force—as part of "government." Government to them was food stamps and student loans.

Thus you can propose to spend $1.518 trillion on defense in five years, not thinking you are in any way increasing the size, scope, and spending of the federal establishment.

And in just the same way, when Jimmy Carter talked about the horrible, bloated, bureaucratic mess, he was largely talking about the cost of the Defense Department, which he promised to cut. He was not thinking of the new departments of education or energy that he helped create. *That* was not increasing the size of the bloated, confused, bureaucratic mess.

It is as if one party had only one lobe of its brain working; the other party has only the other lobe. Neither sees that in both cases they are increasing the size of government.

Let us look at a few numbers. Federal outlays in fiscal year 1982—after the new president got all of the budget cuts he requested—grew by $68.1 billion in 1981. That was a 10.4-percent increase. Can you imagine what a 10.4-percent increase compounded would be? The president's latest budget aims to increase the size of government in the same range for years to come.

A billion is a large sum. A billion minutes ago, St. Peter was fourteen years dead.

I was an assistant secretary of labor when President Johnson assumed office. Like most vice presidents, Johnson had little information about what was going on in the government that he was required to lead. He soon learned to his horror that President Kennedy was scheduled to be the first president to send a $100-

billion budget to the United States Congress.* LBJ was not going
to be that president. One day—Saturday morning—he asked all
the subcabinet officers over to the Roosevelt Room, that room
just outside the Oval Office and across the hall. There were about
thirty of us. He got us seated and gave us coffee, then started
warming to his subject and began bellowing:

> I know that this room is full of mean, scheming little
> s.o.b.'s who've got special plans to put their special little pet
> projects into this budget so I'll be the first damn fool in
> history to send a $100-billion budget to the United States
> Congress.
>
> Let me tell you, you are not going to succeed because
> I'm gonna make you wish you were never born. I'm gonna
> make you so unhappy because I'm never gonna let you go
> easy. It's going to be long, and slow, and hard. It's gonna hurt.

We were terrified.

And we sent up a budget that was 99.9999 billion dollars. It
was actually $101 billion but that didn't really matter.

Now can I tell you that the budget *deficit* for fiscal year 1983
is formally estimated by the Office of Management and Budget
at $182 billion?

The *New York Times* reported on Saturday:

> President Reagan met with Republican Congressional
> leaders (Friday) to plan budget strategy. . . . The White House
> meeting led to a general agreement to use $182 billion as the
> projected deficit without new taxes or spending cuts in 1983.

In our budget legislation, we set aside money for fiscal year
1983 and then indicate what spending will be in 1984 and 1985.
The accumulated budget deficit for the three years is $642 billion.
It took 190 years to get to a trillion dollars in national debt. We

---

* Ronald Reagan sent the first $1-trillion budget in 1982.

estimate that it will take three years to get to one and two-thirds trillion.

I remember the day in 1962 when I first heard an official of the Pentagon, in talking about the budget, refer to a tenth of a billion. I have to tell you, in the budget committee, we have now commenced to talk about tenths of trillions.

Hot Springs, Virginia
May 3, 1982

A Path to Peace

It was time to support the president. In May 1982, in an address to his alma mater, Eureka College in Illinois, he had proposed Strategic Arms Reductions Talks (START) with the Soviet Union. As we were to learn at Reykjavík four years later, he was never strong on the detail of the nuclear arms race—it is a race—but has held to an abiding vision of arms reduction. It could have been his legacy: It might still be.

The occasion was commencement at the State University of New York at Binghamton. Curious as it may seem, speeches such as these are read in the upper reaches of administrations. There are only 100 senators.

I think it may fairly be said that for doctrinal intricacy and duration of debate, Christian theology holds a special place in history. From the earliest times, the debate has been characterized by men of great learning and texts of intimidating complexity. Indeed, there could scarcely have been a greater contrast than that which obtained at the advent of the Middle Ages between clergy who were reading and writing in ancient, unspoken languages, and an illiterate laity. Yet through all those centuries, and to this time, the theologians conceded great authority in matters of doctrine to the *sensum fidelium*, the belief of the

78

faithful. Be it ever so uninformed at a technical level, it was held even so to be a repository of truth.

May I suggest that something comparable is to be encountered in the American people today in their concern about nuclear weapons? There is in this perception of terrible danger a kind of ultimate truth which the experts must acknowledge, and to which they ought in the end defer.

In the history of the race, there cannot ever have been a subject of such importance that was for so long the domain of such a tiny band of intellectuals. Most of them university-based, yet moving in and out of government, they devised the strategic doctrines which guided the development of our nuclear forces during the long post-Hiroshima generation. Interestingly, historians of the subject frequently turn to theological analogies when discussing these men and their work. Thus John Newhouse writes in *Cold Dawn*:

> As in the case of the early Church, contending schools form around antagonistic strategic concepts. The most relevant of these are known as assured destruction and damage limitation, and each can claim broad support and intellectual responsibility. Debates between the two schools recall those between the Thomists and the essentially Franciscan followers of Duns Scotus.

The public was not involved, nor did it feel involved. I offer an example. In the course of 1979, the year the SALT II treaty was submitted to the Senate, I became persuaded that the SALT "process" either had become or was becoming its own nemesis. The Strategic Arms Limitation Talks had been launched in the mid-1960s in hopes that the growth in nuclear arsenals could be capped, then one day reversed. Yet they were producing outcomes opposite to those they nominally sought. The process was hardly limiting, and not at all reducing, nuclear arsenals. Somewhere along the way, or so it seemed to me, there had been a leakage of reality on the part of those charged with arms control. They had commenced to ratify the arms buildup rather than to reduce it.

Now this kind of systemic disorder is not unknown to social science. A reasonable response is to try to shock the system into self-awareness by proposing a wholly new approach to the problem in question. I had such an idea.

One of the concluding articles of SALT II (Article XIV) provided that the next treaty would ordain "further measures for the limitation and reduction of strategic arms." A joint settlement accompanying the treaty spoke of "significant and substantial reductions."

On August 1, 1979, I proposed an amendment to the treaty requiring that these reductions be agreed to by a date certain, else the treaty would expire. (Specifically, December 31, 1981, the end of what was to have been the first phase of the five-year agreement.) I set about testifying, speaking, writing, all to this one plain point. "Freeze," as we would now say, "and reduce."

And the response? During 1979, I received more letters from New Yorkers on the Alaskan timber wolf than on SALT II. The people, simply, were not involved.

Now they are. People, as Michael Polanyi used to say with disarming simplicity, change their minds. The subject is now of the widest interest and most passionate concern. The Senate has responded. The president has responded. Nothing so powerful and potentially important has occurred in our experience of this issue.

Nor, to some, anything so disconcerting. The fear exists, and it should be acknowledged, that a mass movement calling for nuclear arms reductions must inevitably have greater influence on the democratic party to the negotiations than on the totalitarian party.

Such concerns are not to be dismissed. Persons demanding an end to the arms race could usefully be reminded that, in this life, good will is not always rewarded. Some will recall events which occurred during the Holy Year 1500. Cesare Borgia, at the head of the forces of Pope Alexander VI (who happened also to be his parent), had set out to lay siege to Camerion in an outlying region of the Papal States. His march took him in the direction of the prosperous city of Urbino, whose duke happened to possess the finest artillery in Italy at the time. Borgia asked to borrow this new weapon system and the duke, a pious as well as a learned man, agreed. Whereupon Borgia laid siege to Urbino instead and forced the duke to flee into exile.

There is a responsibility, then, to speak to the present movement, as well as for it. It is a responsibility that requires the closest attention to diplomatic history and political science. Inexact and incomplete as both may be, they are all we have.

Three propositions come to mind.

The first is that the Soviet Union is now entering yet another transition crisis. General Secretary Brezhnev, having reigned almost two decades, is old and in ill health. In the West, and for that matter in the East, the process by which a successor emerges is poorly understood, but we know the process is under way. There has been a suicide. A charge of corruption involving a circus performer. A satirical article in a Leningrad literary journal. Names appear—that of Andropov, recently promoted from head of the KGB, is increasingly prominent among them. To emphasize the mystery of the matter, this might be a positive outcome for purposes of arms control, in that such a person might be able to consolidate power more quickly than has been the Soviet pattern. Even so, a period of relative weakness at the center is now inevitable.

Meantime, the United States has proposed that the Soviet Union give up a formidable number of weapons it now possesses, essentially on the understanding that we will neither develop nor deploy their counterparts. To them, in Leslie Gelb's nice phrase, it is a proposal to trade the present for the future. More specifically, of course, it is a proposal to trade their military present for our military future.

In the most democratic of nations, this is a decision in which the military must be involved. But in a totalitarian state such as the Soviet Union, it is a judgment to which the military must assent, and which in normal circumstances must originate with it. Thus it can be argued that the SALT process to date has moved at the pace—and in the direction—the Soviet military has desired. To propose to reverse that direction would involve a huge risk by any general secretary of the Communist party—almost surely an unacceptable or an unsuccessful one for a leader caught up in the four- to five-year period of consolidating power that Soviet transitions seem to require.

I make this argument even to the point of admitting that it casts doubt on the viability of the amendment I proposed in 1979. *By now*, Mr. Brezhnev and an American president might have agreed to the "significant and substantial" reductions in nuclear weapons the amendment would have required. It is doubtful Mr. Brezhnev still has that power, and more doubtful still that anyone will attain to it for some years to come.

So we must tell the American people that arms reduction will be a test of our patience as well as of our will. And to the degree that our will is strengthened by a heightened sense of the danger, it will be a test of our nerve also, for the most hopeful outcome would be to see some results—real results—by the end of the decade.

A second proposition is that in some form the United States must declare its acceptance of SALT II. It is not enough more or less to abide by it, as both we and the Soviets are more or less doing. The Soviet leadership negotiated the treaty with three presidents. President Carter clearly accepted it for the United States, but then the Senate demurred. Now, if we find Soviet ways mysterious, so surely must they find ours. How are they not to suspect a change in United States policy, even perhaps an elaborate, if yet undeciphered, deception?

The Senate is not discharged of its responsibilities with respect to SALT II. As a body, we have never presented, even to our own nation, an account of what we did or, more accurately, did not do. We have never, as a body, even debated the treaty, much less have we voted on it.

The sequence of the Soviet invasion of Afghanistan during

Christmas week of 1979 and President Carter's request that we set the treaty aside continues to obscure the fact that the treaty as such had already failed. I was a member of a small group of senators favorably inclined toward SALT who would meet during 1979 to discuss its progress. Each of us had his own "count" of the probable outcome of a vote. I can tell you that mine never passed twenty votes for ratification, and none that I know of ever passed much above forty. The resolution of ratification, of course, would have required the votes of two-thirds of the senators present and voting, sixty-seven if all were to participate. The Afghanistan invasion in a sense saved SALT, for the treaty was never rejected, as it well might have been, and the parties act as if it had been ratified.

Is not a more positive response possible? Recall that, from the time Adlai Stevenson raised the issue in the 1956 presidential campaign, or for that matter from the time President Truman offered, with certain conditions, to turn the atom bomb over to the United Nations, the United States has been the primary source of ideas and action with respect to nuclear arms control. President Reagan has now made the boldest proposal ever, though this comes in the aftermath of a sharp, sudden break in our previous forthcoming position. Unless we do something to recover the previous momentum, the unratified SALT II will haunt the coming negotiations. We recall Eliot's lines in "The Hollow Men":

> Between the idea
> And the reality
> Between the motion
> And the act
> Falls the Shadow.

Just a week ago, in an address entitled "From Here to There: SALT to START," former Secretary of State Muskie suggested that Congress will pass and the president will sign a joint resolution declaring that we will abide by the treaty as long as the Soviets do so. I suggest that we might go further, that it is possible for the Senate to indicate its willingness to have the substance of the treaty entered into as an interim executive agreement, to be effective during negotiation of a START treaty. Some difficulties would arise if the administration goes forward with the present "dense-pack" proposal for the deployment of an MX missile. But these surely can be overcome through further negotiation.

I would, moreover, propose that Congress express its commitment to arms reductions at an early date—and provide an incentive—by adding to this joint resolution language substantially that of the amendment I proposed in 1979. Such an amendment would provide that the executive agreement on SALT II would expire by a date certain if a START treaty containing "significant and substantial" reductions had not been negotiated.

Would this diminish the authority of the ratification process? Yes. Is that a risk worth taking if the future of nuclear arms control is in the balance? Again, yes.

It is not a step without precedent. SALT I was entered into by the United States in 1972 in the form of an interim executive agreement that was endorsed by both houses of Congress. (In September 1972, a joint resolution "authorizing the president's approval of the five-year U.S.–Soviet agreement limiting offensive nuclear weapons" passed the Senate 88 to 2, and the House of Representatives 308 to 4.) If the president were to propose a similar route, I feel certain the Senate would support him.

So, then, to a third and concluding observation: It is absolutely necessary that this issue be raised above party politics. If it ever divides the parties and hence the people, we shall surely fail. The consequences will be dreadful and the responsibility will be ours.

Such a process of politicization began in the course of the Senate committee deliberations on SALT II. Whereas SALT I had been approved almost unanimously, party dispositions for and against the second treaty were unmistakable. In the Senate Committee on Foreign Relations (on November 9, 1979), the Democrats voted 7 to 2 to recommend ratification of the treaty;

Republicans voted 2 to 4 against. In the Senate Committee on Armed Services, on a motion to submit to the full Senate a report on the "Military Implications" of SALT II that was largely critical of the treaty, Republicans voted 7 to 0 to submit the report; only 3 of 10 Democrats voted to do so (December 4, 1979).

As the 1980 campaign commenced, this division became more pronounced. The Democratic platform supported the treaty. The Republican platform declared it to be a form of "unilateral disarmament." I responded in the "defense speech" to the Democratic Convention by asking whether a "party that careless with words could be trusted with power." Mr. George F. Will took me severely to task for suggesting that Democrats were somehow to be preferred in such matters. He suggested I did not really believe this. I shot off an equally severe rejoinder. DOES ONE GENTLE-MAN, my telegram read, READ ANOTHER GENTLEMAN'S MIND? All of which could have gone on indefinitely save that even American elections come to an end.

Fortunately, following elections, a certain perspective reasserts itself. We have now much increased our defense budget— but we were already increasing it. In that sense, we can offer to trade the Soviets a future for whatever advantages they may have in the present.

Mr. Brezhnev professes to see in President Reagan's Eureka College speech little more than a device "enabling Washington to continue its efforts to achieve military superiority over the Soviet Union." However these defense efforts are to be described, they are the work of both parties and successive administrations. Similarly, we are abiding by SALT II. That is the work of both parties. And the much-abused doctrine of deterrence received a surprising and unanimous vote of confidence from both parties when the Senate Armed Services Committee refused to provide funds to deploy the MX missile in a stationary mode because that would make the missiles vulnerable to attack. The Soviets could consider such deployment a counterforce mode, which is today a manner consistent with a first-strike strategy. We in the Senate are not customarily so alert to Soviet sensibilities. But some matters are too serious to permit us to be otherwise. Finally, leaders of both parties, and of course the president, have declared that our genuine and pressing goal is that of nuclear arms reductions.

The temptation is powerful to distinguish one arms reduction proposal from another, to invent a domestic "linkage" which favors one message over another by dint of association with quite irrelevant matters. Opponents of school busing will be for one "freeze"; advocates of the Alaskan timber wolf for another. This threatens to trivialize a transcendent issue. It is a tendency that can be resisted, and ought to be.

For so much is at stake. The world is at stake. And much will be tested, not least our political institutions. Not long ago, we observed the bicentenary of the battle of Yorktown. We would do well to remember the scale of even epic battles in the age our political institutions were formed. Thirty-eight Americans died at Yorktown; 156 Britons. We thereupon adopted a form of government designed to deal with events of such scale. Time has taken us so far beyond that age as to have brought about a kind of transition crisis of our own. More than good will, something like courage is going to be required if we are to lead the world through this situation.

Binghamton, New York
May 30, 1982

"We Confront, at This Very Moment, the Greatest Constitutional Crisis Since the Civil War"

Time to tell the bar that the New Right had designs on the legal system. The occasion was the commencement at St. John's University Law School.

I hoped that those who disagreed with one or another on the Court's decisions, as I had done with respect to opinions on aid to nonpublic schools and public access to pretrial judicial proceedings, would remember that the Court can change its mind and that there is a legitimate and time-tested way to get it to do so.

But I fear that something else has happened. In the intervening three years, some people—indeed, a great many people—have decided that they do not agree with the Supreme Court and that they are not satisfied to Debate, Legislate, Litigate.

They have embarked upon an altogether new and I believe quite dangerous course of action. A new triumvirate hierarchy has emerged. Convene (meaning the calling of a constitutional convention), Overrule (the passage of legislation designed to overrule a particular Court ruling, when the Court's ruling was based on an interpretation of the Constitution), and Restrict (to restrict the jurisdiction of certain courts to decide particular kinds of cases).

Perhaps the most pernicious of these is the attempt to restrict courts' jurisdictions, for it is both colorably constitutional (at least in the case of inferior courts) and profoundly at odds with our nation's customs and political philosophy.

It is a commonplace that our democracy is characterized by majority rule and minority rights. Our Constitution vests majority rule in the Congress and the president while the courts protect the rights of the minority.

While the legislature makes the laws, and the executive enforces them, it is the courts that tell us what the laws say and whether they conform to the Constitution.

This notion of judicial review has been part of our heritage for nearly two hundred years. There is not a more famous case in American jurisprudence than *Marbury* v. *Madison* and few more famous *dicta* than Chief Justice Marshall's that

> It is emphatically the province and the duty of the judicial department to say what the law is.

But in order for the Court to interpret the law it must decide cases. If it cannot hear certain cases, then it cannot protect certain rights.

As cases produce winners and losers, so do the ideas and principles upon which the cases rely produce supporters and enemies. So I suppose that it is only natural that those who see the courts ruling against them should seek to prevent these rulings by denying the courts the power to decide at all, or, failing that, by denying litigants certain kinds of relief, such as the busing of school children to eliminate illegal segregation.

These court-curbing bills—there are currently thirty-two of them pending in the Ninety-seventh Congress—would deny federal courts the authority to hear cases on a variety of such issues. The Senate, I regret having to report, has already adopted one such measure, having voted 58 to 38, to substantially limit the authority of lower federal courts to require busing as a remedy for the unconstitutional segregation of school children.

These bills are troublesome, not least because they are arguably constitutional. The jurisdiction of the Supreme Court is set out in Article III of the Constitution, which states in Section 2:

> The judicial power shall extend to all cases, in law and equity, arising under this constitution, the laws of the United States, and treaties made, or which shall be made, under their authority; . . . to all cases of admiralty and maritime jurisdiction; . . . to controversies between two or more States, between a state and citizens of another state, between citizens of different states, between citizens of the same state claiming lands under grants of different states, and between a state, or the citizens thereof, and foreign States, citizens or subjects.

> In all cases affecting ambassadors, other public ministers and consuls, and those in which a state shall be party, the supreme court shall have original jurisdiction. In all the other cases before mentioned, the supreme court shall have appellate jurisdiction, both as to law and fact, with such exceptions, and under such regulations as the Congress shall make.

I repeat: "with such exceptions, and under such regulations as the Congress shall make."

The plain meaning of the penultimate clause—the "exceptions" clause—is that Congress may, by statute, set boundaries for the Supreme Court's appellate jurisdiction. Indeed, in *Ex Parte McCardle* (1868), the Court itself *seemingly* bowed to the authority of the legislature. The Court dismissed for want of jurisdiction an appeal based on a law repealed by Congress *after* the case had been argued before the Court, while it was awaiting final decision. Some have suggested that the Court's decision was not truly a test of Congress's powers in the area of jurisdiction in that it merely altered the manner in which a habeas corpus question could be brought before the Court and in no way questioned the Court's ability to hear the case. But it is frequently cited as the leading case in this area by those who would have Congress restrict the jurisdiction of the Court. The Court said:

> We are not at liberty to inquire into the motives of the legislature. We can only examine into its power under the Constitution, and the power to make exceptions to the appellate jurisdiction of this court is given by express words.
>
> What, then, is the effect of the repealing act upon the case before us? We cannot doubt as to this. Without jurisdiction the Court cannot proceed at all in any case. Jurisdiction is power to declare the law, and when it ceases to exist, the only function remaining to the Court is that of announcing the fact and dismissing the cause.

This is not, however, the end of the matter. For the Constitution has other sections, including Article VI which states in part:

> This Constitution, and the Laws of the United States which shall be made in Pursuance thereof; and all Treaties made, or which shall be made, under the Authority of the United States, shall be the Supreme Law of the Land; and the Judges in every State shall be bound thereby, any Thing in the Constitution of Laws of any State to the contrary notwithstanding.

Must we not presume from this, the "supremacy clause," that the Constitution's framers intended that there should be but a single arbiter of this supreme law, rather than the anarchy of a separate interpretation by each state's highest court? Why write a constitutional "supremacy clause" if there were not to be a single supreme tribunal authorized to interpret and pronounce the meaning of the Constitution and of federal law? Indeed, in the case of *Martin* v. *Hunter's Lessee* (1816), Mr. Justice Story said as much.

Thus we have the notion that the Court has certain "essential functions" under the Constitution. And that any power the national legislature might have to limit jurisdiction is itself limited. Professor Leonard G. Ratner of the University of South Carolina suggests that:

> Reasonably interpreted, the [exceptions] clause means 'With such exceptions and under such regulations as Congress may make, not inconsistent with the essential functions of the Supreme Court under this Constitution.'

We find ourselves, then, not knowing if the Supreme Court's appellate jurisdiction is subject to the will of Congress. We have in *Ex Parte McCardle* a leading case, but rather an old one, that suggests that it is. I think it would be fair to say that most modern commentators would say that it is not.

The claim that the Congress makes on the jurisdiction of lower courts though is, I think, more clear. Section 1 of Article III says:

> The judicial power of the United States, shall be vested in one Supreme Court, and in such inferior courts as the Congress may from time to time ordain and establish.

It is held that this section gives Congress absolute discretion to establish lower federal courts and by implication the power to control the jurisdiction of the courts it creates. There are those who would disagree. Professor Theodore Eisenberg of Cornell had said that because of the proliferation of federal law and the dramatic increase in federal court caseloads since the first lower federal courts were established in 1789, these courts have become a constitutional necessity, since the burden of harmonizing conflicting interpretations of federal law by the fifty state-court systems and vindicating federal rights would be more than the Supreme Court exercising its appellate jurisdiction could bear. Others have said that federal courts are constitutionally neces- sary to bar unconstitutional acts by federal officials since state courts are generally without power to afford relief in such cases.

Again we find ourselves in the situation of not knowing for sure what the powers of Congress in this area are. The legislature has repeatedly, and without serious challenge, exercised its power to decide what the lower courts' jurisdiction should be in orga- nizational or administrative matters, such as the minimum dollar amount that must be in controversy before a case can be heard. But it has never tried to say that certain outcomes would not be tolerated or that certain cases rather than classes of cases could not be heard.

If the constitutionality of these jurisdiction-stripping bills is unclear, two things are not. One is that they are a profoundly bad idea that raises the specter of a constitutional crisis that could leave our courts crippled and the Congress diminished. The other is that the Reagan administration has at least tacitly acquiesced in the actions of those who would take away the courts' power to decide.

On October 29, 1981, Attorney General William French Smith spoke before the Federal Legal Council in Reston, Virginia. After saying that "the multiplication of implied constitutional rights . . . has gone far enough," Mr. Smith concluded:

> We intend in a comprehensive way to identify those principles that we will urge upon the Federal courts. And we intend to identify the cases in which to make our arguments all the way to the Supreme Court.

Fair enough. It is the duty of the attorney general to enforce the laws as he sees fit and to interpret the Constitution as best he can. But Mr. Smith also said, "Through legislation and liti- gation we will attempt to effect the goals I have outlined."

Back in October, I had hoped that by this the attorney general meant he had come to accept, in effect, my hierarchy. He had, by the very fact of his address, already begun the debate on the courts' decisions with which he disagreed. I thought he might then seek passage of laws that would bring before the courts those issues he wished to have decided differently, and that he would argue in court for the changes he sought. Debate, Legislate, Litigate.

But it now appears that he had something quite different in mind. For on May 6, 1982, he wrote Congressman Peter Rodino, chairman of the House Judiciary Committee, endorsing the constitutionality of S.951, the Senate-passed version of the Department of Justice authorization bill that limits the power of lower federal courts to order busing. It was clearly his duty to do this, to tell us if he thought the legislation constitutional or not. But the attorney general of the United States has other duties, too. It is his duty to advise on the prudence and the wisdom of matters touching on the Court, of which he must be the first defender.

The attorney general failed in that duty. However much one might disagree, it would be possible to respect a position by the attorney general *supporting* the court-stripping bill. After all, fifty-eight senators did so. But what is one to say of *silence*? The mere assertion, as stated in the accompanying press release:

> With regard to the antibusing legislation, the Attorney General has concluded that this legislation may be enacted consistent with the Constitution.

Indeed, I grant, that might be so. But *should* it be? The American Bar Association declares this to involve "the greatest constitutional crisis since the Civil War." The attorney general declares, in effect, that it is no concern of his.

New York, New York
June 6, 1982

One-Third of a Nation

In 1982, the Reagan administration proposed abolishing Title IV of the Social Security Act, commonly known as Aid to Families with Dependent Children (AFDC), or yet more commonly as welfare, and turning the care of children back to the States. It was as close to a cruel proposal as any that had come from downtown. Yet, it went all but unnoticed; and had it been proposed in the swirl of the first 100 days, as it were, it might well have succeeded. The most urgent thing was to establish just what Title IV was. The editors of the New Republic provided space. Not many would have in the summer of 1982.

The administration's proposal got nowhere, and before long, it was dropped. A few months earlier, Bob Packwood, who headed the Senate Republican Campaign Committee, put it bluntly enough in an interview with the Associated Press.

> Pete Domenici (chairman of the Senate Budget Committee) says we've got a $120-billion deficit coming and the President says, 'you know, a person yesterday, a young man, went into a grocery store and he had an orange in one hand and a bottle of vodka in the other, and he paid for the orange with food stamps and he took the change and paid for the vodka. That's what's wrong.'
>
> And we just shake our heads.

94

From this point, the president's men, or so it appeared, tended to steer him away from welfare anecdotes. Curiously, these years witnessed a slow revival of interest in welfare reform and family policy. The president himself raised the issue in his 1986 State of the Union address.

The story from Albany was puzzling. The New York State commissioner of education had asked the state attorney general to take legal action to prevent the U.S. Department of Education from using 1970, rather than 1980, census figures in calculating New York's share of federal education funds. These monies are allocated by population; in this case, the number of children living in poverty.

New York lost population during the 1970s. There were 1.2 million fewer children living there in 1980 than a decade earlier. At first glance, wouldn't one expect the commissioner to want to use the earlier population data? Well, yes—but only at first glance, because it turns out that although New York did indeed lose over a million children in the 1970s, it gained 158,871 children living in poverty. A decade which saw great and growing efforts to deal with the problem of poverty utterly failed to deal with the problem of dependency.

The dependent family is typically female-headed. The number of such families grew furiously during the 1970s, in all regions of the country. Most such families are poor. During the 1970s, female-headed families became the majority of poor families with children. According to the 1980 census, the proportion of such families is now 53.6 percent. In New York it is closer to two-thirds.

The hidden dynamic in poverty data is changing family composition. For about fifteen years, the Census Bureau has been trying to sort out the question, and is now good at doing so. Simply described, the family composition of a given year—1970—is brought forward to establish what the same composition would mean in income terms at a later year—1980. This is compared with the real 1980 data, and the differences are attributable to family change. Gordon Green and Edward Welniak of the Census Bureau have now done this and will soon publish their results.

In brief, overall changes in family composition accounted for an additional 2,017,000 poor families in the 1970s. This has been a devastating experience for almost every group throughout the country, but especially for minorities. Green and Welniak write that changes in the composition of black families caused their real income to decline by 4.9 percent in the 1970s. Without the changes, the real income of these families would have increased 11.3 percent. Green and Welniak conclude: "These data suggest that, in the absence of changes in family composition, the average income of Black families would have increased much more rapidly than the average income of White families."

No one can say with real confidence just how this transformation got started, and no responsible person could say how it is to be reversed. But one fact is overwhelmingly clear: As long as the condition persists, the single most important federal program dealing with children is the Aid to Families with Dependent Children program, provided under Title IV of the Social Security Act. For this reason, the single most radical change the Reagan administration has proposed in existing social programs is to abolish Title IV and, under the rubric of the "new federalism," to turn the care of dependent children over to those states that give a damn—and to those states that don't.

One would have thought that a program firmly in place for nearly half a century would have acquired a certain acceptance, even an aura of necessity, and that the governors would not be so casual in offering to swap it for this or that program. But no. The life of the AFDC program remains as chancy and skimpy as the lives of the children it supports.

The question goes back to Franklin D. Roosevelt's second inaugural address, in which he saw "one-third of a nation ill-housed, ill-clad, ill-nourished." Whether Roosevelt did in fact "see" that condition in 1937, in the sense that there was a statistical base for his assertion, is problematic. Even so, I doubt he was much wrong; and surely he was rhetorically right.

Roosevelt's ratio has surfaced at various moments in the last four decades, carrying with it profound implications for both political economy and public policy. And it is now reflected in striking data which indicate that one-third of all children born in America during 1980 will likely spend some portion of time on welfare before reaching the age of 18. The notion that one-third of our nation is in need carries large implications as we conduct a national debate on the question of federalism and the role of the national government in caring for the poor.

In July 1963, I was serving as assistant secretary of labor for policy planning in the Kennedy administration. Apart from read-ing the morning papers, I didn't have much to do, as the Labor Department (and, by extension, the administration) had done all the policy planning needed for the moment. The problem was getting the policies enacted into law. President Kennedy's pro-gram was dead in the water. Unemployment had been a recurring theme of his early addresses to Congress, and he had been seeking legislation to create a general youth employment program. As time passed, however, the economy began to recover from the recession of 1959 to 1960, and, inevitably, White House concern with unemployment began to recede.

As my job was to advance the Department of Labor's agenda, especially when our early prominence in the administration's scheme of things seemed to be fading, I had been looking for new arguments for a national youth training and employment pro-gram. Yet something beyond normal institutional interest stirred me as well. I had begun to suspect that the early talk of unem-ployment had been a kind of shorthand, a code in which the administration addressed the problem of economic growth. There was another issue. We did not know much about it, but we knew that social conditions, especially in cities, were not as promising as the generally cheerful 1950s had led many to believe.

One morning, the *Washington Post* carried a brief notice that

General Lewis B. Hershey, director of the Selective Service System, had once again submitted his annual report to the president and Congress, and that once again roughly half of the young men summoned for examination had been rejected for failure to pass the mental examination, the physical examination, or both. General Hershey's ratio was just the sort of thing I had been looking for. Half the eighteen-year-olds in the country were not healthy enough, or quick enough, or both, to serve in the army. Surely this showed the need for a national response. The thought of using the Selective Service System as a national screening device came quickly to mind. To link social issues to military preparedness was, well, an idea.

A cabinet-level group was established, the president's Task Force on Manpower Conservation. An abundance of raw data was available. For two decades, almost half the U.S. population had passed through the Selective Service System's screen, yet almost no analysis of the data had been made. Robert S. McNamara, secretary of defense and an enthusiastic member of the task force, found the figures telling. I was made secretary of the group. After three months, our findings were issued on January 1, 1964, and presented that same week to the president by Secretary of Labor W. Willard Wirtz. The conclusions were succinct, embodied in a report called "One-Third of a Nation: A Report on Young Men Found Unqualified for Military Service":

> One-third of all young men in the nation turning 18 would be found unqualified if they were to be examined for induction into the armed forces. Of these, about one-half would be rejected for medical reasons. The remainder would fail through inability to qualify on the mental test. . . . A nationwide survey, carried out by the task force, of persons who have recently failed the mental test, clearly demonstrates that a major proportion of these young men are the products of poverty. They have inherited their situation from their parents, and unless the cycle is broken, they will almost surely transmit it to their children.

President Johnson was persuaded by the report and adopted the task force's recommendation (really McNamara's) that, starting immediately, all eighteen-year-old males would be tested and informed of their illnesses, if any, and learning disabilities, if any, regardless of whether they were to be drafted. At about this time, the president also established a Task Force on Poverty, with Sargent Shriver at its head. I became a member of that group as well. For historians, I propose that one of the reasons the president's "War on Poverty" seized the day was the powerful body of information assembled by the Task Force on Manpower Conservation. One-third of the nation's youth was not fit for service.

Soon Lyndon Johnson's speeches and informal remarks included references to our report. He commenced to talk about the "peckerwood boys" back in the hollows, with little education and fewer prospects. These were still years of peace in America. As late as 1966, I wrote an article arguing that the armed services were excluding the poor. They were.

Even so, the focus of "One-Third of a Nation" blurred as the War on Poverty unfolded. President Johnson was primarily responsible. The antipoverty program which we presented to the Cabinet in February 1964 included a massive jobs program to be financed by a tax increase on, among other things, tobacco. The president dismissed the proposal. We were, he said, cutting taxes that year, an election year.

Yet our research in the Labor Department continued. In early 1965, I prepared yet another report for President Johnson (the so-called Moynihan Report) describing the emergence of family instability among the poor of America. The report demonstrated that a powerful correlation between minority male unemployment rates and new welfare cases had persisted from 1948, when the statistics were first available, until the late 1950s, but that then the correlation began to break up and suddenly disappeared. Welfare dependency had continued on a steady, independent rise. Or so I thought.

Once again, President Johnson was compelled by the data and persuaded of their importance. Family stability was the theme of his address at Howard University on June 5, 1965, and it promised to remain a major concern of the administration. I had written to warn, and to convince the president of the need for a major initiative. He accepted the warning, as did some others. But the warning was strangely denied or ignored by many, among them those who might have been expected to be the most interested parties.

Despite the controversy, I continued to believe that family policy might be a way in which the national government could approach what seemed to be such large and intractable problems among our people.

During the welfare debates of the 1960s and 1970s, there were two general views about what kinds of reforms were needed. Starting with the administration of President Johnson and continuing to that of President Carter, the presidency tended to think in terms of a guaranteed income, that is, of transforming the original Social Security system into a full-fledged, universal system of income maintenance. The contrary view held that efforts by the state to support family life and encourage family stability unavoidably have the opposite effect. This was stated most intelligibly and compassionately by Nathan Glazer in a series of lectures given at City College of New York in 1970: "The Limits of Social Policy." He observed: "In its effort to deal with the breakdown of . . . traditional structures, . . . social policy tends to encourage their further weakening. There is, then, no sea of misery against which we are making headway. Our efforts to deal with distress themselves increase distress."

At the opposite pole of compassion—and intellect—there is what might be termed the "Welfare Cadillac" school, which disdains family policy and simply holds that much or most welfare is fraudulently obtained or unnecessarily dispensed, and that all would be better off if the program were severely restricted. Somewhere in between, commentators such as George Gilder hold that welfare programs are inherently and unavoidably damaging. In *Wealth and Poverty*, Gilder states: "The most serious fraud is committed not by the members of the welfare culture but by the creators of it, who conceal from the poor, both adults and children, the most fundamental realities of their lives: that to live well and escape poverty . . . the poor need most of all the spur of their poverty."

While the debate intensified between 1961 and 1981, Franklin D. Roosevelt's AFDC program remained the principal formula for child assistance. This is not to say that advocates of "liberal" change in the welfare system brought about no reforms in two decades of prominence. In 1973, a guaranteed income for the aged, blind, and disabled was established as the Supplementary Security Income program, the one part of the Family Assistance Plan (FAP) proposed by President Nixon in 1969 that was enacted. Moreover, the congressional debate over FAP led to the Earned Income Tax Credit, a limited negative income tax for the working poor. Through it all, AFDC has remained in place, the object of "tireless tinkering" but never of basic change. Until now, when it has been proposed for the boneyard.

What has changed is the incidence of welfare dependency. Expenditures for AFDC, expressed as a percentage of the total federal budget, have declined over the last decade. But the number of people dependent on welfare has grown. As I have stated already, one child in three born in 1980 will be on public assistance (AFDC) before the age of eighteen. That is more than four times the 1940 ratio. For New York City, it is now 50 percent.

Clearly, there has been a profound change in the nature of welfare dependency. The original Aid to Families with Dependent Children title of Roosevelt's 1935 Social Security Act (Title IV) was modeled on the widows' acts adopted by various state governments, especially in the Northeast, at the turn of the century. The typical recipient of benefits in the original Social Security Act was seen as the widow of a West Virginia coal miner— or rather, her children, for mothers as such received no direct allowance until much later, in 1950. Society's obligation was primal, almost biblical—to the fatherless child, the orphaned child.

By the 1980s, all this had changed. The welfare population today is associated to a substantial degree not with widowhood but with abandoned female-headed families, or those that never had a father at home in the first place, and these have in turn become the most salient aspect of poverty in America. In 1980, white female-headed families had a median income of $11,908, compared to $23,501 for white husband–wife families. Black female-headed families had a median income of $7,425, compared to $18,593 for black husband–wife families. There has been, then, a "feminization of poverty" that suggests a basis for broad agreement on welfare reform.

Unfortunately, the 1980s are likely to be taken up with skirmishes over "tightening up" existing income maintenance or even abolishing programs rather than with confronting the question of dependency. This need not necessarily be a bad thing. A loose welfare system offends elementary principles of public policy, particularly the requirement that public monies be dispensed with strict propriety. Welfare agencies should understand that they have the most exigent duty to uphold laws and regulations. The widespread charge of "welfare cheating" in the 1960s and 1970s has scarcely helped the condition of welfare recipients who, after all, are mostly children. The duty to care for such children extends to the responsibility to care for the reputation of programs that do so.

Nonetheless, stricter administration is not likely to change our present extraordinary situation. The only clear policy prescription that emerges from the almost half century of experience with the AFDC program is that the time has come to make it a truly national program, as was done with every other provision of the original Social Security Act of 1935. This is to say that the federal government should bear the cost of income maintenance for dependent children, much as it does for the dependent aged. The AFDC program and the attendant Medicaid program should be fully financed by the federal government, providing uniform benefits throughout the nation. The ratio of dependency (one-third of all children born in 1980) shows that the descent into welfare dependency is so chronic a condition that how we deal with it can legitimately be thought of as the question of how the nation will care for its children.

But the present administration is arguing for precisely the opposite direction in policy. Its proposal to return AFDC to the States, as part of some swap for Medicaid programs, is nonsense as federalism and bankrupt as policy. By getting "welfare" out of Washington, the administration hopes to obscure a problem, not to deal with one. There are now twenty titles included under the Social Security Act—Medicaid is Title XIX, AFDC is Title IV. These two serve almost identical populations and should be dealt with at the same level of government. Moreover, there is a fearsome differential in benefit levels among the States. The administration's solution runs the risk of encouraging helpless people in one state to flee to more generous states simply to receive needed benefits.

We surely can devise social institutions that deal with the vulnerability of the "nuclear family" in a postindustrial economy. We must provide ways to support dependent children without introducing incentives to child abandonment. We need to find institutions that generate norms and encourage self-reliance among adults. Most of all, perhaps, we need to recognize that the problem is growing.

I note two encouraging and potentially important developments. First, in December, the Rockefeller Foundation, spurred by its own survey of these questions and urged on by the former chairman of the U.S. Equal Employment Opportunity Commission, Eleanor Holmes Norton, announced a multimillion-dollar program to assist single minority-group women who head households. This action, on behalf of those the foundation described as "the most disadvantaged members of our society," represents a major shift in emphasis for one of our nation's most distinguished philanthropic institutions. Second, the National Urban League, responding to cuts in federal money for its poor black constituents, announced that it would give new priority to four issues. The first two are pregnancy among teenagers and the plight of poor households headed by women. The league's new priorities are all the more significant, considering that it opposed the Family Assistance Plan legislation in the 1970s. What the nation learns from the experiments of the Urban League and the Rockefeller Foundation, one hopes, will help guide the debates over national welfare policy in the years ahead. At the very least, they will help influence public perceptions of what is needed.

What is not needed, in any event, is a response to the dilemma of welfare dependency that repeals the social insurance programs of the New Deal. If we have learned anything from the story of Roosevelt's "one-third of a nation," it is that the perplexity is likely to persist. Just how and why this is so may now be beyond the analytic powers of social science, yet it cannot be kept beyond the realm of public policy.

The *New Republic*
June 9, 1982

Looking for a Kid?

---

*By mid-1982, things were grim enough for any who looked
to the national government for a measure of support on social
issues. There was a degree of organizational panic. Advocacy
organizations simply disappeared from the lobbies and corridors
on Capitol Hill. At times, it seemed the only organization that
had not been scared off or run off was the Junior League of
America, which was founded in New York at the turn of the
century to recruit young matrons to help in settlement houses.
It has never lost touch with this origin.*

*A new group was the North American Conference on Adopt-
able Children, meeting now at its eighth annual convention.*

In the 1930s, the Carnegie Corporation brought not one, but
two Myrdals to the United States to look into major social questions. Gunnar Myrdal was slow with his work and did not publish
his classic study of race relations, *American Dilemma*, until 1944.
As it happened, however, this was just as peace was coming to
the world and America could turn again to great domestic issues.
Alva Myrdal, however, delivered her manuscript *Nation and
Family* right on time and it was published in 1941, only to have
it disappear as war consumed our attention.

In 1967, I persuaded the MIT Press to publish a paperback-edition of *Nation and Family*, which I believe was noticed this time, and well received.

The theme of Alva Myrdal's work is that in the nature of modern industrial society, no government, however firm might be its wish, can avoid having policies that profoundly influence family relationships.

She suggested that an evolutionary process could be discerned, at least in her native Sweden. Social reform, she contended, can be thought of as passing through stages from a paternalistic era, when safeguarding against inequalities through the pooling of risks is enough, to what she called a social democratic era, but which we could probably prefer to think of as postindustrial, when the prevention of ills is attempted.

Surely this sequence can be seen in the field of public health, where the United States has long set a standard for the world.

It can be seen, withal less successfully, in the way we have tried to deal with unemployment; first with relief projects of one kind or another in the nineteenth century; next with unemployment insurance dating from the Social Security Act of 1935; finally with the efforts of modern economics to maintain high levels of employment.

We can even see, if still more faintly, the development of such a sequence in another field of social policy, that of children without families, or without families that can care for them.

We are right, I think, to see this as a modern problem; a problem of cities, a feature of societies made up, in Emile Durkheim's phrase, of a dust of individuals.

In the nineteenth century, there was the orphanage. An institution that endured—as any of you who have the fortune to see *Annie* will know—and indeed continues, for it serves as a necessary last resort. Then there came foster care, as part of Title IV of the Social Security Act of 1935. Last, there was the Child Welfare and Adoption Assistance Act of 1980, which declared a national policy of encouraging and facilitating adoption for all children without families.

I was one of the managers of the legislation. On the date it passed, I emphasized that it was a "limited bill," that we would give the program five years to see if its combination of incentives and disincentives would work; but if we're successful, I said, it would mark a "historic shift."

The problem, of course, is that children get lost in foster care. Even in the most loving and caring foster homes. The National Study of Social Services to Children and Their Families, done in 1978, found that a quarter of all children in foster care had been in three or more foster family homes. As they get lost, and get older, adoption becomes an ever more distant prospect.

And, of course, there are so many such children. The national study estimated half a million in 1977—three times the number in 1951, the last general survey.

Recent years in the United States have not been especially productive in areas of social legislation. It would reasonably be contended, for example, that the Child Welfare and Adoption Assistance Act was the only major piece of social legislation adopted under the Carter administration. The more notable, then, that it was legislation concerning family.

And yet more notable is the fact that almost the first act of the present administration was to propose to repeal it.

In the spring of 1981, the administration proposed to lump adoption assistance in with a general social services block grant. Funds, overall, were to be reduced by a quarter. Far more important, however, the provisions were to be stricken from the Social Security Act. The child without family was no longer to be entitled to some measure of support from the national government. It would be an option of the States.

I am ranking member of the Subcommittee on Social Security. I fought the proposal there: a losing battle, brightened only by the utterly unintimidated defense of the program by the Junior League of America.

The measure came to the floor of the Senate on June 23,

1981. Again, we lost, and again few seemed to notice or care. "I am sorry to say that the lobbies are empty today, the lobbies are empty," I remarked. "The distinguished visitors' gallery has no distinguished visitors. There are but few members in the press gallery. The children are not here. They cannot get here. They have not sent us telegrams. They have no lawyers representing them." The Senate thereupon voted 52 to 46 to abolish rights of citizens so imprudent as not to have lobbyists; worse, not to make campaign contributions.

In the end, we were able in the House–Senate conference to preserve the act, but at a reduced level of funding.

But now the issue recurs as part of the so-called New Federalism, which would abolish Title IV of the Social Security Act altogether.

The only thing more astonishing than this proposal is the absence of any significant public outcry.

The problem of dependency grows ever greater. Here in New York State, during the 1970s, the number of children in poverty increased by 158,871. At the end of the decade, there were 891,842 poor children in New York—surely the largest number in our history.

The same would be true of children in foster care.

As of 1977, 90 percent of these children, in foster care and AFDC homes, were minority children. To what degree have programs designed to ease dependency ended by encouraging it? I cannot say. We owe it to one another to be honest and open on this point.

But we also owe the children something.

It is one thing to tell a twenty-five-year-old adult to be self-supporting. It is another thing to tell that to a twenty-five-week-old child.

If they are to be helped, we all must try to help them. They may be children but they have rights, rights enshrined in the Social Security Act and not to be ripped out of that act.

A simple statistic will tell all you need to know about what is happening in Washington. Last year, fiscal 1981, outlays for means-tested entitlement programs represented about 18 percent of total benefit payments to individuals by the federal government. But these programs accounted for 40 percent of the total reductions in benefit programs.

New York, New York
August 27, 1982

Address to the
Sheet Metal Workers'
International Association

———————

I joined the United Steel Workers in 1943, at age 16, and the labor movement is still to me, well, a labor movement. Here is a typical labor talk of 1982, in the midst of the worst recession—a depression really—since the 1930s.

How much of this was the fault of the Reagan administration? I tend more to look to the Federal Reserve. In the spring of 1982, Robert J. Shapiro of my staff spotted the money supply going negative. A recession was inevitable and it came. Senators Sasser and Riegle joined me in a Budget Committee Resolution asking what the hell was going on. The Republicans would not take our language, but inserted their equivalent in the final Budget Resolution. Too late.

Inflation, of course, would be broken, and the administration would claim credit for that. And why not? Yet the administration gave no discernible thought to the long-term impact on basic industry of the hugely overvalued dollar which fiscal policy now brought about.

Steel production is at 42 percent of capacity. You have to go back to 1935 to find the steel industry at that low level, because we are, in fact, in the first depression in a half century.

The only reason we do not feel the impact is that in the last depression, a series of intelligent, competitive legislative acts provided a buffer for the American people against that experience should it ever happen again. Unemployment insurance, Social Security, bank-deposit insurance, a whole sequence of legislation as no time since has been keeping us from an encounter with the worst economic crash in the postwar experience of the American people.

And the thing we have to get into our heads is that this was a man-made depression, and it was made right here in the United States. You can't blame OPEC, and you can't blame the Russians, and you can't blame the weather. You got to blame that riverboat gamble which was made with our lives and this nation's economy and which lost.

And it lost in the context of two things. We had last year the most expansionary fiscal policy in the nation's history, the largest deficit in the nation's history, which is, by definition, an expansionary policy.

And simultaneously, we've had the tightest monetary policy in twenty years and the highest real interest rates in our history.

I think the side of the economic equation that has been really not addressed has been this whole custom of national monetary policy and what it does to the lives of the American people.

In 1981, in an effort to offset the impact of the deficits, the Federal Reserve kept the growth of money supply 2.3 percent, and at some point it was down below—it was a negative growth with the consequences that there was no alternative but the huge falling-off of investment, huge falling-off of production work all over the economy. They let interest rates go to the highest levels, the real interest rates, as they're called, which is the nominal rate minus inflation rate, the highest levels in the history of the United States economy.

This was not just the highest in six months or the highest in eighteen years—the highest in history. Real interest rates in 1981 were above 11 percent at some point.

Now, there is no way you can—I mean, the people who invested in Pizzaro's expedition in Peru may have made 11 percent on their return, on their investment, but you can't do that in a steel mill, and you can't do that with an office building. It makes any real investment impossible.

And so investment in the corporations began to get more and more difficult. Last week, we had more bankruptcies in the United States than any week since 1932.

Now this is not fooling around. If we don't respond to this, we have the possibility of going over the cliff into an absolute disaster.

I would say, as much as any reputation I would have in labor statistics is worth, we will see the unemployment rate go past 10 percent before this year is out. We're at 9.8 percent now.

We have 10.5 million people out of work; but much more important, we have—I mean in terms of working on the system, you have—got a corporate structure in America which is more and more illiquid and is verging on bankruptcies all through the Fortune 1000, and you have a banking system that is just as precarious.

Last week, in a perfectly, thoroughly responsible action, the Treasury Department found $2 billion to keep the Mexican economy from collapsing; and that was in our national interest; it was certainly in the interest of the Mexicans. There's no interest anybody in the United States has in the collapse of the economy anywhere in this hemisphere; but why did we do it on three days' warning, you might even say?

Because the number of American banks that would have collapsed with the Mexican economy was—even to this point, is—not understood.

Some of the major banks of the United States would have been brought down had that $2 billion not been brought forth in seventy-two hours.

Now this—and one could go on with the catalog of dangers. The important point is that these are man-made events. These things—they're not the weather; and it's not the workings of events in other parts of the world which are beyond our control. It is the result of something very near to quackery in economics.

———

The Federal Reserve has moved its increase of money supply back up to the high rates, the high range of its past, which is 5.5 percent.

Whether they will go beyond that, we begin to doubt, because it has still not heard from the administration. The absolute unwillingness to send this signal from the administration led to an event this spring in the Congress that wasn't much noticed but I think should be recorded. In April, Senators Sasser and Riegle and I introduced in the Budget Committee a sense of the Congress's resolution that the monetary policy of the Federal Reserve Board must be changed and interest rates must be brought down and money supply must be increased. Before June was out, for the first time in the seventy-year history of the Federal Reserve system, Congress adopted a law . . . that said: "Bring interest rates down; move money supply up."

If it doesn't, we could move out of the present situation, which is unacceptable, into one that is absolutely intolerable; and it doesn't have to happen. You don't have to sit down there and say it's—"Just give our program a chance. Give our policy a chance."

We have given that policy a chance, and we brought the worst economic collapse in fifty years. What more do you need to know in the way of evidence?

And one of the great things that inhibits any response is that in the last election, a body of opinion and a group of men and women came to power in Washington fundamentally opposed to the use of government as an instrument of national policy and unwilling to use it in emergencies, as can be done and needs to be done, and unable to see that there is no alternative to government.

Just because you don't know what your monetary policy is doing doesn't mean you don't have a monetary policy which is doing something.

It was rather extraordinary how in seventy-two hours the Treasury could find $2 billion to soar up the Mexican peso; but in eighteen months, we've let the American economy drop to

59-percent capacity production, let unemployment go up to the highest level since 1939, let the rate of our basic industries like steel drop to the bottom of the depression.

They talk about waste, fraud, and abuse. Is there any greater waste than the best steelworkers in the world idle, with the best steelmaking facilities in the world down, automobile industry down, glass, rubber, the basic industries of the country, not just in a business cycle but actually on the edge of disappearing as part of the American economy itself?

Now what is that doing with our future? What is that doing with our abilities? . . . We've got to put Americans back to work. We've got to get on with the things that need doing.

We have got, for example, to start rebuilding the infrastructure of the American economy. One of the most striking things you might find is that in the period 1967 to 1977, in constant dollars, the investment in roads, sewers, water, and basic power-generating systems of the country declined 40 percent.

We have been using up the public capital of the United States, not maintaining it, not adding to it, but using it up and running it down.

Surely the first order of business of the 1980s should be reversing that trend, getting us back into the situation where the public sector, without which you can't have a private sector, is moving again; and that won't happen until you have a change in the attitude in Washington; and it won't happen until we realize once again that we are one nation and one people and we have one set of interests.

New York, New York
September 1, 1982

World Trade and
World Peace

Going around the state in 1982, I met the issue of trade everywhere, but most of all in the small industrial cities. I was once asked to speak at a Steel Workers' hall in a lake town southwest of Buffalo. They were glad I was able to come, glad when I began my remarks, but visibly more glad about my finishing them. For the real event of the Saturday afternoon was the ritual murder of a Volkswagen. No, that's not the right term. The ceremonial murder. It was as if the Iroquois had got hold of a Jesuit fresh out of Fort Niagara. The women got first crack, slowly circling the hapless beetle purchased from some departing college student. First little taps and pinches. Then harder blows. Much noise. Then the braves moved in with sledgehammers. Finally a backhoe beat the alien intruder into a meaningless mass of undifferentiated metal.

I wrote my final newsletter of the year on the subject of trade, and gave this somewhat more detailed talk to Gilbert Kaplan's annual International Roundtable. Again the message: What kind of business-oriented administration allows its businesses to disappear? Note Martin Feldstein's forecast of a trade deficit that "could reach $75 billion in 1983." It reached twice that in 1986.

As with many of my generation following the Second World War, and thanks to the seemingly endless indulgence of the Veterans Administration, I prepared myself for what I hoped would be a career in international affairs. By this I intended, *albeit* a bit vaguely, either working in that branch of my own government, or else in one of the many international organizations that came into being in the war's aftermath.

Thus it was that my education involved considerable study of the many new charters of that time—of the United Nations, of a proposed new international trade organization and its sub-sidiary, the General Agreement on Tariffs and Trade (GATT), of the World Court, UNESCO, and suchlike. As a graduate student, I learned their principles much as undergraduates learn the prin-ciples of the American Constitution. These new worldwide ar-rangements were going to matter much in our future, and they offered much hope.

As with many, my life took unexpected directions, and I became for a time almost exclusively involved with state gov-ernment, or with the domestic side of national government, or with teaching same.

It might have seemed that my education had pretty much gone to waste. I believe I myself thought so. Then in 1962, as assistant secretary of labor, I was sent off to Geneva as part of a three-man delegation sent to negotiate the long-term cotton tex-tile agreement. All of a sudden I was caught up with international matters, but with a wholly unexpected mission.

In brief, President Kennedy had proposed a new round of negotiations to reduce tariffs. Congressional approval was nec-essary, but southern delegations balked. The Carolinas and Vir-ginia, in particular, were beginning to feel the impact of textile imports from, generally speaking, Asian countries. They would not agree to any new tariff cuts unless these nations agreed to limit the volume of exports to the United States.

The trade unions in the garment industry in New York joined in this demand. Their markets were being flooded with apparel from much the same countries. They, too, wanted quotas. Quo-tas? The very concept was an abomination to the persons who had been directing American trade policy for a generation. I use the word "abomination" with care. These were persons of passionate conviction, and they were not wrong to be.

They recalled the consequences of the Smoot–Hawley Tariff Act of 1932, when President Hoover and Congress agreed to huge and wholesale tariff increases. Our trading partners had promptly responded in kind, and in two years' time, American imports fell by two-thirds. So did American exports. All international trade plunged 60 percent, and the world settled into a deepening depression. As things got worse, totalitarianism spread. And war came.

This is the heart of it: Our postwar foreign trade policies were deeply influenced by the conviction that the prewar tariff policies had helped bring about that war. This was a matter that stirred passions and, to repeat, rightly so.

American foreign policy formed during World War II put great stake in creating organizations through which nations collectively could avoid, or at least suppress, the tendencies that had led to that vast catastrophe. The United Nations, of course, and its economic counterpart, the International Trade Organization (ITO), directed particularly against the proliferation of tariffs and quotas.

The ITO never made it through Congress. But the major trading nations of the West did agree to one part of its charter, a General Agreement on Tariffs and Trade—the GATT. The GATT had no organization as such—just a brilliant British civil servant, Eric Wyndham White, who maintained a small villa outside Geneva with the help of three or four attractive French secretaries, and served as GATT's executive secretary. (White died recently, penniless. The man as much responsible as any for three decades of unparalleled world prosperity failed to note that—such was the informality of the GATT arrangements—no provision had been made to provide him a pension.)

For the longest while, GATT seemed to work wonderfully well. The general level of tariffs kept going down. In 1934, the average U.S. tariff rate reached 47 percent. By the opening of the

1962 Kennedy round of negotiations, when I went off to negotiate in Geneva, it had dropped to 12 percent. Today the average U.S. tariff rate is almost half that, 6 percent.

A key device was the most-favored-nation principle, under which every original GATT member automatically received the lowest tariff rate any member had negotiated with any other member. Prior to this, France might charge one tariff rate on Argentine beef, another on American beef, and yet another on Australian beef.

World trade flourished. "Three decades of the greatest growth in history," Leonard Silk called it recently. The industrial world was never so prosperous. Societies regained stability, and relations between industrial nations were never so amicable.

Trouble began as the character of the GATT membership changed, not unlike the change at the United Nations. The UN Charter, I learned as a graduate student, assumed that its members' governments were democratic, or were at least committed to collective security and opposed to the use of force in international affairs, which is to say, much like the United States.

Somewhat later, I would serve as our ambassador to the United Nations. It was by then quite obvious that most members of the UN could not possibly support the democratic principles of its charter, for they were themselves profoundly undemocratic or antidemocratic. Once you accepted this, or so it seemed to me, it was not hard to figure out how to handle yourself in the United Nations. You assumed you were in enemy territory. Which is to say, you saw the world as it was.

In much this way, GATT too had changed. GATT had assumed that its members had something like free economies, in which the overwhelming proportion of commercial decisions was in private hands. Government previously had interfered through tariffs and quotas. If these could be substantially eliminated, the world would have free trade—and more trade.

The twenty-three original members of GATT had basically fit this description. But possibly because GATT has never had much of a formal organization, the change in the character of its members has been less noticed. Today GATT is a world trade organization with eighty-seven members, including four of the Soviet Bloc. And the political economy of the world has changed.

Of GATT's industrialized members, the United States almost alone still subscribes to the economic tenets of 1947 which underlay GATT's formation. In Japan, the powerful Ministry of International Trade and Industry formulates industrial as well as trade policy and facilitates corporate modernization, investment, and technological decisions in accordance with these policies. France has moved from the state-planning principles of the Gaullists' *dirigisme*, embodied in the *Commissariat Général Du Plan*, to the state-directed economics of the current socialist government.

The United States has continued to provide only a minimum of government subsidy for export products—and to resist state direction or planning of matters concerning international trade.

Just as it took us such a long time to recognize—and accept—that the UN had changed, so we were reluctant to recognize that the conditions for world trade have changed.

We persist in speaking as we have for a half century. We conjure up images of a world in free trade, failing to notice that the kind of economies assumed for such trade have, for the most part, passed from the scene.

Many of you will have heard President Reagan's radio address on November 20, entitled "International Free Trade." This was just prior to the opening of the latest GATT ministerial meeting in Geneva. The president said:

> We are reminding our trading partners that preserving individual freedom and restoring prosperity also requires free and fair trade in the marketplace. The United States took the lead after World War II in creating an international trading and financial system that limited governments' ability to disrupt free trade across borders. We did this because history had taught us an important lesson: Free trade serves the cause of world peace.

When governments get too involved in trade, economic costs increase and political disputes multiply. Peace is threatened. In the 1930s, the world experienced an ugly specter—protectionism and trade wars and, eventually, real wars and unprecedented suffering and loss of life.

There are some who seem to believe that we should run up the American flag in defense of our markets. They would embrace protectionism again and insulate our markets from world competition. Well, the last time the United States tried that, there was enormous economic distress in the world. World trade fell by 60 percent, and young Americans soon followed the American flag into World War II.

Cordell Hull could not have said it more eloquently.

The president had reason to be hopeful. It was he, at his first "economic summit" in Ottawa in the summer of 1981, who proposed the GATT conference.

Yet the conference was a near total failure. At the very outset, Michel Jobert, the French foreign trade minister, denounced the United States for "dogmatic liberalism." Free trade, of course, was a profound article of faith with the early-nineteenth-century school of British economists known as liberals (and in their view an article deeply associated with world peace). Alas, the French never forget.

Now, Ronald Reagan has been denounced for much in his career, but rarely for "dogmatic liberalism." But then, to repeat, the world increasingly sees these matters differently. Free trade was, in ways, the economic doctrine of the British and American *imperium*. Which is not to say it was wrong—I happen to believe it to have been profoundly correct and much associated with the political fallout of free markets of which Michael Novak has written so convincingly.

Even so, what do the French care of such matters? (Colbert, chief minister to Louis XIV, founded the state Royal Factory of

Mirror Glass in 1665. Later it was transferred to private owner-
ship as the Saint-Gobain Compagnie and grew to be a major
producer of building materials. Now Mitterand has renational-
ized it. *Plus ça change.*) For that matter, what do the Spanish
care? At yesterday's signing of the Law of the Sea Conference in
Jamaica, the United Nations secretary general, that good man
Javier Pérez de Cuéllar, spoke with ill-disguised disappointment
at the failure of the United States to sign the treaty, urging countries to "reject any mythology in their decision making." To wit,
the mythology of free enterprise. As the *New York Times* reported,

> Many envoys here attribute the American rejection to an
> ideological adherence to free enterprise.

At the close of the GATT meeting, Hobart Rowen of the
Washington Post described the results as "a bitter defeat for free
trade." The *Wall Street Journal* wrote that the GATT "just barely
survived the meeting." And Ambassador Brock, our distinguished
trade representative and a man respected throughout the U.S.
government, returned and told the Senate Finance Committee
that

> we came so close to a disaster that maybe the biggest achieve-
> ment we had was in keeping the system in some form intact.

It was as bad as that.

And why? Because most of the nations in the world just don't
subscribe to GATT's principles. They have political economies.

Now let me take you through a set of troubling and unar-
guable propositions.

There is a rule: Organizations in conflict become like one
another. Think of football teams, of electronics manufacturers,

of navies. World trade is a form of conflict. And as world trade has become more and more directed, or even conducted, by governments, the United States has begun to respond in kind. And will continue to do so.

A few months ago, our International Trade Commission found that several European nations were providing huge subsidies for steel exports to the United States. Last winter, Europeans were selling carbon steel in the United States at $500 a ton, with a government subsidy of $130 a ton.

The GATT already provides that when export subsidies exceed a certain limit, the receiving country can offset the subsidies by countervailing duties.

What did our government actually do? It did what we insist on not doing. Instead of countervailing duties, we negotiated quota agreements with the European governments. That, as I remarked earlier, is an abomination according to the trade doctrine espoused by the president with such eloquence and sincerity just a few days later.

But then how is the president otherwise spending his time? Well, in considerable measure, negotiating the sale of wheat to the Soviet Union, huge government loans to Brazil and Mexico, a complex set of tariff preferences for preferred islands in the Caribbean.

And what is the Congress doing? This week the House of Representatives agreed to bar the use of foreign-produced cement, steel, and manufactured products in projects sponsored under the current road-construction-jobs legislation.

Not exactly what the founders of the GATT had in mind.

What are the alternatives? We can continue to slide towards protectionism, sideways as it were, moving from one industry to another, responding to some bit of damage after-the-fact, with policies that ultimately bring more damage. And watch relations deteriorate between governments forced to oversee sinking economies, ending with misery all around and the erosion of the Western alliance.

Behind the exhilarating rhetoric of protectionism, these are the real consequences.

Or, we can recognize that the world has changed and organize ourselves to make the most of present-day realities. Part of that reality is that our government must play a greater role in trade. We may accept this only reluctantly, insisting it's not so. But accept it we must, because it *is* so.

A greater government role, remember, is the *alternative* to protectionism that the current stage of the world's political economy offers. And an important element arises from the recognition that protectionism is a loser's response to competition. First, we must look long and hard at the conditions for our economy's competitiveness in world markets. And the government's chief part in all this is its overarching fiscal and monetary policies.

Need I tell you that our products cannot be competitive on the world market if our government follows a macroeconomic program that cannot protect the economy from rampant inflation? Nor can we continue to pursue a program that keeps real interest rates at their highest sustained levels in our history. Both erode capital formation and productivity, essential elements— absolutely crucial—for a competitive economy. And it is the failures of macroeconomic policy, both here and abroad, that have helped trigger the worldwide contraction, which in turn is creating mass constituencies for protectionism.

Second, we must insist on the remedies against unfair trade practices provided for in the GATT agreement. Our government hasn't done so, in large part because there is no one organization within our national government which is responsible. Trade responsibilities are spread all over—among the State Department, the Treasury Department, the Commerce Department, the Export-Import Bank, the International Trade Commission, the Office of the U.S. Trade Representative.

This dispersion is not happenstance. The modern era of reciprocal trade agreements, which led to the GATT, was born in the State Department, under the leadership of Cordell Hull. The State Department was the appropriate place then, because the

United States had, or at least acknowledged, few interests abroad except trade.

But America's world responsibilities in the postwar years have changed our State Department in fundamental ways. Not the least of these changes has been its consistent incapacity to insist on its own principles—such as free trade—when it finds any particular nation violating them. And this has been especially true when the violator is an ally. From the State Department's view, some larger geopolitical issue is always at stake, not to be jeopardized by some trade squabble.

The department has not been wrong, but a generation of this has brought us growing protectionism among these allies and trade deficits at home which have averaged more than $30 billion annually over the last five years. This trade deficit, in the view of the president's chief economic adviser, Martin Feldstein, could reach $75 billion in 1983.

We cannot go on in this manner. Fully 15 percent of the products manufactured in our economy, produced by some 5 million American workers, are export-related. The entire world's exports and imports each amount to more than $2 trillion annually, and the United States accounts for more than 10 percent of those totals.

We must organize ourselves. I propose we transform the Commerce Department into a Department of International Trade and Commerce. In its early years, the Commerce Department was enormously useful in helping to create a truly national economy within the United States, out of the regional economies that grew up in the first half of the nineteenth century. That work is done, and in truth, the department doesn't have much to do anymore. It hasn't since Herbert Hoover was secretary under President Coolidge.

So, let it turn to the challenge of our own time, the role our national economy can play in a competitive world. In fact, the department seems to want to do just that. If you open up the *U.S. Government Manual*, its description of the department begins as follows:

The Department of Commerce encourages, serves, and promotes the nation's international trade. . . .

Let it then begin to do so, by consolidating the various related responsibilities strewn across the government.

Palm Beach, Florida
December 11, 1982

1982 was an election year. I carried New York with 66 percent of the vote, and a margin of 1,535,385 voters, a midterm record for the Senate.

Events did this. Argument may have helped.

1983

———

Social Security Secured

The Social Security issue was resolved in twelve days in January 1983. The sequence began January 3 in the course of the opening ceremonies of the new Congress. A few weeks earlier, a National Commission on Social Security Reform had ended a year's work without agreement but not without consequence. A number of Republicans who had been content with the view that the system was on the verge of collapse realized this was not at all the case. Now, January 3, Bob Dole published an op ed article in the **Washington** Post contending that the Republican congressional leadership was getting along just fine with the Republican president. There was this passage.

> Social Security is a case in point. With 116 million workers supporting it and 36 million beneficiaries relying on it, Social Security overwhelms every other domestic priority. Through a combination of relatively modest steps, including some acceleration of already scheduled taxes and some reduction in the rate of future benefit increases, the system can be saved. When it is, much of the credit, rightfully, will belong to this president and his party.

If this were so, why not take these "relatively modest steps"? I went over to talk with Dole. Agreement was reached at Blair

House about 9:30 in the evening of January 15, and just as promptly enacted. I sent out a newsletter.

"The Sun Rises in the West"
That is how the *Los Angeles Times* described the prospect that a bipartisan, comprehensive agreement on Social Security could be reached. An editorial of March 27 began:

> Only weeks ago, the chances of Congress's reforming Social Security in ways both practical and fair seemed about as good as those of the sun's rising in the west.

And yet it happened. In January 1983, after a year's deliberation, the President's Commission on Social Security Reform came up with a set of proposals which the *Washington Post* described as being "as close to absolute fairness as any Social Security revision can ever be." Congress adopted the proposals substantially intact, and the president signed the bill on April 20, 1983.

The signing ceremony took place on the South Lawn of the White House in the presence of twelve of us who were among those involved. I tend to think we were chosen because there are twelve letters in the president's name, and he decided to sign it one letter at a time and give each of the party one of the pens.

Among those present were House Speaker Thomas P. "Tip" O'Neill, Jr., and Republican Majority Leader of the Senate Howard H. Baker, Jr. In that Social Security came to this nation during the presidency of Franklin D. Roosevelt, I note with pride that of the twelve persons present on the platform, three were New Yorkers. Your senator; Alan Greenspan, chairman of the president's commission; and the distinguished ranking member of the House Committee on Ways and Means, Barber B. Conable, Jr., of Alexander in Genesee County. Representative Conable and I were also members of the commission.

Inasmuch as our fellow member, Senator Robert Dole, has

spoken of the event, it is not perhaps unbecoming to describe what happened in reaching this moment.

On January 3, 1983, in the Senate chamber, the newly elected and reelected senators were sworn in. Senator Dole happened to be present. I went over to him and said: "Are we going to let the commission fail?" For it *had* failed. At its last meeting in December 1982, the commission could reach no agreement, and no further meeting was scheduled. The prospect was one of protracted, increasingly embittered crisis.

Senator Dole asked if I could meet with him the next day. I did, with Robert Ball, former Social Security commissioner. The following afternoon, we asked Barber Conable to join us. He probably knows more about Social Security than any member of the Congress, and surely cares about it as only those who have mastered a subject can care.

After several hours' talk, Dole excused himself for a moment. He returned to ask if we could all be at the home of Jim Baker, the White House chief of staff, at 5:30 P.M. White House cars were summoned and we were off. Toward the end of that first meeting, the outcome was in some sense settled. Someone said: "What this comes down to is whether we can govern." And we can, you know. Americans are pretty good at governing.

The details of the Social Security legislation have been widely published and I will only summarize them. But there is one little-known fact about the combined Old Age and Survivors Fund and the Disability Fund. They are short just now, but they will begin to grow rapidly in just a few years. I asked the actuaries at the Social Security Administration when would be the first year the funds decline after going into surplus, and, given their projection of income under the new law, how much would be in the funds at that time. The answer came back: year 2021, surplus $12.1 trillion. I don't ask you to believe this. But it is a change from apocalypse in the morning.

That is what we began to hear as the administration took office two and one-half years ago. "The most devastating bankruptcy in history," if I recall David Stockman's phrase, was about to happen. The whole arrangement, faulted from the first, was now about, finally, to fail.

These were the views of extreme conservatives who really had just never accepted the legitimacy of government-sponsored social insurance. President Eisenhower did, adding disability insurance benefits to the program. President Nixon did, adding supplemental security benefits for the aged and blind. But some didn't. In all truth, Ronald Reagan didn't.

Now he does. Now he has a commitment to Social Security as strong as any a president has ever made. It cannot have come easily to him, and I salute *him* for it. But it was some two years!

Washington, D.C.
May 16, 1983

It is not clear just how much of the details of the agreement the White House negotiators provided the president. It was not a simple affair. But the president now turned completely around on the subject. On April 25, he wrote me, and, I assume, the other negotiators:

> *This law demonstrates for all time our Nation's ironclad commitment to Social Security. It assures the elderly that America will always keep the promises made in troubled times a half of a century ago. It assures those who are still working that they, too, have a pact with the future and that they will receive their fair share of benefits when they retire.*
>
> *This compromise proves that bipartisanship can resolve serious national problems. It is a clear and dramatic demonstration of how effectively our system works when men and women join together for the common good. The Social Security Amendments of 1983 are a monument to the spirit of compassion and commitment that unites us as a people.*

With Social Security behind him, or rather him behind Social Security, and the recession easing, there was nothing now to prevent the reelection of Ronald Reagan. On November 1, 1984, six days before the election, with Republican victory certain, George Will told a business audience in New York that if Democrats had decided to create a Social Security crisis—adding that we could easily have done so—Ronald Reagan could not have hoped to be reelected.

This never occurred to us. Which is to say, it never occurred to us to create a crisis. (It would have been easy enough to make it appear that "The most devastating bankruptcy in history" had in fact occurred and to blame it on the administration, claiming, not entirely without justice, that this is what "they" wanted.) In that sense Democrats were, and remain, a party of government. That is the sense in which the Republicans of 1981 were not. They were learning—Stockman was a master of detail in our round-the-clock meetings—but could never undo the general fiscal crisis they had created in those first crazed months.

The latest estimate of the chief actuary shows the trust funds reaching $12.8 trillion before declining in 2033, a decade later than the agreement envisaged.

Address to the
American Newspaper
Publishers' Association

Thank heaven for one group that takes the Constitution seriously. I don't know that I ever had as much success with the theme of "movement conservatives" as radicals, but these remarks were well received.

My grandfather once said of a man of whom he did not wholly approve that he had "the soul of a butler."

I would like to think there are none such here. Certainly Harold Medina thought so. In defending the First Amendment he told you, "Fight like tigers." But when it comes to defending principles of press freedom, more than great heart is required.

Vigilance is required. A matter our ancestors understood perhaps better than we.

Let me speak to some particulars.

It is something of a routine to decry the insensitivity of successive administrations to issues of freedom of information and freedom of the press. Yet one senses that such insensitivity is growing, much as government grows. It is not irony, I fear, but a general direction of history that we observe in the present administration. It has increased the size of government to unprecedented levels—this coming year, federal outlays will be 25.1

percent of GNP—and it has simultaneously increased pressures on the press.

Consider the Agent Identities Protection Act of 1982. I am vice chairman of the Select Committee on Intelligence. I would wish it understood that the time came when we had to legislate on this subject. Even so, we did not have to violate the Constitution. But when we did legislate, that is exactly what we did do.

One section of the bill makes it a crime to identify a covert agent even if the identity were discovered from publicly available information and even if the person disclosing the information had not the least desire to harm the national interest. Section 601(c) of the National Security Act now provides for the imposition of criminal sanction on a person who discloses the agent's identity.

> In the course of a pattern of activities intended to identify and expose covert agents and with *reason to believe* that such activities would impair or impede the foreign intelligence activities of the United States . . . [My emphasis].

By a vote of 55 to 39, the Senate substituted this language for similar language adopted by the Judiciary Committee which included the crucial distinction that such disclosure had to be done with

> *intent* to impair or impede the foreign intelligence activities of the United States by the fact of such identification and exposure. [My emphasis.]

The final vote on June 10, 1982, was 81 to 4. Four senators voted no, one was paired against. Five senators in all.

Thus, at the urging of the administration, "reason to believe" was made a crime—a standard which is at home in the civil law of negligence, but hardly a basis for sending an editor to jail.

Philip L. Kurland of the University of Chicago Law School

has called this law the "clearest violation of the First Amendment attempted by Congress in this era." I agree, and so stated repeatedly on the floor of the Senate.

Henceforth, a newspaper must proceed at the peril of prosecution if it publishes the name of a covert agent in a news story intended to inform the public and *not* to harm U.S. intelligence operations. The risk that proceeds from the uncertainty of the statutory language is the very essence of a "chilling effect." Has any newspaper publisher challenged it in court? I believe not. I trust this reflects only a sound judgment to let the government make the first move—a step we hope will never be taken. But I do implore you *not* to avoid this risk by imposing self-censorship where none is warranted.

More disturbing yet was the legislation advanced in the summer of 1982 by the senior senator from North Carolina* to deny the Supreme Court jurisdiction over any case relating to voluntary prayer in public schools and public buildings.

Now, clearly, if the Supreme Court can be denied jurisdiction in one aspect of the First Amendment, it can be denied jurisdiction in any aspect. The First Amendment guarantees that Congress shall make no law "respecting the establishment of religion . . . or abridging the freedom of speech, or of the press. . . ."

When the court-stripping bill (the Helms measure) came to the floor, we did not have the votes to defeat it. And so on August 16 last year, four of us, lead by Senators Weicker and Packwood, commenced to filibuster. On September 21, a petition to invoke cloture was rejected 50 to 39. On September 21, a petition to invoke cloture was rejected 53 to 47. On September 22, a petition to invoke cloture was rejected 54 to 46. They were gaining on us. Sixty votes, of course, were needed. But then on the next motion, their majority dropped off by one vote to fifty-three. An election was coming, the season was advancing, and so the proponents gave up. The bill was recommitted. But note: It was never defeated. There was always a majority for it. This despite

---

* Representative Jesse Helms (R).

the fact that it would have profoundly shaken the balance of powers of the American system of government, and in the face of a courageous statement by Attorney General William French Smith, that

> Congress may not, however, consistent with the Constitution, make "exceptions" to Supreme Court jurisdiction which would intrude upon the core functions of the Supreme Court as an independent and equal branch in our system of separation of powers.

It was a close call. And again may I ask, how well was it reported? How *much* was it reported? In my judgment, very little. In the aftermath, Bill Petersen of the *Washington Post* wrote a good analysis:

> The debate was not one of Republicans versus Democrats or Liberals versus Conservatives so much as the moderate center standing up for the Constitution against "the radical right."

But I repeat: How much was it reported?

Now to more recent events. On March 11, 1983, the president issued a directive which requires all government employees with access to classified information of any sort to sign standardized nondisclosure agreements subject to judicial enforcement as a precondition to their access. The directive also authorizes polygraph tests of such employees with respect to suspected leaks. In testimony before joint hearings of the House Judiciary Subcommittee on Civil and Constitutional Rights and the Post Office and Civil Service Subcommittee on Civil Service, Mr. Floyd Abrams, the distinguished authority on press freedom, sought, as he put it, to put the directive in historical context. He said:

> It is not difficult to generalize about these policies. They are unique in recent history. They are coherent, consistent,

and (unlike those of some recent administrations) not a bit schizophrenic. They are also consistently at odds with the notion that widespread dissemination to the public of information from diverse sources is in the public interest. It is almost as if information were in the nature of a potentially disabling contagious disease which must be feared, controlled, and ultimately quarantined.

A singular feature of this directive is that it requires pre-publication clearance of articles and books written by policy-making officials *after* they leave government, if they had access to "sensitive compartmented information"—which is intelligence information to which access is limited to protect sources and methods. Suffice it to say that there are presently about 100,000 people in Washington with such clearances—people who can and do contribute much to public debate after leaving office. Abrams observes:

> Some of the most important speech that occurs in our society would be subjected to governmental scrutiny and, if the government in power decided that something could not be written or said, to judicial review.

He reminds us that in 1980, the last year for which we have statistics, the government placed secrecy classification on 16 million pieces of information. The effect of the new presidential directive could well be to strike at the heart of the ability of the public to be informed about their government.

True, it may spare us some memoirs of presidential aides, but is this sufficient recompense for the silence, or reticence, of the great body of men and women who move in and out of public service in a mode that is in fact unique to the American democracy?

Finally, last Thursday, we also learned that the March 11 directive was based on an interagency study which proposed prison terms for offenders. Now this could readily lead us to the point where at any given moment half the cabinet is in jail. Mind, there have been times in the recent past where we almost reached that point without the aid of any special legislation. Even so, one wonders if the republic is really ready for such an experiment.

With something such in mind, on March 22, I wrote the president enclosing a more or less routine press clipping of the day citing "senior Reagan administration" officials and suchlike letting us in on details of "low-altitude flights by United States spy planes" flying about Central America. I wrote that I assumed there would be "a thorough internal executive branch investigation of this matter" and asked if the Intelligence Committee might be favored with a copy of the findings. I have yet to hear back on the results.

Nor will I. The president won't reply to me. Nor, probably, should he.

He will respond to you. But *I don't think he has heard from you*. Nor has Congress. This is truly a menacing atmosphere gathering in Washington. And it is not at all confined to the executive branch. Freedom of the press, freedom of information, is under attack.

It is time you tigers roared.

New York, New York
April 25, 1983

Commencement Address,
Rensselaer Polytechnic
Institute

More to the theme that it was not our engineers who were letting us down; it was ideologues.

American industry will be a long time recovering from the appreciation of the dollar in the early Reagan years. It will come back, is coming back, but as something different and less American.

There is a passage in *Troilus and Cressida* in which Thersites, watching the goings on between the two lovers in that distant Trojan garden, shares with the audience this memorable commentary on the human condition.

Lechery, lechery,
Still war and lechery,
Nothing else holds fashion.

Perhaps so in olden times, but America, new in so much, has added a third topic of at least recurring fashion, which is to say the state of science and technology. It is the good and deserved fortune of you contemporary Trojans,* graduates now of Rensselaer Polytechnic Institute, to come upon the scene at a moment

---

* RPI is of course in Troy, New York, whose citizens are denominated Trojans.

of mounting interest and concern at what you are not only good at, but, let's face it, best at.

If there is a cycle in such fashion, it is at very least an enduring one, present truly at the first stirrings of what we would recognize as American experience. Our oldest learned society, the American Philosophical Society, was founded by Benjamin Franklin in 1743 "for the promotion of useful knowledge." Science, in its general sense as an extension of culture, was certainly cultivated by Franklin's contemporaries and his heirs. It was David Rittenhouse of the society, who, recording the transit of Venus in 1769, contributed the first American science to draw attention in Europe. But it was the immediately practical that most absorbed them.

Franklin's was an exclusive society, limited then as now to 500 members. The United States had first to be founded and then be committed to an increasingly open and democratic society before a college, a place of teaching as well as learning, was to be established to pursue this theme. This was, of course, RPI, founded by Stephen Van Rensselaer in Troy, "for the purpose," as he put it, "of instructing persons who may choose to apply themselves in the application of science to the common purposes of life."

If you like such things, it is a wonderful continuity. But more came of it than mass production and unequalled abundance of things. What came of it was the American nationality.

We owe this insight to Daniel Boorstin in his great history, *The Americans.* In the final volume, subtitled "The Democratic Experience," he writes:

> No American transformation was more remarkable than these new American ways of changing things from objects of possession and envy into vehicles of community.... Now men were affiliated less by what they believed than by what they consumed.... Men who never saw or knew one another were held together by their common use of objects so similar that they could not be distinguished even by their owners.

I would offer the thought that this perspective on American na-
tionhood helps considerably to understand the sudden, widespread, and deep anxiety which is everywhere to be encountered
concerning the degree to which our own economy is being undermined by foreign imports, and that this reflects a loss of our
competitive position in world technology.

From the moment Boorstin's community of consumption
began until just these past few years, the consumption was of
American products of a distinctly American mode. In the fore-
front, of course, was the automobile, and perhaps quintessentially
the Model-T Ford, which you could have in any color, said the
old gentleman, as long as it was black. I recall reading somewhere
in the works of John Steinbeck that in the beginning of this
century, a generation of young men grew up knowing more about
the planetary system of gears than about the planetary system
itself.

Until, that is, all of a sudden the American automobile was
made in Japan, and also the American television set—the two
most used and unifying artifacts in our national life. This, with
the accompanying discovery that Arab sheiks could raise the
price of gasoline, has given us a state of nerves, which is only to
be understood in the context of Boorstin's thesis, or so I would
submit.

The problem is real enough. We *are* losing our competitive
edge and market share in a good many areas of foreign trade. The
chairman of the Council of Economic Advisors has forecast a
trade deficit of some $65 to $75 billion this year, the magnitude
without equivalent in our history.*

But now to my second thought. This competitive loss has
little to do with technology. It has most to do with the utter
mismanagement of the economy in recent years by a coterie of
half-educated ideologues who seized power in such matters in
the incumbent administration, and, being ideologues, prove im-
pervious to experience.

---

* Again: soon to double.

Thus it came to be held that "the government," as it is generally termed, has no business meddling in money markets. This, combined with the highest real interest rates in history, produced what is known in the press as a "strong dollar." This news stirred many a patriotic heart in Washington, while the industries of the American heartland quietly closed down.

According to the Federal Reserve, between December 1980 and December 1982, the dollar appreciated some 34 percent against a basket of twenty other Western currencies. All other factors remaining equal, these foreign-exchange movements made U.S. exports one-third more expensive elsewhere in the world, while making foreign imports about one-fourth cheaper than otherwise on the U.S. market. This, surely, has nothing to do with the quality of American technology.

There is a larger context, however, in which this issue arises, and that is the plain political fact that most of the nations of the world have opted for economic systems that have large elements of government direction and control: much of it designed specifically to produce favorable outcomes in world trade.

Alan Wolff, deputy U.S. trade representative in the Carter administration, observed recently that "the United States has a trade policy, but no trade strategy." True, but the all-important fact is that our policy is *not to have a strategy*, which is to say ours is a policy of promoting free enterprise and free markets, traditional American beliefs and values. But the policy begins to fail when the world, in a sense, decides to play by different rules.

Do not doubt that this too will prove deeply unsettling to us. There is a rule: Organizations in conflict become like one another. Think of hockey teams, chemistry departments, strategic nuclear forces. Foreign trade, as it becomes more government-directed, becomes less like competition and more and more like conflict.

In this conflict, the United States is likely more and more to become just what we, at least professedly, don't want to be. Which is to say an increasingly centrally directed economy.

There is a sense in which this has all been foretold. A generation ago, Schumpeter described what he judged to be the inexorable "conquest of the private sector by the public sector." That, he said, not revolution, would be the fate of capitalism.

Yet there remains the possibility that, if we would only try a bit harder to understand ourselves and our social processes, outcomes will better. Such, in your various disciplines, has been the faith of scientists and engineers. It is also true of the social sciences.

Saratoga, New York
May 20, 1983

MX Plan Commits U.S.
to First-Strike Policy

Mid-1983 was the season of the MX. The administration had decided to deploy the missile, begun as Minuteman IV, in the Minuteman silos that some fifteen years earlier we'd realized we'd have to get out of because of the sudden appearance of the SS-18 on the other side. It was kind of dottiness—forgetting why it was that the weapon had been wandering about in the desert all those intervening years, looking for a new home—save that the issue truly spoke to ultimate concerns. I spoke and wrote almost daily, as did other senators, notably Gary Hart. We never won. But we would lose by margins that foretold some final if incomplete victory. In July, Hart offered an amendment to the Defense Authorization Bill deleting funds to build the missile. This lost 58 to 41. I followed with an amendment to delete funds for actual deployment. This lost 57 to 42, gaining the vote of Lawton Chiles of Florida.

Newsday *gave me space to record that we would fight again.*

It is now all but certain that the Senate will vote tonight to proceed with construction of the first of 100 MX missiles, for deployment in unimproved Minuteman silos, as President Reagan has proposed. After a generation and more of nuclear peace based on the doctrine of "deterrence," the United States will have changed its strategic policy to one of "launch on warning." The

145

result will be a world set on a hair trigger, ready to be catapulted into holocaust one day on about nine minutes' notice—like as not by accident, because a Russian computer will have momentarily gone down.

From the time Americans learned that the Soviets had developed the capacity to deliver a nuclear bomb to the United States, deterrence has guided both our thinking about how to build nuclear weapons and our planning about how to avoid nuclear war.

Deterrence is a simple idea, and it is defensive in character. It calls for the nuclear power to deploy its forces so they are able to survive a preemptive attack by the other side in sufficient strength to inflict unacceptable retaliatory damage on the aggressor. War is deterred by making it clear that war cannot succeed.

Although it clearly would work best if both sides accepted the premise, and acted accordingly, we have never been given any reason to think the Soviets had adopted deterrence as a working proposition. To the contrary, Soviet military leaders speak frequently about launching preemptive strikes, about fighting nuclear wars and expecting to "win" something. They conduct training exercises along these lines. And, until quite recently, they have relied almost exclusively on a nuclear force that is not very survivable, consisting almost entirely of large, powerful, evermore accurate—and stationary—land-based missiles. Sitting ducks, you might call them. The Soviet force has seemed designed for the purpose of launching a first strike, not at all capable of launching a second strike.

Somehow it has always seemed to be in the nature of things that this asymmetry should exist. After all, as long as we were able to threaten a credible second strike, there was not going to be a first strike. We're us, and they're them. We knew this; they knew; we knew that they knew.

Crucial to this "second strike" concept at the heart of deterrence is the requirement that our nuclear forces be deployed in ways enabling them to survive attack. American policy therefore evolved toward a strategic triad, in which our nuclear weapons are deployed in airplanes, at sea, and in land-based silos. Each has strengths and weaknesses; the diversity, moreover, makes it still more difficult for the Soviets to be certain they could destroy them all simultaneously.

Almost fifteen years ago, our intelligence agencies began to sense that the Soviets were developing a new class of missile large and accurate enough to destroy our Minuteman sites in a first strike. These, in the main, constituted the land-based leg of our triad. (The Soviet missiles known as the SS-17, SS-18, SS-19 began to be deployed in 1974.)

America had to respond if deterrence were to survive as a working doctrine. In 1972, the United States set out to develop a new intercontinental ballistic missile. All parties concurred in the Air Force judgment that it would have to be based in a survivable manner. When reports surfaced that the Air Force might be straying from this course, Congress asserted (in the defense authorization bill for fiscal years 1976 and 1977) that "studies will not be conducted for a fixed-base ICBM because of its questionable survivability."

Yet, in April of this year, after reviewing thirty-four basing modes and examining the state of the American deterrent force, the president's highly regarded Commission on Strategic Forces recommended that we deploy the new MX missile in the very Minuteman silos whose vulnerability had caused us to look for a new basing mode in the first place. Reagan passed this extraordinary recommendation to the Congress with his endorsement, and this week the Senate will complete its consideration of the legislation that will authorize that the scheme be put in place.

For the first time, the United States will have deployed a nuclear weapon in a fashion we know—and they know—cannot survive a first strike. (Already there are at least two Soviet warheads dedicated, as they say, to each Minuteman silo.) And this is not just any nuclear weapon we will be placing in these silos; the MX, at 195,000 pounds, with 10 warheads on each of the 100 missiles and the best in inertial guidance systems, will be the most powerful weapon we have ever produced—for effectiveness, range, and accuracy.

The MX is so powerful and so accurate, in fact, that it possesses "counterforce" capability—that is, the ability to destroy a heavily fortified, or hardened, Soviet missile silo. A counterforce weapon, deployed in sufficient numbers, can undermine deterrence regardless of how it is based. It can, if known to be powerful and accurate enough, raise the possibility that it will be used to conduct an effective first strike, knocking out all Soviet missiles in one blow and eliminating the ability to retaliate.

Thus the MX, a weapon that had the capacity to be used to great advantage in a Soviet first strike, is going to be deployed in a fashion in which it can only be used as a first-strike weapon.

"For what purpose have the Americans done this," Soviets will ask themselves, "after ten years of development and billions of investment?"

They will have no choice but to conclude that the United States has abandoned deterrence, and resorted to the long-standing Soviet posture, based on heavy, vulnerable missiles suited to a first strike. Under the most outspokenly antiCommunist president yet elected, ironically, the world has witnessed the Sovietization of American strategic policy!

But the irony is richer still, the gaping sense of opportunities lost far greater. For in the same period in which the United States has moved for the first time to deploy a first-strike weapon system in the Soviet style, the Soviets have provided evidence that they may finally be willing to come to terms with deterrence.

In the past year, the Soviets have begun testing two new missiles, the SS-X-24 and the PL-5. The distinguishing characteristic of the two is that both are solid-fuel missiles. Solid fuel is a condition for mobile missiles.

Small, mobile missiles are the way of the future in intercontinental ballistic missiles, and also the way to stability in nuclear balance. For they are infinitely better suited to deterrence than are the behemoths of which the Soviets have hitherto seemed so fond. Small, mobile missiles are better suited to deterrence than the MX.

Indeed, the President's Commission on Strategic Forces, which recommended in passing that the United States deploy the MX in Minuteman silos, devoted more lengthy and more persuasive analysis to a proposal that we accelerate efforts to develop and deploy such a small, mobile missile. Being mobile, it could be hidden much more easily and so would not be as vulnerable to attack. Being small, with fewer warheads, it would make a less attractive target.

I will offer an amendment that, while halting the MX deployment, would double the money spent on research and development of a small, single-warhead ICBM. It won't pass. The Congress will go forward with the president's proposal to deploy the MX as a first-strike weapon.

This means that on that day in the not-far-off future when the Soviet leader is told that their computer indicates that a missile attack has been launched at Moscow, he will know two things: that the computer issued false reports before, and that the United States recently deployed an MX good for nothing but a first strike. He will have only nine or ten or twelve minutes to give the order to launch a retaliatory attack. In that kind of pressure—especially if the moment should arrive in the midst of a global political crisis—what will that Russian leader think about an American decision to deploy the MX? What can he possibly think? And what order will he give?

What order will our own strategic command be inclined to give when our computer indicates we are under attack? With a weapon as capable and as defenseless as the MX in our arsenal (the American queen of the nuclear chessboard?), will there be added pressure to unleash it early, before it is destroyed on the ground? This is precisely the scenario the chairman of the Joint Chiefs of Staff, General John W. Vessey, Jr., set forth for a Senate committee on May 5. Yes, he said, the MX in Minuteman silos could not be defended from a first strike by the Soviets. But, he said, "the Soviets have no assurance that we will ride out the attack." Translation? That we too will "launch on warning." A warning we may not have time to double-check, triple-check. Machines, not men, will decide.

Though this is reason for the gravest concern, it is not quite time to despair. Happily, it is the nature of the American political system that decisions are rarely made irrevocably—more money will have to be appropriated; elections intervene; popular sentiment, which government tends in the end to reflect pretty well, shifts or becomes energized. Our hope is that, at some point before the first MX missiles are lowered in their silos at Warren Air Force Base in Wyoming in the middle of 1986, this dreadful course can be reversed, and deterrence reestablished.

Newsday
July 26, 1983

My amendment lost, of course. And the first of fifty MX missiles were deployed in Minuteman silos in late 1986—I went out to Wyoming to watch. But in the main our argument did prevail, and as I write, the Midgetman is going forward.

Reagan's Bankrupt Budget

By the close of 1983, I knew the early Reagan deficits had been deliberate, that there had been a hidden agenda. How did I know? The people who did it told me: now, that is, that the plan was not working. Of this period David Stockman later wrote:

> The 1983 deficit had . . . already come in at $208 billion. The case for a major tax increase was overwhelming, unassailable, inescapable, and self-evident. Not to raise taxes when all other avenues were closed was a willful act of ignorance and grotesque irresponsibility. In the entire twentieth-century fiscal history of the nation, there has been nothing to rival it.

Stockman ascribes this mostly to the president: "Ronald Reagan . . . a terminal optimist." In this New Republic article, I happen on a somewhat different idea. Mr. Reagan had made big government cheap. For seventy-five cents worth of taxes, you got a dollar's worth of return. I mention the farm program, which, if "hog wild" by 1983, attained to a generalized dementia by 1986 when we learned that the largest recipient of grain subsidies in Texas was the Crown Prince of Liechtenstein, and that, as the year closed, 144 dairy "farmers" had received $1 million or *more in payments for not milking cows, or slaughtering them, or something.*

In his first thousand days in office, Ronald Reagan increased the national debt of the United States by half. If he should serve a second term, and the debt continues to mount as currently forecast by the Congressional Budget Office, the Reagan administration will have nearly tripled the national debt. In eight years, one Republican administration will have done twice, you might say, what it took 192 years and thirty-eight Federalist, Democratic, Whig, and Republican predecessors to do once. The numbers are so large they defy any ordinary effort at comprehension, but for the record they are as follows. On President Reagan's inauguration day, January 20, 1981, the national debt stood at $940.5 billion. In the next thirty-two months, $457 billion was added. The projected eight-year growth is $1.64 trillion, bringing us to a total debt, by 1989, of $2.58 trillion.*

Debt service, which is to say interest on the debt, will rise accordingly. It came to $75 billion in fiscal year 1980. By the end of this fiscal year, it will be something like $148.5 billion. And so it might also be said that the Reagan administration will have doubled the cost of the debt in four years.

A law of opposites frequently influences the American presidency. Once in office, presidents are seen to do things least expected of them, often things they had explicitly promised not to do. Previous commitments or perceived inclinations act as a kind of insurance that protects against any great loss if a president behaves contrary to expectation. He is given the benefit of the doubt. He can't have wanted to do this or that; he must have had to do it. President Eisenhower made peace, President Kennedy went to war, President Nixon went to China.

Something of this indulgence is now being granted President

---

* The debt ceiling eventually went to $2.8 trillion, treble the amount the Reagan administration inherited.

Reagan. Consider the extraordinary deficits, $200 billion a year, and continuing, in David Stockman's phrase, as far as the eye can see. This accumulation of a serious debt—the kind that leads the International Monetary Fund to take over a third-world country's economic affairs (or in olden times would lead us to send in the marines to collect customs duties)—is all happening without any great public protest, or apparent political cost.

As such, this need be no great cause for concern. If Ronald Reagan is lucky, good for him. There is little enough luck in the business. But, unfortunately, something much larger is at issue. If nothing is done, the debt and the deficit will virtually paralyze American national government for the rest of the decade. The first thing to be done, to use that old Marxist terminology, is to demystify the Reagan deficit.

If I may say so, what I now write, I know. That is not and should not be enough for the reader. I will ask to be judged, then, by whether the proposition to be presented is coherent, and whether any other proposition makes more sense.

The proposition is that the deficits were purposeful, that is to say, the deficits for the president's initial budgets. They were thereafter expected to disappear. That they have not, and will not, is the result of a massive misunderstanding of American government. This is not understood in either party. Democrats feel uneasy with the subject, one on which we have been attacked since the New Deal. Republicans are simply uncomprehending, or—as Senator John Danforth of Missouri said in a speech on the debt ceiling in November (referring to the whole Senate, but permit me an inference)—"catatonic."

Start with the campaign. Although we may be forgiven if we remember otherwise, as a candidate, Mr. Reagan did not propose to reduce federal spending. Waste, yes, that would be eliminated, but name a program, at least one of any significance, that was to go. To the contrary, defense spending was to be considerably increased. That was the one program issue of his campaign. It was the peculiar genius of that campaign that it proposed to increase defense expenditures while cutting taxes. This was the

Kemp–Roth proposal, based on Arthur Laffer's celebrated curve. As a candidate, Mr. Reagan went so far as to assert that this particular tax cut would actually increase revenues.

What follows is crucial: No one believed this. Obviously, a tax can be so high that it discourages the taxed activity and reduces revenue. This is called price elasticity and is a principle that applies to pretty much everything from the price of the *New Republic* to the price Justice Holmes said we pay for civilization. But any massive reduction in something as fundamental as the income tax was going to bring about a massive loss of revenue. And this was intended.

There was a hidden agenda. It came out in a television speech sixteen days after President Reagan's inauguration, when he stated, "There were always those who told us that taxes couldn't be cut until spending was reduced. Well, you know we can lecture our children about extravagance until we run out of voice and breath. Or we can cut their extravagance by simply reducing their allowance." The president genuinely wanted to reduce the size of the federal government. He genuinely thought it was riddled with "waste, fraud, and abuse," with things that needn't or shouldn't be done. He was astute enough to know there are constituencies for such activities, and he thought it pointless to try to argue them out of existence one by one. He would instead create a fiscal crisis in which, willy-nilly, they would be driven out of existence.

If *his* understanding of the government had been right, his strategy for reducing its size would have been sound. But his understanding was desperately flawed. There is waste in the federal budget, but it is of the kind generic to large and long-established enterprises. Thus we have an army, a navy, and an air force. They compete, they overlap, they duplicate. Well, yes. But they also fight, in no small measure because these uniforms mean something to those men and women, and have, in the case of the army and navy (and of course the Marine Corps, which is part of the navy), for more than two centuries. A management consultant might merge them. I sure as hell wouldn't, except perhaps way at the top. For the rest, well, there is the FBI at $1 billion; the Coast Guard (equally long established) at $2.5 billion; and so on. Welfare? In the sense of welfare mothers? The Aid to Families with Dependent Children program comes in at about 1 percent of the whole budget. (The *Washington Post* has half-seriously proposed that it be abolished altogether so that people will stop talking about it.) There are areas in the budget where expenditure is indeed growing at enormous rates, principally that of medical care. But for the most part, and especially in the case of medical care, expenditure is growing at similar rates in both the private and public sectors. Large social forces are at work, not simply a peculiarly pathological tendency of government.

A notable area of miscalculation, or rather misinformation, among the Reaganites was that of foreign affairs. President Reagan has acted much as his predecessors have done in foreign affairs, and for the elemental reason that he is faced with much the same situations. Invariably, this has meant spending money. This fall the president had to plead with Congress to increase appropriations for the International Monetary Fund, something he cannot have expected ever to be doing, but there you are. As I write, the Kissinger Commission on Central America is no doubt drawing up a massive "Marshall Plan" for the area. Is there any doubt that in the next session, the president will be pleading with Congress to increase this particular form of foreign aid? (Just as, had his supporters in the Senate been successful in blocking the Panama Canal treaties in the Carter years, Reagan would be pleading today with the Senate to consent to their ratification.)

President Reagan's tax cut—the largest tax reduction in history—became law in August 1981. Critics, if they are members of Congress, typically must begin by explaining why they voted for the tax cut. I am one. (There were only eleven senators who voted no.) I have an explanation, but no excuse.

After years of intense inflation and the accompanying "bracket creep" in the income tax, we did need to reduce personal tax rates. A year earlier, the Senate Finance Committee, controlled by the Democratic majority, had reported out just such a bill, but Mr. Carter's White House would not hear of it. This helped lose the Senate for the Democrats, but the lesson was not lost.

The great recession of 1981/82 made it painfully clear that the tax cut was too small for the first year, when a neo-Keynesian stimulus was in order. At the time, however, a bidding war broke out in the House, sending the parties into senseless competition to offer loopholes to special interests. The result was a tax cut much too large for the later years. Thus the $200 billion annual deficit.

Enter the Federal Reserve Board which looked at the huge tax cuts in the midst of high inflation and decided to create an economic downturn. Of all the structural anomalies of American government, the arrangements for setting macroeconomic policy are the most perverse. Although fiscal policy (the amounts of money the government spends, receives, and borrows) is made through a painfully elaborate public process by an elected president and an elected Congress, monetary policy (the total amount of money in the economy and the cost of borrowing it) is made in secret by appointed officials. The Reserve Board tightened the growth of the money supply so strenuously that it actually declined in the third quarter of 1981. Real interest rates reached the highest levels in our nation's history, and the economy fell off the cliff. At the end of September 1981, the steel industry was operating at 75.9 percent of capacity; by the end of 1982, it was operating at 34.0 percent of capacity.

To be sure, the Federal Reserve does not control the precise money supply and cannot precisely determine interest rates. But it can set the direction and range for both, and this it did. Anyone who tried to dissent was soundly rapped. Its two dozen or so central bankers decided to bust the economy, and bust it they did. In a White House appearance in October 1982, Nobel economist George Stigler used the term "depression" to describe the economy.

There is a tendency for any government to live beyond its income. The Reagan administration transformed this temptation from a vice into an opportunity. Put plainly, under Ronald Reagan, big government became a bargain. For seventy-five cents worth of taxes, you got one dollar's worth of return. Washington came to resemble a giant discount house. If no tax would balance the budget, and no outlay would make it any worse, why try?

A boom psychology moved through government. Defense came first, from space wars to battleships—the latest defense appropriation reactivates the World War II–vintage U.S.S. *Missouri*. "Hog wild" is the only way to describe the farm program. Jimmy Carter left behind a $4-billion enterprise, somewhat overpriced at that and the object of incessant right-wing criticism. Whereupon the fundamentalists and their political brethren took over. Within thirty-six months, they increased the annual cost of the farm program more than fourfold. Their most recent enthusiasm, signed into law by President Reagan, is a program paying dairy farmers not to milk their cows.*

What is to be done? The economy is at stake. The country can bankrupt itself. According to the latest budget projections, prepared by the Congressional Budget Office under the impeccably conservative new director, Rudolph G. Penner (formerly of the American Enterprise Institute), the deficit for the six years from 1984 to 1989 will come to approximately $1,339,000,000,000. In order to support and service this debt, the government will have to absorb more and more of the capital that is becoming available in the nation's credit markets. Direct federal borrowing for the deficit and federally guaranteed loans absorbed 62 percent of all credit raised on the nation's financial markets this year, compared to an average absorption rate of 8.3 percent in the 1960s and 15.3 percent in the 1970s. This "crowding out" was not much felt, because few others were borrowing to invest. But when the day comes that business, consumers, and government all compete for the same funds, interest rates will go up, with predictable consequences.

Under these circumstances, the only thing a Republican administration and a Republican Senate will be able to consider

---

* The cost of the farm program reached $25.6 billion in 1986.

doing will be to revert to their original agenda: use the budget deficit to force massive reductions in social programs. This time they will be able to cite not mere illusions but necessity. Even if interest on the debt climbs to $200 billion a year, as now seems likely, presumably there will still be an army, an FBI, and some kind of customs service and border control. What then will be left to cut?

Entitlements, or more precisely, Social Security.

The word is already the rage. There is scarcely a Republican member of the Senate who does not know that entitlements must be cut, and cut deeply. Many Democrats agree; almost none dissent. Remember, at least twenty senators are millionaires, living at considerable social distance from those who would be most affected. It will be much the same in the House. The budget deficit in the year ahead will threaten any sustained recovery. The members of the House, as a rule, are not millionaires, but they know their street corners. The street corners will say, "Cut. Something must be done."

Cut back Social Security in desperation, and you abandon a solemn promise of the Democratic party and of American society. This promise, once broken, will fracture a little bit of society. (Moreover, cutting Social Security will not improve the deficit problem. As Martin Feldstein, chairman of the Council of Economic Advisers, has noted, Social Security is funded by separate payroll taxes and contributes not a cent to the deficit.)

There is an alternative. There is the possibility of a historic compromise that can bring the now dominant branch of the Republican party to grips with reality, while shaking the now dominant branch of the Democratic party from its illusion that no one will listen to Republicans for very long. Such a compromise cannot await a change in the political culture. It must be negotiated. We need a structure, a forum in which negotiations can take place. A presidential commission might be such a structure.

The National Commission on Social Security Reform would provide a model. It was established by President Reagan in December 1981, after Congress rejected his original plan to sharply reduce Social Security benefits. One point in particular is crucial. Alan Greenspan, who chaired the commission, adopted a simple rule: Each member was entitled to his own opinion but not his own facts. Within a year, Mr. Greenspan had established the facts, which showed that the problem was neither trivial nor hopeless. The commission as such could reach no agreement. But with the facts established, we put together a bipartisan legislative package last January in exactly twelve days.

The budget crisis presents a harder problem, but it can be approached in the same way. Martin Feldstein made a good beginning in a speech to the Southern Economic Association on November 21. He agreed with the Congressional Budget Office that by 1988 the deficit will absorb 5.1 percent of the nation's GNP. Of this, Feldstein noted, 2.4 percent will come from increased defense spending, 1.7 percent from the tax cut, and the remaining 1 percent from higher interest payments. The facts about the structural deficit flow readily from such quantification.

The members of the budget commission—representatives from the administration, Congress, the Federal Reserve, and the Congressional Budget Office—would determine the actual effects of deficits on employment, real interest rates, capital formation, investment, and the prospects for vigorous economic growth. Then they would propose the steps to reduce the deficit, making certain that the burden of these reductions did not fall disproportionately on any economic or social group. Delaying tax indexing, reforming corporate tax law deductions and credits, cutting defense spending, and reducing farm price supports, among other proposals, would have to be considered. Medicare, secure in the short term, will be in deep trouble before the end of this decade. The deficit commission must face up to this problem. Democrats should agree to do so in return for assurances that the Social Security agreement will be respected and that the Social Security trust fund will not be raided (the plain purpose of those who say entitlements are the problem).

Moreover, a solution to the deficit crisis will require more than adjustments in spending and taxation. It will demand change in the way we make fiscal and monetary policy and the way those policies are coordinated. Monetary policy and the operations of the Federal Reserve must be an integral part of any fiscal resolution. Nothing can be achieved without a joint monetary-fiscal effort to promote an expanding economy and an approach to full employment—a one-percentage-point drop in unemployment alone reduces the budget deficit by $30 billion.

But let's stop here. I have my own thoughts. The reader will have his or hers. On the final day of the last session of Congress, I introduced legislation to establish the National Commission on Deficit Reduction. Now, can we get the president to join?

The *New Republic*
December 31, 1983

Low inflation rates of the mid-1980s eased interest costs, which peaked at $136 billion in fiscal year 1985. Still a huge sum.

1984

Letter to New York: 1984

1984 began with a New York Times/*CBS News poll report-*
ing that for the first time in ages, Americans thought things were
better off than they had been and would soon be better off than
they were. So much for the election year. I wrote 1.2 million
New Yorkers asking how they themselves felt, with first a dollop
of Orwell.

Dear New Yorker:

1984 has come at last! George Orwell chose *1984* as the title
of his classic depiction of a dreadful age to come simply by reversing the last two digits of the year he began writing the book,
1948. He attached no particular significance to the year as such.
He was writing, really, of the changes that had already taken
place in life as a result of three central developments of the
twentieth century.

First, the advent of the modern form of tyranny, the totalitarian state, which first appeared in Soviet Russia. This was a
form of government altogether different from the tyrannies of
old, which only required that you *behave*, which is to say that
you not challenge those in power. These new regimes required
that you *believe*: that you love Big Brother. Control becomes
total; privacy utterly disappears. (In this sense, terrorism is to-

talitarian: One murders children to oppose a government in power, there being no distinction between the individual and the state, no realm of the personal and private.)

The manipulation of language, especially the inversion of meaning, becomes a state industry. War is Peace, proclaimed Winston Smith's state of Oceania. (UNESCO conferences begin speaking about "peoples' rights" as against human rights. "Peoples' rights" turn out to be the rights of governments.) This manipulation of belief was made possible by our century's second central development, the information revolution. Technological changes in electronics have made it possible to record—and erase— billions of bits of information about everybody and everything.

The final pivotal development of our century was the splitting of the atom and development of atomic weapons which, in Orwell's vision, made one kind of war (nuclear) so vastly destructive and threatening that another, lower-level kind of hostility (conventional) became continuous between the three empires of *1984*: Oceania, Eastasia, and Eurasia.

Orwell, the simplest of men, was in fact a genius when it came to envisioning the gadgetry of the "1984" future. Buck Rogers and his space ships had nothing on Big Brother's police installing surveillance cameras in everybody's bedroom. (Have you happened lately to notice how often you are being silently watched by a slowly arcing, tireless lens tucked up in the corner of your supermarket, or bank, or United States Capitol?)

Again, Orwell was uncanny in foreseeing the possible disappearance altogether of any *person* as the head of a totalitarian state. Consider Yuri Andropov, ruler of all the Russias. He has not been seen in public since last August. And yet he rules! (As I recall, it is never clear in *1984* whether Big Brother, the ruler of Oceania, actually exists.) But the main point about *1984* is that it was more warning than prophecy.

Orwell, at intervals, would immerse himself in the life of English working people, and came utterly to trust *their* judgment of things, as against that of his own class. (He was, of course, an Etonian.) In 1943, when the Yanks began to arrive in England in serious numbers, the word went around the fashionable, leftist circles of London that the soldiers were there not to help mount an invasion of the Continent, but rather to put down an expected general strike. Orwell observed that you have to have a college education to believe such a proposition. No London taxi driver would give it a moment's credence.

You can overdo this. No group is infallible. And you can't hold it against a person that his parents sent him to a "good" school. But granting Orwell his quirks, he really did believe in democracy, in the good sense of people.

This is why those who follow such things truly began to worry about our country some twenty years ago when, starting in 1964—the year after the assassination of President Kennedy— opinion polls began to show a sharp decline in public trust in government. In the 1930s, American social scientists learned the techniques of opinion polling and began a regular measure of our attitudes about what kind of country we have, and where we seemed to be headed. In 1958, the Institute of Social Science at the University of Michigan began to measure what it called "trust in government." People were asked whether they saw "the government in Washington" as honest and trustworthy; whether they thought it knew what it was doing and was run for the benefit of the people—or perhaps just the opposite.

The early findings reflected everything we (somewhat belatedly) now recognize about the Eisenhower era. A solid 60 percent and more of the public trusted their government. Then in 1964, confidence broke and went down and down, until we entered the 1970s with Americans hardly trusting their government at all; not a quarter of whites, not 15 percent of blacks.

In a 1971 national study, the institute found that the proportion of people who believed "life in the United States" was getting worse (36 percent) was twice as large as the number who thought it was getting better (17 percent). That year, a respected research organization concluded from its data that "the peoples' assessment of the state of the nation in 1971 was unquestionably the most pessimistic recorded since the introduction of public opinion polling . . . in the midst of the great depression of the 1930s."

This is why it was such good news to pick up the papers on the first day of 1984 and find Adam Clymer, a greatly gifted journalist, reporting that a *New York Times*/CBS News poll found that for the first time in a very long while, Americans, asked to rate "the way things are going in the United States," how they had been five years ago, and would be five years hence, said things were better than they were and will be still better in the future.

What does it all signify? My thought would be that it does not necessarily mean we are all happy and getting happier. That trivializes the results. For a long while, over the past twenty years, individuals would report that *they themselves* were better off and expected to be still more so—but they didn't think our country was. They didn't think our democracy was working as it should. Now, once again, most of us do. Which means we can look to the political process to respond to what we think.

This is good news *if* we all decide to think a little harder about that process. For the changing character of our politics requires more of us than it once did, and 1984 in the United States is very much a political year.

Benjamin Ginsberg of Cornell University argues that politics in the United States is shifting from a labor-intensive to a capital-intensive activity. Sophisticated communications technology is supplanting mass organization "as the ultimate weaponry of American electoral conflict."

From the time, at least, of the Jacksonians, labor-intensive campaign techniques—the torch-light parade, the monster rally, the precinct worker—had given a certain advantage, or at least strength, to groups "nearer the bottom of the social scale. . . ."

Any such advantage now shifts to those able to deploy the new technology, which is to say those able to pay for it—forces usually, in Professor Ginsberg's view, "found on the political right."

He proposes that the displacement of mass organization by the new technology may prove to be the equivalent of "a critical electoral realignment, substantially redistributing power and profoundly transforming political possibilities in the United States."

In a nice image, he writes that the new technology is to money "what the invention of the internal combustion engine was to oil—a development that substantially increased the utility and importance of this resource by permitting a fuller utilization of its inherent potential."

I would prefer to withhold judgment on the issue of ultimate party advantage. There is money to be had by both sides—by all sides. But I have seen the transition; I have taken part in it. When I first entered a political headquarters in New York City in 1953 (Liz was a year ahead of me!), I entered a world hardly changed from that of Martin Van Buren.

Generally speaking, we knew our people and what they thought. Our job was to "turn *them* out." The "others" we didn't know, and had no way of knowing. It is in this regard that things have most changed, and the opinion poll has most changed them. It is here that money, in combination with the new technology, is acquiring the power to defeat not so much one political party or another, but the political process itself.

Until the advent of reliable and regular polling, now being supplemented by focus groups ("downscale, blue collar, northern New Jersey") and other techniques for learning what people feel and how they are moved, candidates for office pretty much presented themselves to the electorate as the persons they actually were.

Party platforms reflected more or less genuine intentions—wishful perhaps, but at a significant level true. None of this need any longer be so, and more and more it is not so. Candidates and organizations can adapt to the finest nuance of the opinions of the many publics that make up the American electorate, and increasingly they must.

Deceit becomes possible, and, in a sense, necessary if a candidate or party has views incompatible with whatever is needed to put together a majority. The hidden agenda becomes the rule; an uneasy echo of the totalitarianism of *1984*.

I do not assert there was a time when candidates for office were always upright and honorable. Some were; some weren't. But they had a limited capacity to dissimulate. However much they tried, they could not finally know what the electorate was thinking. Now they can.

Further, this new technology imposes itself on political campaigns much as new weaponry imposes itself on the military. The voter profile, the media "buy" (who is watching which channel at what hour?), the mass "personalized" mailing and the daily sampling, now are as common as volunteers are scarce.

What does this require of us? A steady grasp of the principles of American government, first and foremost those of the Constitution, which speaks to the objects of government as establishment of justice and domestic tranquility; as provision for the "common defense" *and* promotion of "the general Welfare." (Not one *or* the other.) Beyond that? A certain wariness is in order, a certain vigilance. It may be that more is demanded of a citizen these days. Distrust is one thing, vigilance another.

And a happy 1984 in spite of it all!

Washington, D.C.
January 2, 1984

This newsletter invited readers to score themselves. Not everybody can cope with a Cantrill Self-Anchoring Striving Scale, but 12,000 New Yorkers could. We turned out, as individuals, to be less optimistic; women especially so. Age didn't matter much. Still, the essential profile was not that different. New Yorkers thought things were looking up.

U.S. Has Abandoned
International Law

That winter (1983–84), the Senate Intelligence Committee, with Goldwater as chairman and me as vice chairman, kept tugging at the CIA to tell us what was going on in Central America. Something was. The most likely explanation—we still don't know for sure—is that the argument within the administration for a direct assault on the Sandinista regime finally prevailed and operations commenced. This transition should not be lost to subsequent history. The first requests by the Reagan administration for covert aid in the area were to interdict Nicaraguan arms shipments to El Salvador. The United States had every right to do this, and arguably a duty. I took authorization bills to the floor stating that we were acting under international law, as indeed we were.

This now changed. We commenced activities which were neither legal nor logical.

The mining of the harbors was especially painful: concussion bombs that would not give a Bulgarian ship captain five seconds' pause, but which would raise hell with Lloyds and suchlike insurers of Panamanian tankers. The Senate Intelligence Committee ought to have been informed in advance as it was in any number of serious operations. We were not. In the second week of April, Barry Goldwater sent an open letter to Director William Casey at the CIA saying that we were "violating international law" and that this was an "act of war." On

169

Thursday of that week, Robert C. McFarlane, as national security advisor, went to the Naval Academy and gave an address in which he stated that the committee had been informed and what was the matter with us.

Goldwater having left for Asia, the Easter recess having begun, I was ranking member of the committee and announced I would resign as vice chairman. (Allow me to note here that the greatest part of the most sensitive matters the intelligence community passes on are provided simply to the chairman and vice chairman. It is a heavy load to carry about if you are in politics.) Three weeks later, Casey apologized in writing to Goldwater and things were patched up. But I never did hear from Mc-Farlane.

I wrote a short account for Newsday. *May I call attention to the argument that adherence to law is, or can be, the foundation of bipartisanship in foreign policy? Tedious stuff, I know. But have in mind just where contempt for it got us.*

As a young man, just after World War II, I studied what was then called international relations, and I suppose still is. My hope was to join the foreign service, or something of that sort, and my purpose was still plainer. I wanted to take part in the great challenge and destiny of my generation. Some of my classmates had been deeply touched by the war; some, such as I, only slightly. But all of us were convinced that it was our duty and destiny to help build a world of peace based on law.

More than any other, the reason that era now seems so distant, at least to my view, is because the idea of law—international law—has faded from our collective memory.

But that *is* what we studied: the works of the great international legal scholars; the great tribunals and the somewhat meager cases they had decided; the Covenant of the League of Nations and the Charter of the United Nations; above all, the long history of U.S. devotion to principles of international law. The Constitution provides in Article VI that, "all treaties made, or which shall be made, under the authority of the United States, shall be the supreme law of the land."

The UN Charter, for example, is a treaty. Accordingly, it is as much a part of American law as the speeding regulations of the Long Island Expressway.

I flunked the Foreign Service examinations, but grew up to become a UN ambassador in the mid-1970s. By then our understanding of the charter had quite changed: It was an instrument used by others to harass *us*. The idea of the *force* of law, international law, that is, had quite vanished.

I began to think more about the subject when I went to the Senate.

In February 1979, I suggested in an address to the Council on Foreign Relations in New York City that the disorientation in American foreign policy derived, at least in part, from our having abandoned the concept that international relations can and should be governed by a regime of public international law— without having replaced it with some other reasonably comprehensive and coherent notion as to the kind of world order we do seek. Since then, I have spoken and written steadily on this theme during two presidencies. Not four weeks ago, I published a small book largely on this subject. I gave it the title *Loyalties*, making clear that I think we have been drifting away from early loyalties that ought still to command us.

More recent events in Nicaragua, Washington, and The Hague persuade me still further.

The sequence began on Thursday, April 5. I addressed a distinguished gathering sponsored by Georgetown University on the topic "Forging a Bipartisan American Foreign and Defense Policy." As the "Democratic" speaker, I offered the thought:

> To the degree that law is seen to be and is the basis of our international conduct, a bipartisan foreign policy does not require a party out of office to agree with policies of the party in power, but rather simply to agree with the principles of law on which those policies are based.

The following day, President Reagan spoke at lunch to the same conference, saying that "an effective foreign policy must begin with bipartisanship. . . . The sharing of responsibility for a safer and more humane world must begin at home."

Fair enough. But what of law? What of the fact that that very afternoon, faced with the prospect that Nicaragua was about to take a case against us to the International Court of Justice at The Hague, the administration said it would not accept the compulsory jurisdiction of that court with respect to "any dispute with any Central American state" for the next two years.

No one at the Department of State seemed to know or wish to acknowledge that when the United States accepted the compulsory jurisdiction of the court in 1946, we explicitly committed ourselves not to do precisely what the administration now sought to do: evade the jurisdiction of the court when a complaint is about to be filed against us.

President Harry Truman announced in August 1946 that the United States "recognizes as compulsory ipso facto . . . the jurisdiction of the International Court of Justice in all legal disputes hereafter arising."

The declaration included three reservations and then stated that the undertaking would remain in force "until the expiration of six months after notice may be given to terminate this decision." The report of the Foreign Relations Committee on the resolution ratifying Truman's declaration stated: "The provision for six months' notice of termination . . . has the effect of a renunciation of any intention to withdraw our obligation in the face of a threatened legal proceeding."

A former cabinet officer here in Washington had described the administration's action to me as a "preemptive statement of guilt." I prefer to think of it as part of that lapsed memory I spoke to earlier. We seem to have forgotten what we once believed.

How far better it would have been for the United States to have taken Nicaragua to court. Managua charges the United States with violating Article 19 of the Charter of the Organization of American States, which holds:

No state may use or encourage the use of coercive measure of an economic or political character in order to force the sovereign will of another state and obtain from it advantages of any kind.

Surely it is Nicaragua that violated the charter first. Promptly on coming to power, the Sandinistas began shipping arms to like-minded insurgents in neighboring countries of the region. Congress found, in the 1984 Intelligence Authorization Act, "that by providing military support . . . to groups seeking to overthrow the government of El Salvador and other Central American governments, the government of Nicaragua has violated Article 18 of the Charter of the Organization of American States."

It was therefore the duty, or at least the right, of the United States to respond to these violations of international law and uphold the charter of the OAS.

Theodore Roosevelt, a Nobel Peace Prize recipient, recommended to the Nobel Committee in 1910 that "those great powers bent on peace . . . form a league of peace, not only to keep the peace among themselves, but to prevent, by force if necessary, its being broken by others."

A commitment to law ought to be understood not as a commitment never to use force, but rather to use force only as an instrument of law.

A great many people seem to think of law as a kind of self-imposed restraint on America's ability to act decisively or with force in world affairs. This misstates what law is, and obscures the fact that international law can actually enhance the national security of the United States.

John Norton Moore, once counselor on international law at the Department of State and now professor of law at the University of Virginia, wrote in *Foreign Affairs* magazine some years ago about the "misleading image of law as a system of negative restraint. . . .

"The legal tradition complements the realist approach precisely where that approach is weakest, that is, in preoccupation with short-run goals at the expense of long-run interest."

By "realist approach," I take him to refer to that of the macho strategists, much to be encountered in Washington just now, who let it be known that in their view the law is for sissies.

Yet, no less a patriot than Senator Barry Goldwater (R-Arizona), chairman of the Intelligence Committee, wrote—in a letter to William Casey, the director of central intelligence, stating the committee had not been informed that the CIA was mining Nicaragua's harbors—that "this is an act violating international law."

On the day following the administration's withdrawal from the jurisdiction of the World Court, it was revealed through the press that the CIA had gone beyond its congressional mandate. Even we on the Senate Intelligence Committee have been startled to learn that the CIA has been actively engaged in the mining, endangering the innocent passage of commercial ships of third parties.

This goes considerably beyond the law—both American law as the Senate meant it to be understood, and international law as the world understands it.

The president seems not to think this matters, but it does. Having rejected the authority of the World Court to review the legality of American policy (because "the Soviet Union, and other communist countries" reject it, too), he shall find that Congress will not permit so clearly illegal a program to continue.

In an unusually strong expression of bipartisanship, eighty-four senators—forty-two Democrats and forty-two Republicans—voted Tuesday that the mining should stop. The rest of the president's Nicaragua program is in ruins.

Newsday
April 13, 1984

"It Gets Down to One, Little, Simple Phrase: I Am Pissed Off!"

A few days before Ronald Reagan became president, Barry Goldwater became chairman and I vice chairman of the Senate Select Committee on Intelligence. Thus it came to pass that we were at the center of the events that would lead to the ruin of the Reagan administration.

The Intelligence Committee was meant to be bipartisan, with a chairman from the majority and a vice chairman from the minority who, in the absence of the chairman, presides at committee meetings (something never done on regular standing committees). During our four years it was bipartisan. Barry and I were friends, having first met in the Kennedy years. I knew him as a man of unbreachable integrity.

The intelligence committees had been established in 1976; both of us had been appointed to eight-year terms in 1977, and so had watched the process evolve. It seemed to be working. As most any political scientist would have predicted, the moment the "intelligence community" got a pair of congressional committees to look after it, things started looking up. This is not a cynical observation. Intelligence, like defense, had run down badly during the late 1960s and early 1970s and only began to recover under Carter. But whereas the armed services were more than comfortable with the armed services committees, the intelligence community didn't know what to expect of us. Slowly they came to see that we could help them and would. More, that we could keep secrets; better than the executive branch. Last, not least, they began to trust our oversight role. A congressional committee not only authorizes the budget of the agencies it is responsible for, it oversees the activities of those agencies. In the intelligence community, communications and satellites are by far the most important of such activities, but by far the most sensational are the covert operations. Or thought to be.

The statute provided that save in circumstances of great urgency, the committees would be informed in advance of any such "significant anticipated activities." This commenced to be routine, more than once eliciting sounds of incredulity from the chairman such that the particular proposal was heard of no more. I think the career service began to value this review process, which often was confined to the chairman and vice chairman, leaving it to us to judge whether the full committee needed to be bothered. Occasionally, there was a touch of drama. I was hauled off a lecture platform at the Smithsonian to be advised of the decision to invade Grenada. (I asked, in what sense was that to be a covert operation?) But mostly it was tedium. Intelligence mostly is.

Then, of course, came Nicaragua. What we encounter here is the incapacitating complacency of persons with limited intellects but seemingly unlimited success. The British author Robert Byron observed of England in the latter half of the nineteenth century: "Misfortune comes to the complacent, brought not by some moral law, but because complacence is the parent of incompetence."

By 1981, it was clear enough that the Sandinistas, in the best Leninist fashion, had betrayed the revolution which outsiders, not least the United States, had helped them win. A new administration in Washington might, for example, have moved swiftly by setting up a rival provisional government on the Caribbean coast (where English is spoken), cutting the two (!) roads that cross the country, bringing in the Eden Pastora, legitimate

176

Democrats, holding elections, publishing La Prensa, *sending ambassadors, sending trade unionists, sending money. Hanging in while the Managua Regime revealed itself. Such a strategy had a chance.*

Ours had none. Our equivalent of their "talk and fight" was talk and dawdle. By 1983, we had commenced to support a group of exiles in Honduras who had been under training by officers sent there by generals of the Argentine junta. (Which Margaret Thatcher, not given to dawdling, overthrew in a month's time.) Our staging area was the equivalent of Dien Bien Phu.

The president became anxious. Had they in fact dawdled? "I've got to win one," he would tell career ambassadors. In July 1983, the decision was made to mine Nicaraguan harbors. It was a decision of incompetents. To wit. We must interdict Soviet arms shipments. But if we use real mines, we might sink a Soviet ship. Therefore use pretend (i.e., percussion) mines, which would not in the least interfere with Soviet shipping, but would land the United States in the World Court.

The committee, in the meantime, had grown uneasy. Just what was going on down there? In May 1983, we asked for a new Presidential Finding that would set forth any new developments. A new finding was presented to the committee on September 20, 1983, by Casey and, sorry, George P. Shultz. No mention was made of the forthcoming mining, it having been decided to withhold this from Congress. Yet inevitably we would learn—the Sandinistas would know!—and then the committees would feel betrayed and the policy would be in ruins.

The first mines were laid, by an American vessel, on January 7, 1984. The contras *announced this the next day as something they were doing. Only slowly did it dawn on us that we were directly involved. Dim of us, you might say. Well yes, but then we trusted them. Even so, on March 27, I wrote Kenneth W. Dam, deputy secretary of state, asking for a legal opinion about mining harbors.*

On April 6, the Wall Street Journal *carried the full story.*

Barry Goldwater was outraged. I was stunned: Could no one down there think? We agreed he would send a public letter to Casey:

April 9, 1984

The Honorable William J. Casey
Director of Central Intelligence
Central Intelligence Agency
Washington, DC 20505

Dear Bill:

All this past weekend, I've been trying to figure out how I can most easily tell you my feelings about the discovery of the President having approved mining some of the harbors of Central America.

It gets down to one, little, simple phrase: I am pissed off!

I understand you had briefed the House on this matter. I've heard that. Now, during the important debate we had all last week and the week before, on whether we would increase funds for the Nicaragua program, we were doing all right, until a Member of the Committee charged that the President had approved the mining. I strongly denied that because I had never heard of it. I found out the next day that the CIA had, with the written approval of the President, engaged in such mining, and the approval came in February!

Bill, this is no way to run a railroad and I find myself in a hell of a quandary. I am forced to apologize to the Members of the Intelligence Committee because I did not know the facts on this. At the same time, my counterpart in the House did know.

The President has asked us to back his foreign policy. Bill, how can we back his foreign policy when we don't know what the hell he is doing? Lebanon, yes, we all knew that he sent troops over there. But mine the harbors in Nicaragua? This is an act violating international law. It is an act of war. For the life of me, I don't see how we are going to explain it.

My simple guess is that the House is going to defeat this supplemental and we will not be in any position to put up much of an argument after we were not given the information we were entitled to receive; particularly, if my memory serves me correctly, when you briefed us on Central America just a couple of weeks ago. And the order was signed before that.

I don't like this. I don't like it one bit from the President or from you. I don't think we need a lot of lengthy explanations. The deed has been done and, in the future, if anything like this happens, I'm going to raise one hell of a lot of fuss about it in public.

Sincerely,
Barry Goldwater
Chairman

The statement that this was "an act of war" was Barry's. I had offered the further thought that it was "an act violating international law." It was in substance a joint letter.

On April 12, Robert C. McFarlane, national security advisor to the president, gave an address at the Naval Academy in which he said, in effect, that what Senator Goldwater had written was not true. The Washington Times *reported:*

> *Every important detail of United States secret warfare in El Salvador and Nicaragua—including the mining of Nicaraguan harbors—was "shared in full by the proper congressional oversight committees," insists President Reagan's assistant for national security affairs, Robert C. McFarlane.*
>
> *Mr. McFarlane said he "cannot account for" Sen. Barry Goldwater's contention that he was kept ignorant about the CIA-sponsored harbor minings.*

I read this on April 13. Senator Goldwater was on his way to Asia, the Easter recess being at hand. It was my watch, and here was the national security advisor in effect calling the chairman of our committee a liar. Did he realize this was not so? Had he allowed himself to be lied to: told that we had been informed? What was going on in the White House basement?

Three years later, McFarlane would tell the Joint Hearings on the Iran–contra Investigation that had he "been in the Congress" at the time, and watched the mining, he "would have reached out with the only instrument I had which is law and enacted Boland Two. . . ." That is to say the second Boland amendment prohibiting further aid to the contras and, in effect, putting an end to the covert Central American policy. This was done in October 1984. In the meantime, I used the only instrument I had at hand. Two days after the reports of McFarlane's speech appeared, I announced I would resign as vice chairman, issuing the following statement.

April 15, 1984

I have announced today that I will resign as Vice Chairman of the Senate Select Committee on Intelligence.

This appears to me the most emphatic way I can express my view that the Senate committee was not properly briefed on the mining of Nicaraguan harbors with American mines from an American ship under American command.

An employee bulletin of the Central Intelligence Agency issued April 12 states that the House committee was first briefed on 31 January, but the Senate committee not until 8 March. Even then, as Senator Goldwater has stated, nothing occurred which could be called a briefing. The reference is to a single sentence in a two-hour committee meeting, and a singularly obscure sentence at that.

This sentence was substantially repeated in a meeting on March 13. In no event was the briefing "full," "current," or "prior" as required by the Intelligence Oversight Act of

1980—a measure I helped write. If this action was important enough for the president to have approved it in February, it was important enough for the committee to have been informed in February.

In the public hearing on the confirmation of John J. McMahon as deputy director of Central Intelligence, I remarked that with respect to intelligence matters, the "oversight function necessarily involves a trust relationship between the committee and the community because we cannot know what we are not told and therefore must trust the leaders of the community to inform us."

I had thought this relationship of trust was securely in place. Certainly the career service gave every such indication. Even so, something went wrong, and the seriousness of this must be expressed.

I will submit my resignation when Senator Goldwater returns from the Far East.

This further exchange took place in the Iran–*contra* hearings:

MR. SARBANES. Did you know about the mining of the Nicaraguan harbor?
MR. MCFARLANE. Yes, sir.
MR. SARBANES. Did you think that should have been consulted with the Intelligence Committees?
MR. MCFARLANE. Yes, sir.
MR. SARBANES. It wasn't done.
MR. MCFARLANE. No, sir.

The episode brought great attention, but few seemed to understand what I was trying to say. A general impression was that I was covering up for not having spotted the mining earlier. Editorial comment was decisively unfriendly.

Two weeks later, Casey apologized to us in a handsome, manly manner. I stayed on.

Honor satisfied and the point made—the point that under the Constitution and under statute, Congress is part of the foreign policy process—we set out to see if some good could come of it all.

The statute spoke of "significant anticipated activities." Very well, then, what did "significant" mean? I came up with a simple working definition: Anything the president signs is significant. Only so many pieces of paper reach his desk; within the executive branch there are things you would never do without first getting presidential approval, or after receiving a presidential order. Agreed, then. If you see the president's initials, tell the committee.

We put this in writing. The president agreed through Mr. McFarlane. On June 6, 1984, Barry and I and the director of Central Intelligence signed the first of "The Casey Accords," as they came to be known.

PROCEDURES GOVERNING REPORTING TO THE
SENATE SELECT COMMITTEE ON INTELLIGENCE (SSCI)
ON COVERT ACTION

The DCI and the SSCI agree that a planned intelligence activity may constitute a "significant anticipated intelligence activity" under section 501 of the National Security Act of 1947 (the "Intelligence Oversight Act of 1980") even if the planned activity is part of an ongoing covert action operation within the scope of an existing Presidential Finding pursuant to the Hughes–Ryan Amendment (22 U.S.C. 2422). The DCI and the SSCI further agree that they may better discharge their respective responsibilities under the Oversight Act by reaching a clearer understanding concerning reporting of covert action activity. To this end the DCI and SSCI make the following representations and undertakings, subject to the possible exceptional circumstances contemplated in the Intelligence Oversight Act:

1. In addition to providing the SSCI with the text of new Presidential Findings concerning covert action, the DCI will provide the SSCI with the contents of the accompanying scope paper following approval of the Finding. The contents of the scope paper will be provided in writing unless the SSCI and the DCI agree that an oral presentation would be preferable. Any subsequent modification to the scope paper will be provided to the SSCI.

2. The DCI also will inform the SSCI of any other planned covert action activities for which higher authority or Presidential approval has been provided, including, but not limited to, approvals of any activity which would substantially change the scope of an ongoing covert action operation.

3. Notification of the above decisions will be provided to the SSCI as soon as practicable and prior to implementation of the actual activity.

4. The DCI and the SSCI recognize that an activity planned to be carried out in connection with an ongoing covert action operation may be of such a nature that the Committee will desire notification of the activity prior to implementation, even if the activity does not require separate higher authority or Presidential approval. The SSCI will, in connection with each ongoing covert action operation, communicate to the DCI the kinds of activities (in addition to those described in paragraphs 1 and 2) that it would consider to fall in this category. The DCI will independently take steps to ensure that the SSCI is also advised of activities that the DCI reasonably believes fall in this category.

5. When briefing the SSCI on a new Presidential Finding or on any activity described in paragraphs 2 or 4, the presentation should include a discussion of all important elements of the activity, including operational and political risks,

possible repercussions under treaty obligations or agreements, and any special issues raised under U.S. law.

6. To keep the SSCI fully and currently informed on the progress and status of each covert action operation, the DCI will provide to the SSCI: (A) a comprehensive annual briefing on all covert action operations; and (B) regular information on implementation of each ongoing operation, with emphasis on aspects in which the SSCI has indicated particular interest.

7. The DCI and the SSCI agree that the above procedures reflect the fact that covert action activities are of particular sensitivity, and it is imperative that every effort be made to prevent their unauthorized disclosure. The SSCI will protect the information provided pursuant to these notification procedures in accordance with the procedures set forth in S. Res. 400, and with special regard for the extreme sensitivity of these activities. It is further recognized that public reference to covert action activities raises serious problems for the United States abroad, and, therefore, such references by either the Executive or Legislative Branches are inappropriate. It is also recognized that the compromise of classified information concerning covert activities does not automatically declassify such information. The appearance of references to such activities in the public media does not constitute authorization to discuss such activities. The DCI and the SSCI recognize that the long-established policy of the U.S. Government is not to comment publicly on classified intelligence activities.

8. The DCI will establish mechanisms as provided by paragraphs 1 through 4, and that the Committee is fully and currently informed as provided by paragraph 6. The DCI will describe these mechanisms to the SSCI.

9. The SSCI, in consultation with the DCI when appropriate, will review and, if necessary, refine the mechanisms which enable it to carry out its responsibilities under the Intelligence Oversight Act.

10. The DCI and the SSCI will jointly review these procedures no later than one year after they become operative,
in order to assess their effectiveness and their impact on the
ability of the DCI and the Committee to fulfill their respective responsibilities.

William J. Casey
DCI

Barry Goldwater
Chairman, SSCI

Daniel P. Moynihan
Vice Chairman, SSCI

*A year went by, but the scheduled review kept being put
off. It was not until June 1986 that the second accord was signed
(by our successors Senators Durenberger and Leahy, and, again,
Mr. Casey). It was solemnly agreed that ". . . the Procedures
have worked well and that they have aided the Committee and
the DCI in the fulfillment of their respective responsibilities."
It was further provided that the committee should be informed
when "significant military equipment actually is to be supplied
for the first time in an ongoing operation, or there is a significant
change in the quantity or quality of equipment provided."*

*This was done five months after the president had signed a
finding providing for the shipment of arms to Iran and stipulating
further that the intelligence committees not be informed.*

*What we had here, however unwitting, was an effort to sub-
vert the Constitution of the United States. Such is the fruit of
contempt of government.*

Commencement Address,
New York University

I had my voice now, even if few heard it. The administration, Soviet-obsessed, was missing more important things in the world.

The theologian, Georges Bernanos, once observed that "the worst, the most corrupting lies are problems poorly stated." This is in a way a kindly view of the human condition, but it makes a special claim on those whose education is much concerned, as yours has been, with the art of problem solving.

It would appear that once again, as a nation, we are in the process of defining the nature of our problems with the Soviet Union. This is a recurrent process; things change. An early period of intense hostility was followed by a measure of normalcy, next by a wartime alliance, thereafter by a period of alternating co-operation and competition accompanied by the accumulation on both sides of unimagined levels of nuclear weaponry, which now presents itself as the central concern of mankind.

This period of redefinition has been brought about by a number of events, some transient, as in the styles of political rhetoric, but some far more real. Of these, the single largest fact is the obsessive accumulation by the Soviets not just of more nuclear weapons, but ever newer weapon systems. This behavior seems unrelated to anything we do. A recent secretary of defense put it, "When we build, they build; when we don't build, they build."

186

Of late, the Soviets have begun to deploy these weapons in ways that have no conceivable military purpose but are, rather, singularly political. In Europe, they have deployed far more SS-20 missiles, or rather warheads, than there are targets they might wish to destroy. Here on the east coast of the United States, our week began with an announcement by Marshal Ustinov that the Soviet Union has deployed an increased number of nuclear-armed submarines off our shores, with missiles aboard capable of reaching their targets in "ten minutes." President Reagan has replied that there is nothing new in this; that if there were, he would not have slept in the White House Tuesday night.

Now, indeed, there is nothing new in the deployment of Soviet submarines close to our shores. Their Yankee Class boats began to appear there some fifteen years ago, and in fact they have been moving further off shore ever since. Their newest submarine, the Typhoon Class, half again as large as our Trident, will spend much of its time under Arctic ice.

Even so, the question arises how it has come about that our relations have deteriorated to the point that responsible Soviet officials talk of war as if it were coming, and, as in Europe, direct their remarks not to governments but to the publics. This is new and ominous.

In less dangerous times, it would be sufficient that if something ominous developed in our relations with the Soviet Union, it was because they wanted it to. Certainly that is the experience of the last forty years. But at this moment, it seems necessary to ask the degree to which the United States shares some responsibility. Such a case can be made.

In the aftermath of World War II, finding ourselves the ascendant, indeed almost the only economic and military power in the world, the United States, under a succession of presidents of both parties, conceived a world politics based on a remarkably enlightened perception of our own national interests. (Which is to say interests not inimical to others and thus having the potential of forming an enduring system.)

These world politics were based on three central concepts.

In the order they emerged: first, the idea of law governing the conduct of nations; second, the doctrine of nuclear deterrence; and third, growing out of the first two, the quest for arms control agreements so that the world might back away from the nuclear brink.

The Soviets came to understand these to be our politics, and to a degree participated in them.

Then, all of a sudden, it began to appear that the United States was abandoning these former positions. Certainly our friends began to ask whether we were. We must assume our adversaries had done so as well.

In the realm of law, the United States seems almost to have forgotten our once deep and abiding commitment to the rules of international conduct. In Washington, where toughness and ignorance are frequently confused, the view is heard that for us to abide by such rules when the Soviets do not is to submit to a permanent and possibly fatal disadvantage. Former Ambassador Richard N. Gardner, now teaching at Columbia, has described this as a contention "that we must be free to 'fight fire with fire,'" and admits its undoubted political appeal, even, in such cases, its utility. But, he asks, if nations such as the United States "accept the Soviet standard of international behavior as their own, do they then forfeit any claim before the rest of the world to stand on a higher plane of morality?" And, of course, we do. And if such a claim is thought not to matter, then indeed we have changed.

The doctrine of strategic deterrence emerged in the 1950s when it became clear that the Soviets, also, would have nuclear weapons and missiles. It was a simple doctrine: The United States would defend itself, a right, incidentally, fundamental to international law.

We would never use our strategic weapons first, but we would deploy them in such a manner that if attacked, we would always attack back. And yet a year ago, as if no such history existed, the administration proposed, and Congress agreed, to deploy the giant MX missile in the old Minuteman silos in Wyoming and Ne-

braska, the very sites which, having become vulnerable to a Soviet attack, led to our decision to build the new missile and deploy
it elsewhere.

The MX in Minuteman silos can be instantly destroyed by
a Soviet first strike. Which means that in a crisis, our only choice,
as the phrase goes, is to "use 'em or lose 'em." Which the Soviets
know is our only choice, and which allows them ten minutes to
preempt. The moment those missiles are deployed, the world
goes on a ten-minute trigger, called "launch on warning." Wise
men protest. McGeorge Bundy of this university has written that
the MX decision

> violated the fundamental rule first laid down in the Eisen-
> hower Administration: The object of any new strategic sys-
> tem is to deter, and to deter safely it must be able to survive.

Professor Bundy goes on to echo Ambassador Gardner's remark. True, he writes, the Soviets deploy their land-based missiles in a first-strike mode; it has ever been such. It follows that
"the most important thing we can do, is not imitate the Russians." But with an amnesiac innocence, we seem bent on just
that.

Arms control agreements got off to a fast start in the 1960s,
beginning with the Limited Test Ban Treaty negotiated under
President Kennedy; then the critical Non-Proliferation Treaty of
the Johnson administration, culminating in the SALT I agreement reached under President Nixon. Then, all of a sudden, the
momentum broke. The Soviets have watched us sign, in succession, the Threshold Test Ban Treaty of 1974, the Peaceful Nuclear
Explosions Treaty of 1976, and the SALT II Treaty of 1979—but
not finally ratify any of them. For the moment, we are not even
negotiating. That the United States is prepared to negotiate, no
one doubts. But we can no longer bring the Soviets to do so. And
we don't know why.

And so the question arises: Are we stating the problem poorly?
Let me offer the thought that the desired outcome of the

world politics the United States pursued in the period of its great ascendancy a generation ago is that the ascendancy would gradually merge into an ascendant world community of like-minded, above all democratic, nations. This has happened. Our politics worked. Now this change, of course, causes problems too. We have now to pay a great deal more heed to other nations than we once did. Fine. That is the mark of our success. But somehow of late, we seem to be mistaking it for a sign of weakness and attributing that weakness to the rise of Soviet strength.

What pitiful stuff that is. The truth is that the Soviet idea is spent. It commands some influence in the world; and fear. But it summons no loyalty. History is moving away from it with astounding speed. I would not press the image, but it is as if the whole Marxist-Leninist ethos is hurtling off into a black hole in the universe. They will be remembered for what? The death of Andrei Sakharov? Yelena Bonner?

Are there Marxist-Leninists here and about in the world? Yes: especially when the West allows communism to identify with nationalism. But in truth, when they do succeed, how well do they do? And for how long?

We should be less obsessed with the Soviets. If we must learn to live with military parity, let us keep all the more in mind that we have consolidated an overwhelming economic advantage. The twenty-four members of the Organization for Economic Cooperation and Development, known as the OECD—a quintessential initiative in world politics of the postwar United States—now produce 60 percent of the world's GNP. The Soviet block produces 19 percent. What is the rest of the world to think?

The historical outcome is certain if we can keep the nuclear peace and attend to our own arrangements in a manner in which they continue to improve. The world monetary system, which the United States put in place forty years ago, is badly in need of adjustment, lest it become an instrument for draining wealth from the nations that are least wealthy.

The culture of terror, a peculiar mutant of the totalitarian age, threatens democratic societies across the globe: in my own ancestral home of Ireland; in Italy; Israel; now India. That the governments and peoples of these nations show surpassing resources of firmness and courage does not make of terror any less a trial. (The Soviets, of course, contribute greatly to terrorist movements. Here we have no choice but to confront them. But, surely, with a sense of proportion.) And, last, a kind of latent tribalism is sweeping much of the earth, challenging the traditions of modernity in which we have invested so much hope. This, too, is to be understood and confronted. But now, are these not challenges enough for one generation?

I suggest they are, and I offer a closing thought: Our grand strategy should be to wait out the Soviet Union; its time is passing. Let us resolve to be here, our old selves, with an ever surging font of ideas. When the time comes, it will be clear that in the end freedom did prevail.

New York, New York
May 24, 1984

Preserving a Pillar of
Crisis Stability

By mid-1984, we were back to the MX, as once again au-
thorization bills came to the floor. Lawton Chiles, our late re-
cruit of the previous year, now joined me in the amendment
prohibiting deployment. This was not a symbolic measure. The
United States needed a new land-based ICBM. We had not de-
ployed a new system since the Minuteman III was put in service
almost two decades earlier. There were other perfectly good, if
expensive, deployment modes besides fixed basing, which Pres-
ident Carter had advocated, but which the new administration
rejected because of public opposition in Nevada, home of "first
friend" Senator Paul Laxalt. This was not a decision quite in
accord with the administration's much advertised commitment
to defense, but there was no point getting personal. We won on
the merits.

On this occasion, the Christian Science Monitor *provided*
space.

The president's proposal to deploy 100 MX missiles in Minuteman silos will never come to pass. This became clear on June
14 when forty-eight senators voted for an amendment Senator
Lawton Chiles of Florida and I proposed to prohibit deployment.
This was, by five, the greatest number of votes gathered against
the president's MX proposal. We lost that day; the Senate dead-

locked 48 to 48, and Vice President George Bush cast the deciding ballot in favor of the program. One absent senator had voted with us before; another announced he would, for the first time, vote against the MX.

The next Senate vote on this could well mark the end of the program.

Our argument against the administration's MX deployment scheme is that it would undermine the doctrine of deterrence, which has for more than a generation served to keep the nuclear peace.

From the time Americans learned that the Soviets had developed the capacity to deliver a nuclear bomb to the United States, that policy of deterrence has guided both our thinking about how to build nuclear weapons and our planning as to how to avoid nuclear war. It has been followed with great faithfulness by every president since Eisenhower. Until now.

At the heart of deterrence theory is the proposition that war is deterred by making it clear that war cannot succeed. We seek to deploy our nuclear weapons in ways that make them invulnerable to a first strike, so the U.S. is in a position always to strike back in force if attacked.

It happens I was a member of the Cabinet fifteen years ago when that distinguished secretary of defense, Melvin Laird, began regularly to inform us that the Soviets were developing large land-based missiles with a degree of range and accuracy such that our Minuteman missiles, not originally vulnerable to a first strike, were becoming very much so.

If this continued, Laird said, we would have to get out of those silos if our land-based missiles were to continue to be deployed in a deterrent mode. In time, it was decided—reluctantly, and with no great rush to judgment—that a new missile would have to be developed and deployed elsewhere in a comparably invulnerable mode.

What emerged was the M (for missile) X (for experimental). Because the Strategic Arms Limitation Talks (SALT) limited the number of missiles the Americans and Soviets could have, it was thought necessary to pack as much power as possible into them. With ten warheads, each with almost ten times the power of the warhead that destroyed Hiroshima, MX became very powerful indeed: also a very valuable target.

Having so designed the missile, we set out to find a way to deploy it. For a decade, the MX wandered in the desert, searching for an invulnerable basing mode. Thirty-two basing plans were considered, but each was found unacceptable. To overcome this seemingly insuperable problem, President Reagan appointed a commission, chaired by General Brent Scowcroft, a man of unquestioned integrity and knowledge in this field. In April 1983, the commission proposed we move as rapidly as possible to deploy a mobile single-warhead intercontinental ballistic missile (ICBM) of approximately 15 tons. This ICBM is called the Midgetman, and its explicit purpose is to maintain our deterrent posture. Unfortunately, the report also suggested we build and deploy the MX missile *in the very Minuteman silos whose vulnerability had forced the search for a new missile.*

Let us be clear about what this means. The MX in Minuteman silos can be instantly destroyed by a Soviet first strike. Which means that in a crisis, the Soviets must think that *our* only choice is to "use 'em or lose 'em." This knowledge allows them ten minutes to preempt us. The moment those missiles are deployed, the world goes on a ten-minute trigger, called "launch on warning."

The world also loses one of the pillars of what is known as crisis stability. In situations of international tension—most recently in Lebanon—Soviet leaders have known what to expect from us. *We* will not begin a nuclear exchange. It is *their* choice whether to commence one. They know our doctrine is to respond. Have they ever had to ask themselves: Is the United States thinking we are about to start something? Do the Americans feel they had better launch their Minuteman missiles? Does Soviet security require a preemptive launch on warning? One easy answer to all questions: No. But put the MX in those Minuteman silos and all the answers become: Yes.

The amendment Senator Chiles and I offered would not have allowed us to put ourselves on that ten-minute hair trigger. Instead, it would have refocused our strategic modernization in a stability-enhancing direction.

The MX does not do this; Midgetman does. It has the virtues of a deterrent weapon; it is widely dispersible; it can be mobile. It would get us out of the holes that represent the basic tactical vulnerability of fixed ICBMs.

Perhaps, if we choose this course, the Soviets in time may also judge that there is greater strategic security to be got out of mobile, small, single-warhead missiles. Half the U.S. Senate evidently agrees. Half plus one could restore to American policy a commitment to deterrence.

The *Christian Science Monitor*
July 9, 1984

On December 19, 1986, the White House announced it would request funds for some 500 Midgetman missiles, and another, final, 50 MXs to be based on railroad cars. In an article in the Washington Post, *Brent Scowcroft, John Deutch, and R. James Woolsey described this as "one of the most important strategic weapons decisions . . . any administration has ever made: the decision to move decisively toward mobility and survivability for the U.S. ICBM force." From that moment, they summed up, "the SS-18s began to become a wasting asset for the Soviets." You can't lose 'em all.*

The Deficit—
The Real Crisis

Audiences vary. Here is an effort to walk the New York State Association of Counties through the arithmetic of the structural deficit in Washington which had now clearly emerged. This was information they, as local government officials, needed to have and although most were, and are, Republican, I do not recall much resentment. I was still talking as if something could be changed, citing Tryon Edwards: "Hell is truth seen too late." Did I really think that? Looking back, it is so clear that the basic events of the Reagan administration were over by his seventh month in office and no argument thereafter changed anything with respect to public finance. The Congress, with the initiative coming largely from the Senate, enacted hidden tax increases ("revenue enhancement") in 1982 and 1984, and there was a tax increase also in the Social Security legislation of 1983: but all on the margin.

This month, Congress reconvened after a lengthy recess for the Republican convention—there was an equally lengthy break for the Democratic convention. Howard Baker described the reconvening of Congress as "its final hours." Congress is scheduled to adjourn October 4 *sine die*, which means "forever and ever." Of course, Congress does not intend to disappear. The Ninety-ninth Congress will convene next January. But the unfinished

196

business of this Congress, the budget deficit, has taken on a *sine die* character. It is a central issue of the presidential campaign, and may well be the central matter for politics through the rest of the century.

This Congress, the Ninety-eighth, has strained to its limits trying to respond to the deficit. In 1982 and again this year, Congress did what it likes least to do—raised taxes and cut spending for domestic programs. Despite this, the deficit continues to climb. Something is happening here, something wholly new, something we have not understood. And it is no wonder, because it's no fun.

The president has told Congress the deficit is falling, from $195 billion in 1983 to $174 billion this year, and that these deficits don't matter much; the situation is not a critical one. But the Congressional Budget Office, the nonpartisan analytical branch of the legislature now directed by an economist of impeccably conservative credentials, Rudolph Penner, says the deficit is something to worry about. By 1989, CBO says the deficit will be more than $260 billion, and the total national debt will reach a numbing $2.6 trillion. It's difficult to remain unconcerned.

By that year, 1989, annual interest payments on the federal debt will reach $214 billion. By then, almost half of the personal income tax receipts will be required just to pay this interest bill.

All this matters for the economy—the nation's and your counties'. We have to take money—credit—away from private investment for the federal debt, but even that is not enough. We have to borrow from abroad too. According to the Economics Department of Morgan Stanley, in the latter part of this decade, more than $30 billion a year will go abroad to pay the interest on this foreign borrowing for the federal deficit. That's more than the federal government will spend this year on all education, training, and employment programs—and certainly more than we will be able to spend for these programs in 1989.

It matters. On February 14, Paul Volcker, the chairman of the Federal Reserve Board, told the House Banking Committee:

The net investment position of the United States overseas, built up gradually over the entire postwar period, will in the space of only three years—1983, 1984, 1985—be reversed. The richest economy in the world is on the verge of becoming a net debtor.

It is said the public can't understand the deficit. I think we can, if we get the terms of the new problem straight.

In thinking about this wholly new situation, it helps to separate the deficit into two parts. First, what the experts call the primary deficit. That's the amount of money spent on all federal programs, minus federal revenues. Second, the amount paid in interest on the outstanding debt.

Contrary to what we hear, and what most of us think, until recently, primary deficits have been relatively rare. There were two in the 1950s, two in the 1960s. They were relatively small. Those in the 1960s averaged $300 million, or one-fifteenth of what the Treasury now borrows each week. There were six in the 1970s, but still not large ones, save for the $40 billion primary deficit in the postrecession year, 1976.

This pattern continued in 1980 and 1981, until the walloping $105-billion primary deficit in the depression year 1982. But the primary deficit has now slacked off. It is some $61 billion this year, in a total deficit of $172 billion, and the Congressional Budget Office projects it will average about $46 billion for the rest of the decade.

In the meantime, interest begins to go out of control. In the economist's term, it becomes "unstable." In 1980, the Treasury paid out $52 billion in interest payments; this year the interest bill will reach $111 billion. By 1989, $214 billion.*

Here's why. What Keynes called the "magic of compound interest" works with debt as well as with savings. It starts slowly—seemingly so—and then explodes. It is these interest costs, not the primary deficit, that are behind the explosion of the budget

* Not now likely, but not impossible.

deficit and the national debt. Once again, while the primary deficit is stable for the rest of the decade, the interest costs will continue to soar.

Here's how it works. If the debt today is $1 trillion—and it's more—and the interest rate paid on this debt is 10 percent—and that's more too—in five years with *no* new primary deficits, the debt would soar to more than $1.6 trillion.

This means that, more and more, we will be borrowing largely to pay the interest on the debt, not to finance an imbalance between federal revenues and spending for federal programs. This always happens when the growth in interest payments is greater than the growth in the primary deficit. The result is the exploding deficit but, in point of fact, an exploding interest deficit, not a program deficit.

This is new. We have never experienced anything like it. If we do not get a hold on this, we will face a crisis unlike any we have ever known.

You are already facing serious problems, as Congress and the administration work to pare some of the responsibilities of the federal government—because that often can mean increasing the burdens on county government.

You know the facts; you live with them. Here are the figures. From 1981 to 1983, federal grants-in-aid to the fifty states fell by almost 20 percent, in inflation-adjusted terms. Revenue sharing fell even more sharply across the nation, from $6.8 billion in 1980 to $4.6 billion last year. It will not rise this year or next. Here in New York, I am told by the Office of Revenue Sharing at the Treasury Department, you will receive $3.5 million less in 1985 than you get this year—which was even less than you got in 1982, when New York got $464 million in revenue sharing.

Another example. In 1981, New York communities received $459 million in Community Development Block Grant funds to help build industrial parks and the like. Last year, New York's share fell $36 million—an 18-percent cut over two years when you adjust for inflation. And *you* have to adjust for inflation, because you have to make up the difference.

All this increases your burden and the pressures on your most important source of income, the property tax. Most of the rest of the country can finance more of their local services through federal grants-in-aid than through the property tax. In California, which provides a lower level of services per capita than does New York, for every $10 collected in property taxes, the state receives about $12.90 in federal grants-in-aid. Not so in New York. Here, for every $10 collected in property taxes, you receive less than $9 in federal grants-in-aid.

Let me say that again. New York received $9 billion in federal support for local projects and services in 1982—and had to collect more than $10 billion in property taxes for many of the same purposes.

Property taxes are not enough. You have to borrow, too. But as you know, the federal deficit is pushing up all interest rates.

Long-term general obligation bonds in New York today pay more than 10-percent interest; medium-term obligations yield more than 9.25-percent interest—which you pay. And your interest burden will compound much like the federal government's, cutting into your ability to pick up the services the federal government is cutting, yes, to pay the interest on the federal debt. The result is a politics of misery, allaround.

Deficits do matter, and we cannot eliminate them by simply cutting spending. You are forced to try to pick up much of these cuts. At the same time, the stock of federal debt has taken on a life of its own. It is an independent economic force, absorbing capital, channeling more of our national resources to pay interest—increasingly to foreign investors. This is a cycle of economic decline.

Tryon Edwards, the nineteenth-century New York theologian, wrote, "Hell is truth seen too late." I will say it again. Unless we see this particular truth, we will find ourselves in a crisis unlike any we have ever seen.

Grossinger, New York
September 16, 1984

Richard Rovere

This essay on Richard Rovere is somewhat out of place in a book of political argument. And yet it was *political argument. Was* meant *as such. I was by this time a bit estranged from a greatly gifted circle of New York writers who first came together in dismay at the "liberal" politics of the 1960s. Many had gone over to the Republicans; many had entered the new adminis- tration or assertively supported it. I hadn't, didn't, wouldn't, don't. Neither had Dick Rovere, who in a final memoir wrote of his background on the left which was not general knowledge. It seemed to me his history of the 1930s told much about the 1980s.*

On or about June 20, 1790, Thomas Jefferson, then secretary of state, Alexander Hamilton, the secretary of the Treasury, and James Madison, member of the House of Representatives for the Fifth District of Virginia, met over Jefferson's dinner table at 57 Maiden Lane, in Manhattan, and reached one of the momentous agreements of American political history. Depending on how you look at it, it was the last of the great constitutional accords, such as that which gave the small states equal representation in the Senate, while the more populous states would prevail in the House of Representatives. Alternatively, it was the first major conflict resolved by the newly established government, and, as such, marked the beginning of the American political system.

Two issues were involved. First, whether the new national government would assume the debt incurred by the sates during the Revolutionary War. Hamilton had proposed this five months earlier, in his Report on the Public Credit. Here was a classic regional conflict. Virginia, which pretty much spoke for the South, had arranged to repay its debt. It would gain little if the national government were to pay off the debt of others. The Northern states had not paid theirs (and also had more debt—nearly a third of the battles of the Revolutionary War were fought on New York soil). Northern financiers had bought up a good deal of this debt, in the form of much-discounted bonds, and stood to make a bundle if Hamilton could deliver.

The second issue was whether the capital would remain in New York or move south. The Constitution had left the matter unresolved, providing only that the seat of the government of the United States be located in an area "not exceeding ten miles square." Not just region but mores were at issue. Was ours to be a country run by Southern farmers or by Northern financiers? Never mind that the Southern farmers concerned were not quite plowmen, while the Manhattan financiers had to deal with an already developed urban democracy that was not notably disposed to an oligarchy of position. Something large and enduring was at stake. Jefferson and Hamilton understood. Jefferson made the deal. The war debt would be assumed. In return, the capital would move to a swamp on the banks of the Potomac which turned malarial in April. (Any congressman who lingered on into May might not be back in December, when Congress then convened.)

A hundred and fifty-eight years later, the *New Yorker* decided to establish a "Letter from Washington" as a regular feature of the magazine. A "Letter from London," written by Mollie Panter-Downes, and a "Letter from Paris," written by Janet Flanner, were already well established. With the plain precision that marked all his work, Richard Rovere, who was to write the new "Letter," describes the assignment in his posthumous memoir *Final Reports*. As with London and Paris, Washington was to be written about "as if it were a foreign metropolis."

I would hold that the Compromise of 1790, as historians refer to the Jefferson–Hamilton agreement, was essentially constitutional in nature—a separation of powers as important in its way as that between the executive and the legislature. The decision was made that the seat of government was to be removed from the otherwise natural capital, the soon-to-be-biggest city in the country, the center of commerce and finance and culture. The decision had great consequences. The economy began to grow on an axis moving west from New York to Chicago, scarcely touching Washington in any sense of the word. (Well into the second half of the twentieth century, national associations, such as the Association of State Governors, routinely had their headquarters in Chicago, where the railroads met.) All else was in New York. The port, Wall Street, the Opera, the *New York Times*, *Time*, NBC, Madison Square Garden, Madison Avenue, the Village, Fifth Avenue—where to stop? The culture in the largest sense was in New York: Government was somewhere else. Among other things, this meant that when the forces of the twentieth century required the two to become deeply intertwined, neither was ready. Neither *knew* the other. Consider the prolonged reluctance by American business to accept the necessary roles of government in a modern economy; or the incredible resistance in Congress, just twenty years ago, to civil-rights legislation. For thirty years, Richard Rovere recorded this encounter. There is no œuvre equal to it in American annals.

His memoir recreates experience with the compression and audacious truthfulness that we came to assume in his writing about others but only now encounter in writing about himself. He kept a journal, at least intermittently, from the early 1930s to his death, in 1979. "My formative years," he writes, "were the 1930s." Normal. These were the years he attended college, got his first job, wrote his first articles. But what is noteworthy is that his formative years were spent in *New York* of the 1930s.

This is to say, New York of the era of the Communist party, and its assorted offshoots and "fractions," as the term came to be known in the not always flawless English of the varied participants. It is an experience now all but forgotten. It barely (although importantly) touched Washington, and was never at all understood there. On the other hand, as with any powerful generational experience, it did not go away; rather, it passed on in ways usually unrecognized but not less real. (Not the least quality of Rovere's memoir is his sense of the continuities here.)

Robert Warshow, writing in *Commentary*, in December 1947, summed up the 1930s in New York:

> For American intellectuals, the Communist movement of the 1930s was a crucial experience. In Europe, where the movement was at once more serious and more popular, it was still only one current in intellectual life; the communists could never completely set the tone of thinking. . . . But in this country there was a time when virtually all intellectual vitality was derived in one way or another from the communist party. If you were not somewhere within the party's wide orbit, then you were likely to be in the opposition, which meant that much of your thought and energy had to be devoted to maintaining yourself in opposition.

Rovere did not escape; did not try. He writes that in his junior year at Bard, "I decided to become a Communist." His journal of June 15, 1936, records, "Joined Communist Party under assumed name of Dick Halworth—same as my *New Masses* name." (Halworth was his middle name, the nom de guerre was ritual.) He wrote a bit; spent the winter of 1937/38 with Granville Hicks and his family in a no-frills farmhouse far up the Hudson Valley; returned to New York in the spring to become a literary editor of *New Masses*. (Come to think of it, for the rest of his life he would follow this pattern of moving upriver and down.) Some of the scenes from his life then are mordant, irresistible. (He was obviously writing better for his journal than for his magazine!) There is Granville Hicks, the leading Marxist literary critic in the United States, earnestly immersed in a Marxist study group with the six Communists of Rensselaer County, New York. Or the sudden appearance at *New Masses* of Huntington Hartford, the A.&P. heir, fresh from Harvard:

> Hartford was quietly installed in one of our dark and musty cubicles and assigned the task of reading unsolicited fiction and poetry. We junior editors were assigned the task of making life as pleasant as possible for him. . . . I did my share of lunching, often paying the check since, like so many of the rich, he seldom seemed to have any pocket money on him. . . . *New Masses* got not one penny of the $40 million he was then said to be worth, and I estimate that he still owes me something in the neighborhood of twenty or twenty-five dollars, which compounded over forty years would be a respectable sum.

But it was not to last. Rovere, in "that dreadful autumn of 1939," was to encounter the defining political experience of his generation—the Molotov–Ribbentrop pact, in which the Soviet Union emerged on the world scene as the ally of the Nazis. He conveys the depth of the personal shock: "It is strange—or perhaps it is not—that I have so little memory, almost none, of August 24, 1939, the day the Soviet–Nazi nonaggression pact was made known to the world." He records that in his life "this was an event as stunning and as consequential as Pearl Harbor." But while he can recall precisely where he was on December 7, 1941—and precisely where he was when Franklin D. Roosevelt died, precisely where he was when John F. Kennedy was shot—August 24 remains "a blank, a nullity, a cavity in time. . . . My memory begins to return three or four days after the news, and it is largely a memory of walks." Now came the critical decision. He could have got over the shock, denied what happened. Many did. He could have turned to political opposition, as many also did. But he did neither. He was a writer, and decided to remain one, with one great lesson learned: "Don't surrender your independence to anybody." He never did. Even to the extent of not moving to Washington when he began to write his Letter, remaining instead in Dutchess County with his wife, Eleanor, and making the occasional trip to Washington by train.

His first Letter, dated December 20, 1948, described, with a measure of glee, the capital and its seers getting over the shock of Truman's reelection. From the first, he had a genius for spotting the illuminating detail. Anticipating a Dewey victory, the Republican Eightieth Congress, with the particularly penny-pinching Illinois Senator Charles Wayland (Curly) Brooks handling the matter, had appropriated a huge sum—"only a trifle less than a hundred thousand dollars"—to build a platform on the east side of the Capitol, where the swearing in would take place. "It is the most impressive lumber pile of its sort ever erected," Rovere said, and added that it was now known as the C. Wayland Brooks Memorial Stadium.

Still, the past had not left him. That first Letter referred to the Hiss–Chambers affair; there was an apt passage from *Pravda*; Henry Wallace was "a neo-Marxian reformer." But then the past wasn't yet past: Its meaning was still being fought for. Shortly thereafter, in his introduction to *The God That Failed*, R. H. S. Crossman was to write, "No one who has not wrestled with Communism as a philosophy, and Communists as political opponents, can really understand the values of Western democracy." Rovere felt that. And he knew shadows; heard voices. This never left him. Nor, in truth, any of those who'd had his experience. How to describe the American cultural encounter with Marxism and the sundering of the group of immigrants who mainly brought it here? In 1946/47, Lionel Trilling wrote his novel *The Middle of the Journey*. It can be read only as an account of the relations between Alger Hiss and Whittaker Chambers. But while Trilling knew Chambers slightly, he was not aware of the existence of Hiss. The Hiss case, as it came to be known, broke some months after the novel was published. And yet Trilling *did* know. Because somewhere out there, the things he wrote about *had* to be taking place. That is the difference between that generation and all the generations that preceded it and all that have followed or will follow.

In his personal politics, Rovere became a Democrat: for him the party of the center. Toward the end of his memoir, he writes of his friend Joseph Lash, "Like him I was a Stalinist forty years ago. The two of us are among the few who did not move from the far Left to the far Right, or away from politics altogether." Rovere's politics were seasoned and restrained—the mark of that earlier trauma—but nonetheless felt. He was a liberal, and he was a liberal Democrat. He did not much like Republicans. There were exceptions. In this memoir, he writes with great affection of Robert A. Taft. But in his first Letter, for example, he is so *pleased* that all the stuffed shirts were wrong, and that the Republicans lost, that there is no room for the sort of detachments he was capable of in other matters. In retrospect, Truman's victory may or may not have been such a good thing. The Democrats had had sixteen years in office, it was time the Republicans had a turn, not least in order to learn what modern government requires of those who would govern. They had worked at it in the Eightieth Congress—the first they had controlled since 1931—and had done well, enacting the Marshall Plan, for instance. But only to be denounced by the president as "do-nothings," and to lose their majority to boot. A bad lesson. Dewey's defeat discredited the "Eastern" Republicans, with consequences that are more in evidence today than ever.

Rovere's weakness in this respect was also a strength. None knew better than he when the Democrats went wrong. The 1960s— that "slum of a decade"—were wrenching for him. He hated the Vietnam War; despised Nixon. Even Truman diminished with time. He came to think that the Korean War, which he had much supported, began the militarization of American foreign policy. (Yes and no. We might have avoided the North Korean invasion; but to have acquiesced in it would have had miserable consequences. Vietnam did *not* logically follow. Even so, it can be granted that, as he writes, "in Korea, as in Vietnam, we . . .

confused the national interest with an ideological preference.") His final Letter, dated March 12, 1978, recounts the muddle the Carter administration was getting itself into. (Although Rovere suggests that even he had been surprised by the outcome of the 1948 election, it is clear what he would have called the 1980 one.) The bureaucracy? An "ungainly monster." The Party? Well:

> Common sense may call for a new farm program or the closing of obsolete shipyards or the elimination of wasteful and environmentally destructive hydroelectric projects, but there is nothing in the Constitution or in the 1976 Democratic platform that requires the President to do anything at any time merely because common sense seems to call for it.

Having helped to draft that platform, I can but agree. The passage is revealing, however. This is where he came out in the end—for common sense, however uncommon a virtue. There is nothing heroic in this, and, accordingly, only a strong will can cleave to it. He sums up: "My generation has a lot to answer for."

And also much to be proud of. Men and women like him saved us from the totalitarian temptation. And *kept* saving us, even to the point of numb weariness. (Near the end of his book, he writes, "No longer any point in asking Mary McCarthy why compassion led her to celebrate virtue and strength of character in Hanoi that she had never discerned elsewhere—not in Saigon, not in New York or Paris, not on Cape Cod or in the groves of academe.") Yet resorting simply to common sense bespeaks an exhaustion of ideas and, in turn, a decline of energies. He would, I think, be writing about that in this presidential year.

There are two other large themes that, had he lived, he would have addressed, and that someone ought to address. The first may be thought of as the breakdown of the Compromise of 1790. In Rovere's professional lifetime, the division of powers between New York and Washington—and it was just that: a quasi-constitutional arrangement arising from specific political ideas and with definable political purposes—began to collapse. When illness had finally prevented him from making his trips to Washington, he wrote of "the follies and occasional splendors of that awesome center of imperial power—a city I first got to know when it seemed an outpost of empire rather than a center." In the half century, the power of New York has declined almost in proportion to the imperious, if not altogether imperial, ascent of Washington. Consider that the day came when the city—the center of the wealth and the financial institutions of the nation—was as near as makes no matter to being bankrupt, and the capital had to "bail it out." New York is still a great city; but slowly, inexorably, Washington becomes the greater one. Yet Washington, deprived of the diversity of New York, is not prepared to be great. The power is unrefined. There are too few filters of sensibility through which ambition must pass toward fulfillment; too few standards that must be met. A president of the United States, for example, can state propositions about important matters in which he is simply *wrong*. No one is embarrassed; no one is surprised. That is "inside the Beltway," where standards are lower.

The second theme is a political transformation that, by contrast, Rovere seems not to have noticed—a failing he may have imposed on himself. His first Letter, in the aftermath of Truman's 1948 victory, essentially concentrated on how wrong the experts had been. In their "first, fine flush of humility," he wrote, "they sounded as eloquent and emphatic as Horace Walpole, one of the best of all political observers, when he learned of the coalition that had been formed by Pitt and Newcastle—an event as unthinkable to him as an invitation to Dewey and Wallace to enter Truman's Cabinet would be to us. 'I renounce all prophesying,' Walpole wrote Sir Horace Mann. 'I will never suppose that I can foresee politically.' " Rovere wrote of Washington as "shocked and incredulous at first, like every other community that had been penetrated by the false doctrines of opinion research." Here his literary and historical bent misled him. (Arthur M. Schlesinger, Jr., in his graceful foreword to the book, writes that throughout his life Rovere was fascinated by writing and by writers—much more than by politics and by politicians.) Opinion research—polling—was just beginning (and, in truth, wasn't all that bad in the Truman–Dewey contest). In short order, it became a highly accurate measuring device.

Jim Farley knew what folk were thinking in the brickyards of Rockland County, and a succession of Republican presidential candidates not only did not, but didn't know anyone who did. All that has changed. There is a vanguard in politics, all right, but it is not the vanguard of the proletariat dreamt of in Rovere's youth. It is, rather, a vanguard of small groups with lots of money, a good pollster, and the best commercials.

The *New Yorker*
September 17, 1984

The rest is too personal to bear repeating. Rovere had died in Vassar Brothers Hospital in Poughkeepsie. A rare New York sensibility would no longer explain Washington.

Tax Changes That Would
Devastate New York

In August 1984, I wrote this brief op ed article for the New York Times *asking if they would run it in late November when the elections would be over and attention would be turning to the next Congress. I more or less knew, but couldn't properly say, that the administration's tax reform measure would propose that state and local taxes no longer be deductible. This would be devastating to federalism and not just incidentally to New York. As I had to look after my sources, my specific charges were directed against Representative Jack Kemp and Senator Robert W. Kasten, Jr. Treasury I, as it came to be known, was published six days after this piece appeared and the battle raged for two years. Legions joined the cause. But again: the mindless inconsistencies of this time. How could an administration committed beyond endurance to the rhetoric of federalism and states' rights propose in an all but absentminded manner to devastate the capacity for local innovation and variation?*

Congress is about to embark on a major attempt at tax simplification. The principal thrust of the various proposals, including one that is to come from the administration, is to lower tax rates by cutting back the tangle of deductions, credits, and different treatment for different kinds of income that has grown up in the current code. That this needs doing, there is no doubt. But if the present deduction for state and local taxes were to be eliminated or sharply reduced, the effect on New York State would be devastating.

It is no news that taxes are high in New York, especially in the city. It may not be generally realized, however, just how high our taxes are, and how precarious our state's tax system is. No other state comes close to matching New York's combination of an enormous state and local tax burden—income, property, and sales taxes—resting on a surprisingly and increasingly narrow tax base.

For some years, the Advisory Commission on Intergovernmental Relations has kept track of the "tax capacity" and "tax effort" of the different states. Tax capacity measures how much a state could collect on resources that by common practice are taxed. Tax effort is the burden the state chooses to place on its tax capacity. Each is measured against a national index of 100.

As recently as 1967, New York taxes were higher than the national average—but so were our resources, and the mix wasn't too much out of line. In that year, our tax capacity was 108, or 8 percent greater than the national average, and our tax effort was 138. By 1981, however, our tax capacity had declined to 89 while our tax effort had risen to 171.

New York and Texas have almost exactly opposite patterns. In New York, tax effort is twice tax capacity; in Texas, tax capacity (132) is more than twice the tax effort (65).

The effects of this disparity would be vastly more painful than they are without the deductibility feature of the federal tax code. By allowing state and local taxes to be deducted from income for federal tax purposes, the code enables us to pay such taxes in much discounted dollars. Given the miserable level of federal outlays in New York, the deductibility of taxes is one of the chief features of the federal system that enables New York to maintain the public services we think necessary.

Put plain, if a New York taxpayer is in a 50-percent federal bracket, he pays state and local taxes with 50-cent dollars. If in the 40-percent bracket, 60-cent dollars, and so on. In all, the federal deduction is worth more than $4 billion a year to New Yorkers, with the average New York taxpayer "saving" $892. By contrast, the tax deduction is worth only $329 to Texans, because they pay much lower state and local taxes.

The larger effect, naturally, is on persons with larger incomes. In New York City in 1982, a couple with taxable income of $100,000 paid on average $12,179 in state and local taxes. However, federal deductibility cut the real cost of these taxes to $6,211.

In these circumstances, the "Fair and Simple Tax" proposed by Representative Jack F. Kemp, Republican of New York, and Senator Robert W. Kasten, Jr., Republican of Wisconsin, which eliminates all state and local income tax deductibility, would be ruinous to our region. The low-tax states would be vastly better off; average-tax states, about even; and New York, devastatingly worse off. No other state is damaged to the same degree.

It may not be easy to stop this particular provision in Congress. In taxation, as in a number of matters, New York has let itself get so far "off the curve" that it gets more and more difficult to pick up allies against proposals that do us particular damage.

There is an interest here beyond New York's. As everyone knows, there are great differences among the states in the public services they provide. Some of this is a matter of plain political preference—Westerners are different from Easterners. Some of it arises from the competition of, say, Southern states for Northern industry, and so on. Fair enough. It is an arrangement called federalism.

The tax code makes the different levels of social provision feasible. To make them infeasible would be as large a change in social policy as any this administration has contemplated.

The *New York Times*
November 21, 1984

1985

President Reagan
and Chairman Morrill:
A Constitutional Reflection

This address to the League of Cities was the first opportunity
I had to make the case for retaining the deductibility of state
and local taxes in the larger context of federalism.

I point out that the administration's proposal, so at odds
with its rhetoric, was more the work of the "permanent govern-
ment" at Treasury than of the political elements in the admin-
istration. Still, it speaks to attentiveness to details; even, in my
view, to their understanding of what their policies were supposed
to encourage and discourage.

I expect you will spend much of your meeting here talking
about proposed federal program cuts, and asking how to prevent
them, or limit them. This is what you are supposed to be doing.
The Republican leadership of the Senate is doing much the same.
In all likelihood, we will all still be doing this a decade hence.

There is an irony here. Because the debt has grown so great,
the cost of the federal government, as a proportion of gross national product, is now larger than it has ever been in peacetime
history. But the domestic budget, especially the portion allocated
to cities, is now under permanent pressure and will remain so.
Small victories come in terms of programs kept from being cut,
or cuts kept from being too great. As for the chance of major
policy changes, my friend George Will recently estimated their

likelihood as having gone from "not very" to "are you kidding?"

This is why I would take the opportunity presented by your invitation to draw attention to one subject, about which our cities can and ought to make a difference. I am talking about an event of constitutional dimension that has not yet happened, but may well occur.

A year ago, in his State of the Union message, the president proposed to present Congress with a major overhaul of the tax system. This work was finished in November and published in three volumes, with the title *Tax Reform for Fairness, Simplicity, and Economic Growth*.

In a hundred ways, the proposal is altogether admirable. Call it the pure theory of taxation. Call it a *festschrift* for Stanley Surrey, President Kennedy's renowned assistant secretary of the Treasury who preached the gospel of a tax code that would be neutral with respect to individual or corporate economic choices.

Part of the proposal, however, embodies a profound constitutional error, or so I believe. This is the proposal to eliminate the deduction of state and local taxes for the purpose of assessing federal tax.

It would be the huge irony of Mr. Reagan's administration if, having started out to reduce the size of the federal government, he ended by putting in place a principle that can only vastly enlarge its scope, but that is what is at issue here.

The framers of the Constitution had more thoughts about power than merely its limitation. They recognized and accepted the reality of the power embodied in government, and they sought not only to ensure that it was limited, but to ensure also that it was shared. This was the system we call federalism. It was not copied from anyone. It was wholly an American innovation, and it is precious.

In the debate to come, much is going to depend on our getting this straight in our heads. Federalism is not a managerial arrangement that the framers hit upon because the country was big and there were no telephones. Federalism is not a form of decentralization with which large corporations occasionally experiment when things get clogged at the top. Federalism is not an arrangement of necessity forced upon the men at Philadelphia by the cantankerous parochialism of the Yankees and the Yorkers and the Southern gentry.

In some measure it was those things, but it was larger than any. As Daniel J. Elazar shows in the current issue of *This World* magazine, federalism was a fundamental expression of the American idea of covenant.

Americans rejected "the notions of the general will and the organic state common among their European contemporaries." In our formal Constitution, we opted instead for the principle declared in the Mayflower Compact, which is that we solemnly entered a covenant, one with the other, that we would govern *together*. The word "federal" derives from the Latin *foedus*, which Elazar tells us is simply the Latin for "covenant."

This concept of covenant, of a lasting yet limited agreement between free men or between free families of men, entered into freely by the parties concerned to achieve common ends or to protect common rights, has its roots in the Hebrew Bible. There the covenant principle stands at the very center of the relationship between man and God and also forms the basis for the establishment of the holy commonwealth. The covenant idea passed into early Christianity only after losing its political implications. Its political sense was restored during the Protestant reformation, particularly by the Protestant groups influenced by Calvin and the Hebrew Bible, the same groups that dominated the political revolutionary movements in Britain and America in the seventeenth and eighteenth centuries. Much of the American reliance upon the covenant principle stems from the attempts of religiously inspired settlers on those shores to reproduce that kind of covenant in the New World and to build their commonwealths upon it. The Yankees of New England, the Scotch-Irish of the mountains and piedmont from Pennsylvania to Georgia, the Dutch of New York, the Presbyte-

rians, and to a lesser extent, the Quakers and German Sec-
tarians of Pennsylvania and the Middle States were all nurtured
in churches constructed on the covenant principle and sub-
scribing to federal theology as the means for properly delin-
eating the relationship between man and God (and, by extension, between man and man) as revealed by the Bible
itself.

The essence of the federal idea is that there are spheres of
government which must not be invaded by other governments.
Now this is not a rigid compartmentalization. All membranes in
the federal system are permeable. But they are not to be ripped.
(Nowhere is this more important than in the sphere of taxation,
wherein the initiative and independence of different levels of
government commences.)

Yet this is what the Treasury proposal would do.

Last year, the deduction for state and local taxes reduced
federal taxes by $28.5 billion; in 1988, according to the Treasury,
it would reduce federal taxes by $34 billion. This is a large sum,
and it introduces a question of first importance: how much the
actual burden on state and local taxes would increase, if the
deduction were repealed.

We don't have precise figures, but state and local governments raised, in round numbers, about $310 billion through taxes
last year. The proposed change in the federal tax code, then,
would increase the real burden of these state and local taxes by
about 10 percent.

The arithmetic is easy. The federal deduction reduces the
"real" cost of state and local taxes by upwards of 10 percent. For
persons in higher tax brackets, the cost is correspondingly greater.
This would certainly lead to a good deal of migration out of high-
tax jurisdictions, and indeed the Treasury proposal states outright
that those who don't like the extra costs the administration proposal would impose "are free to locate in the jurisdiction which
provides the most amenable combination of public services and

tax rates. Taxpayers have increasingly 'voted with their feet' in recent years." (*Tax Reform for Fairness, Simplicity, and Economic Growth*, Office of the Secretary, Department of the Treasury, p. 63.)

Last November, I wrote a short article on the subject for the op ed page of the *New York Times*. My first draft began: "If you are looking for an apartment in Manhattan, help is on the way." On second thought, I decided this was too alarmist, and took the sentence out. I wish now I hadn't.

The proposal will convulse the finances of school districts, that most quiet, efficient, and public-regarding of all levels of American government. And it will work perversely. More and more, the nation will turn to the federal government for the resources it needs, the very opposite of the principle of the Reagan Revolution. (In 1979, California passed Proposition 13 and had to cut local property taxes. The year previous, the state had contributed 40 to 45 percent of all local school district revenues. The year after, the state was called on to contribute 65 to 70 percent of all school funding.)

This also is the very opposite of the principle of federalism. Nothing is so revealing as the language of the Treasury proposal. Over and again the deduction for state and local taxes is referred to as a federal "subsidy":

> The deduction is sometimes defended as a subsidy. . . . There is no more reason for a Federal subsidy for spending by State and local governments than for private spending. . . . There is no reason to provide implicit Federal subsidies for spending of State and local governments by allowing deduction for their taxes. . . . Moreover, the deduction for State and local taxes is not an efficient subsidy. . . . In order to be even-handed and avoid (a) distributionally perverse pattern of subsidies, no itemized deductions should be allowed for taxes and fees paid to State and local governments. . . .

The Treasury would have us believe the most fundamental activities of state and local governments are in some significant sense activities paid for by the federal government.

A century ago, we understood this. On July 1, 1862, President Lincoln signed the Revenue Act of 1862, the first national income tax, a 3 to 5 percent tax to finance the Union effort. Section 91 of that revenue act said that "all other national, state, and local taxes . . . shall first be deducted" to determine a taxpayer's liability for the income tax—and this under the most pressing emergency conditions our country ever has faced.

The then-chairman of the House Ways and Means Committee was Justin Smith Morrill. (In the same year, Representative Morrill wrote what we know as the Morrill Act, providing federal lands to establish state land-grant colleges.)

Chairman Morrill, reporting the tax bill, explained that as a matter of simple logic, the deduction would be necessary both to avoid double taxation and to preserve a principle of federalism:

> It is a question of vital importance that the General Government should not absorb all [the states'] taxable resources—that the accustomed objects of State taxation should, in some degree at least, go untouched. . . . Otherwise, we might perplex and jostle, if we did not actually crush, some of the most loyal States in the Union.

Will not this proposal perplex and jostle, if not actually crush? Will it not produce this huge and final irony: that the transfer of revenue resources to Washington inevitably concentrates more resources in the federal government, which will grow ever larger?

You don't have to accept this. What is at issue are your budgets, your basic services, and your fundamental relationship to the national government. All in the service of an abstract theory of taxation.

Yesterday, you passed a resolution on this issue. It begins:

222

The provision of the Federal income tax code that allows taxpayers to deduct their state and local tax obligations from their Federal taxable income is a fundamental statement of the historical right of state and local governments to raise revenues and of individuals not to be double taxed.

The resolution describes this provision of the federal income tax code as the largest single federal "tax expenditure" item directly affecting cities.

Now "tax expenditure" is a term that implies that if the federal government lets you keep some of your income, it is somehow giving you that income. A curious proposition from the present administration. But that's what it says: If we let you keep it, it's something we've given you; it somehow belonged to us in the first place.

I don't believe this. I don't think that's what they had in mind in Philadelphia in 1787. I don't think you should call it a tax expenditure, and I don't think you should let the Treasury get away with calling it a federal "subsidy." In diplomacy this is known as semantic infiltration: If the other fellow can get you to use his words, he wins.

I began on a large theme and will close on one. Thirteen days after Mr. Reagan stated his theory of federal spending, he presented an equally large proposition about federal taxes. In an address to a Joint Session of Congress on February 18, 1981, he said:

> The taxing power of government must be used to provide revenues for legitimate government purposes. It must not be used to regulate the economy or bring about social change.

May I offer the view that this is not possible? It sounds good. It doesn't happen. *Any* tax affects the economy and changes society: a little bit, a lot, something in-between. A "neutral" tax proposal such as the Treasury has offered will have pervasive effects on the economy and the society. There is no avoiding this;

only disguising it. I happen to prefer John F. Kennedy's formulation, that to govern is to choose, and I would choose not to assault federalism in the manner the Treasury proposes.

Washington, D.C.
March 24, 1985

Letter to New York:
The Dollar and Eastman
Kodak Company

Walt W. Rostow has recently suggested that the world is entering a stage of economic development in which the United States will face the challenge of maintaining its own standard of living in the face of competition from the developing nations. We began to experience this in the 1980s. History was helped along by mindlessness.

To my knowledge, the Kodak Company (with headquarters in Rochester, New York) was the first major American enterprise to speak out.

Dear New Yorker:

The time could come when about the only thing American below the hood ornament of an American automobile will be a license plate made by prison labor.

If it does, it will because of decisions made in Washington and Detroit, *not* Tokyo. Let me give an example. Early this year, lobbyists for the Chrysler Corporation were all over the Hill talking down a bill to place a fixed quota on the number of Japanese automobiles that could be imported into the United States. Suddenly the signals reversed. What happened? As best I can follow it, General Motors decided to start importing many or most of its small engines from Japan, and put them in an

225

"American" frame. Chrysler saw itself losing this option if quotas were imposed. And so a Chrysler representative told the House Ways and Means Committee:

> Up to this moment, Chrysler has been advocating a freeze for ourselves and other importers of Japanese vehicles at current levels. However, given the running rules dictated by GM and the administration, it is now clear that Chrysler will have to make the hard choice of adopting a parallel "Far East strategy" of its own. It's apparent to us that GM wants a lion's share of the auto trade deficit. Well, I'm here to say that Chrysler is forced to demand *its* share of the trade deficit, too.

This came several weeks before the Senate unanimously passed a resolution telling the president to *try* to do something about the trade deficit—$37 billion last year—with Japan. Next, the Senate Finance Committee, which is responsible for trade matters, voted 12 to 4 in favor of a bill that would *require* the president to reduce the trade deficit with Japan, by either increasing exports or cutting imports. I should tell you I was one of the four who voted "No." I said at the time that the Japanese had plenty to account for and needed to be pressed, but that the main problem was here at home and this was no time to divert attention by "Japan bashing" as they say down here.

I have been expecting trade to become one of the great political issues of the 1980s. It has taken longer to do so than I expected, and has done so in different ways, but it has now happened.

If you have a little patience, international trade is a fascinating subject. Columbus wasn't looking for the Bahamas, where he first landed, when he sailed west from Spain. He was looking for India, where he could sell European goods for the manufactures of Asia. It is worth recalling that Asia was then the low-cost producer of high-quality goods. Three centuries later, *we* were selling *them* herbs. The "Empress of China" sailed from

New York for Canton in 1789 hoping to bring back, as it did, manufactured Chinese wares in return for ginseng root dug up in the Catskills. (The trade continues to this day.) Trade changes history: makes history.

Another example? In the decades after the Civil War, the railroads spread across the Great Plains, and wheat shipments began pouring back east and thence across the Atlantic to Europe on steamships. Now this was the time of the great political struggles against the surviving, still feudal power of the great landlords. Many a speech was made, many a pamphlet written. More than a few bombs thrown. But what brought the old regime down? Kansas. In his wonderful book *The Americans*, Stanley Lebergott writes: "The small capitalist farmers of North America hacked away at the economic base of the ruling landed classes in Europe more destructively than all the revolutionaries on the Continent."

The absolute American economic preeminence of the post–World War II years couldn't last, shouldn't have, and didn't. What didn't have to happen was for us to start getting complacent, which is what we did. One of the best measures of an economy is output per man-hour in iron and steel. We passed the British in this regard long, long ago. Then in 1973, the Japanese passed us. Mind, the Japanese were getting their ore from Australia, their coal from West Virginia, and their technology from Austria. Nature didn't give them their new eminence. Hard work did.

Even so, we held our own more or less through the 1970s, but then disaster struck at the beginning of this decade. Owing to mindless mismanagement in Washington—I don't believe I use such words often in these newsletters—in the space of four years, we turned ourselves into a debtor nation with a currency so overpriced that we could literally cease to be an exporting economy.

What happened?

Running huge deficits, the government has had to borrow huge amounts of money. The national debt all but doubled in four years. A huge chunk of this money was lent to us by foreign investors. . . . The result was that a month ago, or thereabouts, the United States owed more money abroad than we were owed. The savings, you might say, of three generations gone in four years. (We were first out of debt to foreigners in 1914 when the European countries liquidated their assets to pay for their war.)

An article in the *Financial Times* of London put the matter succinctly:

> 1985 is the year when the United States, the richest and most powerful nation on earth, becomes a debtor to its poorer neighbors.

You've heard me on the subject of interest costs. The federal government is now borrowing money to pay interest, much of which goes abroad. An indirect result is that the value of the dollar rises. Investors abroad bid for dollars in order to lend them to the U.S. government at the high interest rates we maintain in order to encourage them to do so. But this in turn bids up the "price" of the dollar in foreign currencies. (Since 1980, the price of the dollar has increased some 80 percent against the currencies of ten major trading partners.) One of the reasons this subject is hard to follow is that when this happens, the dollar is said to "strengthen" against other currencies.

A "strong dollar" *sounds* good, but leads to ruin. At least at the levels the administration has sanctioned.

Take our relationship with Canada, the country most like us of any country in the world. The American dollar is now "stronger" than the Canadian dollar. One dollar U.S. equals $1.37 Canadian.

Here now comes the trade issue. New Yorkers grow onions. Canadians grow onions. Not as good as ours from, say, Orange County, but good enough, I'm sure. And sooner or later, some food wholesaler in the Bronx discovers that for a dollar he can buy $1.37 worth of onions across the border. Result: Canadian onions start pouring into this country like Japanese cars. Last year, our trade deficit with Canada was $20 billion. Comparing their 25 million people to Japan's 120 million, the per capita trade deficit with Canada is *three times* as great as with the Japanese. In the meantime, Mexico has begun to buy wheat from China, and the Argentine to sell wheat to the United States. There are some things even Kansas farmers can't overcome, of which the most important is a hugely mismanaged economic policy in Washington.

All this led to an unusual event in Rochester, the home of the Kodak Company, one of the largest and finest of American manufacturers. Kodak's name is known the world over: a standard of quality and a technological leader. It is our nation's 10th-largest exporting company. And it is, in no small measure, responsible for Monroe County's economic importance.

In 1983, the last year for which a Commerce Department estimate is available, New York exported manufactured goods valued at $13.1 billion. A full 40 percent, or $5.3 billion, was produced in Monroe County. Kodak accounted for more than $1.2 billion, 9 percent of the state total.

Kodak also produces the world over. It has been in Japan for some 50 years, now has some 15 to 18 percent of the Japanese film market, and plans more. It goes toe-to-toe with Fuji on price, and isn't asking any help from anybody.

What it can't do is overcome the effect of the overpriced dollar. (Here again that problem of words. Typically, we say "strong dollar." Strong dollar, strong America, right? Wrong. But there you are. "Overpriced" is the right way to say it. If the dollar is overpriced, American exports are overpriced, imports are underpriced.) In 1984, Kodak's purchases of foreign parts and products doubled from the previous year, while exports stayed level. The situation is becoming threatening.

Kodak estimates that the overpriced dollar has cost it $1 billion in earnings since the summer of 1980.

And so, in April, the company took the unprecedented step of writing its 183,000 stockholders a letter on the subject. It lays out the issue more clearly than anything I've seen. Here is an extract:

The strong dollar has resulted in a decrease of several percentage points in U.S. economic growth, helped to produce a trade deficit of $123 billion in 1984, and according to some, eliminated more than 2 million manufacturing jobs. At Kodak alone, some 20,000 jobs depend upon exports.

Kodak, as a multinational company with about 40 percent of its sales outside the United States, has not escaped the impact of the artificially strong dollar. . . .

In 1984, Kodak net earnings totalled $923 million, an increase of 63 percent over the depressed levels of 1983. . . . Yet the upward surge of the dollar actually reduced our earnings by about $.60 a share in 1984 alone. If the dollar remains at its current value, 1985 earnings will be adversely affected by more than they were in 1984. . . .

This challenge is affecting all U.S. companies operating in global terms. Kodak believes in free trade: We do not advocate protective tariffs and import quotas. But while the company welcomes fair competition in a healthy worldwide marketplace, the abnormally strong dollar encourages imports while restricting the ability of U.S. producers to market their goods and services at home and abroad. In effect, this abnormality provides our competitors with an unearned opportunity.

The danger here is that our large manufacturers will slowly cease to produce here in the United States and instead become marketing companies that sell products made abroad.

That is what I meant by my opening remark. Those shiny new automobiles may have American names, may even be assembled here, but they won't have American engines.

The worst of it is that, at first, these changes present themselves as a break for the consumer. Goods are cheaper. One of the reasons inflation has come down so rapidly is the flood of imports. But this catches up with a people who, in effect, are living on borrowed money. Yesterday the Senate Finance Committee held hearings on "the dollar."

Our opening witness was Mr. Colby H. Chandler, chairman of Kodak, who described in grim detail the international trading scene from the point of view of an American manufacturer, and then brought it home to downtown Rochester. A retailer friend of his had asked this question: "What good will it do to have lower-priced merchandise if I have no consumer with jobs and dollars to spend?"

Protectionism—tariffs, quotas, closed trading systems—seems an easy answer to this. Keep the foreigner out of your market. It surely seemed a good idea in 1930, after the stock market crash. In a frenzy still remembered around here, Congress enacted the Smoot–Hawley Tariff Act of 1930. Tariffs were raised on, well, everything by the time every member of Congress had got his amendment attached.

And did it do the job. Within two years, American imports were cut by half. But so were American exports: European nations had retaliated against us instantly. This set in motion changes that led to a general trade war, as tariffs went up and the depression of the 1930s deepened.

It ended with World War II. In the United States and United Kingdom, a group of men of great patriotism and courage were persuaded that the trade war had led to the real war, the most awful carnage known to human history: from Auschwitz to Hiroshima. These men determined that at all costs, the postwar world must avoid the awful simplicity of trying to stay prosperous while making your neighbor poor.

Under the leadership of Secretary of State Cordell Hull, an American trade policy team began working in 1943 on a postwar trading system.

For decades the new system worked wonderfully. World trade doubled, then redoubled. The trading nations prospered as never in history.

It is breaking down again. The breakdown is starting here. *This* morning in the Finance Committee, we held a hearing on a new proposal making its way around the Hill. It is to impose a 20-percent "surcharge" on all imports until our trade deficit clears up. Rudolph G. Penner, director of the Congressional Budget Office, testified:

> The proposed import surcharge would actually raise the average tariff for all imported goods above the average level attained by the Smoot–Hawley Tariff Act of 1930.

There are many things we can do. First, second, third is to reduce the deficit in a responsible way. We can restrain the dollar's rise by building a "Strategic Foreign Currency Reserve." Certainly the major trading nations need to work together to keep their currencies in line. Most assuredly, the United States must drop its *policy* of doing nothing. But above all, we must not go crazy with tariffs.

Washington, D.C.
April 24, 1985

Letter to New York:
The $35,000 Telephone,
A Spy Story

A spy story with a moral!

Dear New Yorker:

I was named U.S. ambassador at the United Nations in the late spring of 1975. Nelson Rockefeller, then vice president, asked if I would look in on him when I was next in Washington, which I was happy to do. I was working on what were then (and I suppose still are) called North–South economic issues which he cared a lot about and knew a lot about, but that was not what was on his mind.

I showed up at his suite in the old State, War & Navy building next to the White House. He took me into a back room, summoned coffee, and told me that the first thing I must know about the UN is that the Soviets would be listening to every telephone call I made from our mission or from our suite in the Waldorf Towers. They had installed increasingly sophisticated equipment for doing this in their mission on 67th Street, in their compound at Glen Cove on Long Island, and most important in a new 22-story building they had built on the high ground of Riverdale in the Bronx and from which their intercepts swept the whole of Manhattan.

I thought he was telling me something deeply secret and

treated it as such. Only just recently did I learn that it wasn't secret at all. He had *tried* to make the matter public. But no one seemed interested.

In January 1975, President Ford had appointed him chairman of the Commission on CIA Activities Within the United States. (Ronald Reagan was a member.) There were wild charges being made against the agency in those days; and some not entirely wild. The Company, as they call it, had not always been as careful or even as sensible as it ought to have been. Still, the more lurid charges were baseless. The CIA was never involved in "large-scale spying on American citizens," nor yet grossly "engaged in illegal wiretaps." Rockefeller's report dismissed these charges straight out, and then took the offensive, stating that while the CIA wasn't, the Soviets most assuredly were.

A section on "Foreign Invasions of United States Privacy" began:

> This Commission is devoted to analyzing the domestic activities of the CIA in the interest of protecting the privacy and security rights of American citizens. But we cannot ignore the invasion of the privacy and security rights of Americans by foreign countries or their agents. This is the other side of the coin—and it merits attention here in the interest of perspective.

They had found out what the Soviets were up to in New York. They said so about as plain as you could ask:

> While making large-scale use of human intelligence sources, the communist countries also appear to have developed electronic collection of intelligence to an extraordinary degree of technology and sophistication for use in the United States and elsewhere throughout the world, and we believe that these countries can monitor and record thousands of private telephone conversations. Americans have a right to be uneasy if not seriously disturbed at the real pos-

sibility that their personal and business activities which they discuss freely over the telephone could be recorded and analyzed by agents of foreign powers.

If no one in Washington seemed to care that we were being listened to, I did. I had just come from India where you learn the importance of knowing who's after you. Palestinians had got Cleo Noel in Khartoum a few weeks after I arrived. I was apparently next on the list. By the time my tour was up in New Delhi, I had developed the not unreasonable judgment that it was owing mostly to the Indian plainclothesmen who looked after me that I was leaving in Clipper Class and not in a box.

Anyway, it turned out to be important. About six months later—Friday, December 5, 1975, if anybody wants to know—a member of the mission staff asked to see me. He came into the office, closed the door and reported that Arkady Nikolaevich Shevchenko, under secretary general of the United Nations, had told an American in the secretariat that he wished to defect.

Impossible. Shevchenko was the ranking Russian at the UN, a protégé of Gromyko, who took him to meetings of the Politburo. At forty-seven, he was already touted for deputy foreign minister as his next assignment. It would be the highest-level defection of a Soviet official in their history. A trap? Had to be. Yet you don't use a Shevchenko for bait. We would have to find out and we did and it worked. *And we did not use the telephone.* I took to meeting people at hockey games in Madison Square Garden. It may have made a difference. Anyway, Shevchenko did defect (secretly at first), and this year, ten years later, published his book, *Breaking with Moscow*. It has one passage I sort of wish Nelson Rockefeller was around to read.

He writes of his early assignments as a member of the Soviet Mission to the United Nations and the mushrooming of KGB agents specializing in science espionage:

At Glen Cove alone, the escalation was striking. When I first came to the United States in 1958, there were three or four KGB communications technicians and their gear sharing the former servants' quarters in the attic. By 1973, the specialists in intercepting radio signals numbered at least a dozen, and they had taken over the whole floor. Their equipment occupied so much space, in fact, that one of the two large unused greenhouses had been commandeered to store it. These quarters were off limits to other personnel.

The rooftops at Glen Cove, the apartment building in Riverdale, and the Mission all bristled with antennas for listening to American conversations.

Next thing you know, I was in the Senate, and Nelson Rockefeller wasn't, and it seemed to me we owed him something. At the outset of the Carter administration, I put in a simple bill: "Whenever the President has reason . . . to believe . . . that . . . any individual on whom diplomatic immunity has been conferred by the United States is willfully engaging in electronic surveillance on behalf of a foreign power, the President shall . . ." tell them to stop, and if they don't stop, send them the hell home.

At a news conference on June 12, 1977, the president of the United States was asked about this. What did he think? Well, said Jimmy Carter, because of microwave transmission of telephone conversations, "the intercept on a passive basis of these kinds of transmission has become a common ability for nations to pursue. It's not an act of aggression or war; it's completely passive." He wandered on a bit and left it: "I would not interpret this use by the Soviet Union . . . to be an act of aggression."

Thanks, Chief. I never said it was an act of aggression. I said it was a violation of the constitutional rights of American citizens. I wasn't asking him to declare war. I was asking him to uphold the Constitution. Which he had sworn to do. So have senators.

The government had another plan. It began to bury its own telephone cables. Did they realize they were saying that the government has interests different from those of the people? The *New York Times* did. An editorial commented:

When a United States Government agency is found to have been doing illicit wiretapping, the expected response from law-enforcement officials is not to make the job more difficult but to order the agency to stop. If the Soviet tappers are being treated as though this were some sort of a game, it is probably because the intelligence arms of our two countries are linked in just such a game. We are probably getting valuable information from tuning in on Russians in Russia, and perhaps some of that information is deemed so vital as to justify turning a blind eye or deaf ear to Soviet activities here.

But for a nation that prizes individual privacy and public accountability, the presumption must be otherwise. If a member of the Soviet Embassy were caught stealing and shipping economic data back home, our authorities would, we hope, see to it that he was shipped back home. The blunt fact is that a foreign government on American shores is prying on American citizens. And notwithstanding the niceties of diplomatic immunity and extraterritoriality and rigamarole, the response should be equally blunt.

The public must be fully informed as to the extent to which their privacy has already been invaded and the Russians must be made to remove their monitoring equipment from this country.

But the Carter administration wouldn't touch the bill. The Foreign Relations Committee was dissuaded from even holding hearings. By this time, I was on the Select Committee on Intelligence and contrived to raise the subject with CIA officials in a public hearing. Wouldn't the agency agree that this "passive" practice violated the Fourth Amendment rights of American citizens? To wit:

The right of the people to be secure in their persons, homes, papers, and effects, against unreasonable searches and seizures, shall not be violated. . . .

No, replied the general counsel of the CIA. No? That's right: You see, senator, the Fourth Amendment only protects you from invasions of privacy by your *own* government, not by foreign governments.

Administrations changed. But the position with respect to Soviet telephone espionage did not.

Toward the end of 1981, the FBI decided to speak up. Theodore Gardner, special agent in charge of the Washington field office, described for the press just what those funny looking antennas and wooden shacks on the top of the Soviet embassy on 16th Street really were. He estimated that 40 percent of the Russian embassy personnel in Washington were occupied with eavesdropping. The press began to note that by 1984, the Soviets would be moving into a new embassy on Mount Alto, 350 feet above sea level, one of the highest points in the city.

Next, the National Security Agency went public. In October 1984, the press reported: 500,000 More Spy-Proof Phones Proposed By Top Security Agency. Walter G. Deeley, the senior officer in charge of protecting government communications, gave an interview in which he stated that electronic eavesdropping by the Soviet Union posed a genuine threat to the United States:

> I want the country to be aware that if we don't protect our communications, it can do a great deal of damage to us. This is a problem that goes to the very fabric of our society. It is not just a worry of the national security agencies.

Rare. The NSA was set up by President Truman in a secret executive order in 1952 to conduct electronic intelligence abroad as well as to protect our worldwide communications. For the longest while, it was referred to as "No Such Agency." They don't give interviews.

With the new Soviet embassy coming on line, concern within the American government continued to surface. Deeley's interview was with David Burnham of the *New York Times*. Three weeks later, *Time* reported that President Reagan had "quietly" signed National Security Decision Directive No. 145 setting up the president's policy on telecommunications and computer security. The magazine estimated the cost of implementing the directive's program at $6 billion to $8 billion, including an increase in the number of secure telephones. The following May, Burnham reported that "at the insistence of President Reagan . . . the 86 limousines used by top American officials in the capital got scramblers on their phones." These would cost $35,000 apiece. (Oh well, in other parts of the Pentagon they pay $9,000 for a 12-cent Allen wrench.)

Soon the Washington press was alive with speculation about the new embassy:

SOVIETS TAKE THE HIGH GROUND
New Embassy on Mount Alto Is a Prime
Watching—and Listening—Post

(You have to admire the Soviet spokesman who, when queried, replied: "We did not capture the site. We were given it." True. It was the site of a VA hospital. In 1969, we swapped it for a site on the mud flats of the Moscow River.)

I was still at it. I had reintroduced the wiretapping bill at the outset of Mr. Reagan's first term, and now did so yet again as S. 12, the Foreign Surveillance Prevention Act of 1985. The *Wall Street Journal* came to my support in an editorial "Is Moscow Listening?" (It was well understood that the Soviets focus particularly on banking and financial traffic.) "We hope," said the *Journal*, "that this time around, Congress will send a loud and clear message to Moscow that such breaches of U.S. laws and electronic eavesdropping on government, industry, and private citizens cannot be conducted with impunity."

The editorial had no sooner appeared than the administration informed the Foreign Relations Committee that it opposed S.12. In June, the Department of State Authorization Act came to the floor and I offered the bill as an amendment. The managers accepted it, and it became Title VII of that measure, which thereupon went to conference with the House. All looked well until at the very last moment, the administration intervened and Title VII was dropped. A letter to the chairman of the Foreign Relations Committee explained that "the President already possesses all of the authority that the Moynihan amendment would grant."

If you are a diligent reader of newspapers, you will already have learned everything you've read here so far. Now for a secret. I think we have begun to be afraid of these people.

I grant it was difficult for Jimmy Carter to be tough. He didn't understand the Soviets—to his credit he said so when they invaded Afghanistan—and had relied on the soft edges of our party to beat Scoop Jackson. But what of the present lot? All that talk. Evil Empire. Noise about the UN sailing off into the sunset. (Landing in Hoboken.) Have Shevchenko to lunch at the White House. Tell us more about how those Russkies plot to export revolution. But say a word about the KGB agents swarming in the UN Secretariat? Not in the script. Show Dobrynin how tough we are: Take away his parking spot in the State Department basement. But tell people to stop spying? Dear heavens no. That would be a provocation. It might even interrupt wheat sales. Again, the letter to the Foreign Relations Committee chairman:

> The President already possesses all of the authority that the Moynihan amendment would grant, and diplomatic personnel have and will continue to be expelled from this country when such action is appropriate.

But such action would scarcely be appropriate for a mere criminal act directed against some 10 or 12 million New Yorkers!

The danger is that we invite contempt. The Soviets know that we know they acquired something close to effective control of the American telephone system. AT&T figures that 70 percent of its domestic and 60 percent of overseas traffic is transmitted by microwave, and so is readily sucked into the Soviet computer. (They have a big dish in Cuba, also.) They know that years ago

Nelson Rockefeller warned that such control could lead to blackmail and to Americans' "recruitment as espionage agents."

Hold it: This is a spy story, not some article for the *New
Right Review*. Let's play "Supposing Rocky was Right?" How
come the most assertively anticommunist administration in our
history supinely submits to Soviet subversion?

Has ten years of electronic spying taken its toll? Every day,
we seem to be indicting our first-ever FBI agent, a CIA employee,
a Navy petty officer, an Army lieutenant colonel. Has the rot
gone higher? Blackmail, said Rocky.

To be continued.

Pindars Corners, New York
August 10, 1985

*In 1986, the Reagan administration expelled a number of
Soviet "diplomats" at their UN mission. The Soviet foreign minister complained to our secretary of state that one of the expellees
never even left the Soviet compound!*

The Potemkin Palace

Was this an argument with Reagan? Or Kennedy? Johnson? Nixon? I suppose it is an argument with the last quarter century, and a strong case for language training! It was given as the Feinstone Lecture at the United States Military Academy, and later reprinted in the National Interest. *The cadets listened with a high order of interest, reflecting more, I think, than their accustomed good manners. I was talking, after all, about what my calling had done to their profession.*

A visitor to Panmunjom in Korea undergoes a succession of experiences. First one senses the tension, unlike anything to be encountered on other borders between the communist and non-communist world. A Military Armistice Commission meets here. The fighting has stopped; the peace is still to come. Next one notices the tiny temporary buildings in which the commission meets: little more than Quonset huts, the sort of thing put up to last out a three- or four-year war, but now in use for a third of a century. Then suddenly, looking up, out, something different. There, looming over the tin roof shacks is a massive white masonry palace put up by the North Koreans. It is hard to place architecturally. Late Stalinoid doesn't quite do, for there are slight oriental touches about the three doorways that intersperse twelve large windows along a second-story balcony. But any architec-

242

tural interest is quickly displaced when one learns that the building, a full 34 meters long and 9 meters high, is 4 meters deep.

Off in the middle distance is a thriving village at the center of which is a flagpole some 160 meters tall. As the Washington Monument is 169 meters in height, we can safely say this is the tallest flagpole on earth, and the 15 by 30-meter red flag flying there may be safely assumed to be the largest of its kind. The village itself would accommodate hundreds of contented collective farmers, save for the problem we encounter at Panmunjom itself: The buildings are all facades; nobody lives there.

A visitor thinks immediately of the Potemkin villages said to have been erected for the edification of Catherine the Great of Russia and the foreign ambassadors who accompanied her on a celebrated journey down the Dnepr River in 1787. (Historians have quite rejected the tale of a hoax perpetrated by Prince Potemkin, the governor of the newly acquired southern territories through which the party travelled. It seems he did apply a touch of paint here and there, but the villages were not stage props carted downstream one after the other, nor were the villagers Lithuanians conscripted for the festivities, as was anonymously reported in the German press by the Saxon envoy von Helbig, whence the myth began. To the contrary, it appears the Czarist conquests were doing well enough. Only in contemporary Soviet satellites is the need for dissimulation total: brave and yet so pathetic.)

Such a sight brings to mind not just the long history of deceptions, including at times self-deception, by which various despotic governments have sought to advance their causes, but also the difficulty that free peoples sometimes have in perceiving those deceptions.

I have been in government for a long while now—long, that is, for someone who serves in appointive or elective office. I have served in the cabinet or subcabinet of four presidents, have been an ambassador for my country on several occasions, and now serve in the Senate. And so I have been involved with American government during a long period when American power, the strength of the political ideal of freedom, has been repeatedly tested.

I went to Washington with John F. Kennedy, which was a complex fate. Early on, one was to experience the assertion of American ideals in the most stirring terms, and the ready acknowledgment that if ideals are of any consequence they must be defended, which is to say that American ideals required American power. Next, one learned the limits on American power imposed by the growing nuclear strength of the Soviet Union. Finally, slowly, and well past Kennedy's death, one learned in Southeast Asia something of the inherent limitations on American power which those very ideals impose.

I thought at the time, and think now, that this latter point impressed itself on Kennedy as time passed. I believe he was referring to this almost paradoxical aspect of democratic government in an address he made at Dublin Castle in Ireland in June 1963, the last year of his life. In a particularly poignant passage, he said: "Democracy is a difficult kind of government. It requires the highest qualities of self-discipline, restraint, a willingness to make commitments and sacrifices for the general interest, and it also requires knowledge."

It is that last point I wish to dwell upon: knowledge. Knowledge, and the various decisions or nondecisions that led us, beginning with Kennedy, into a war in Indochina that proved the most serious setback we have ever encountered as a nation, at least since the British burned the capital. (Military correctness requires that I note that we had first burned what is now Toronto.)

I admit to a certain fatalism about the war at the time. My generation had reason to think of violence as a normal condition of life. I was in the navy at age seventeen, and save for the nuclear bomb, would be long since dead on the beaches of Kyushu or some such bastion of the Japanese archipelago. Serving in the Johnson and Kennedy administrations, I knew, without significant exception, the persons who made the initial decisions to enter the conflict and then to intensify it to the point where a presidency was lost, and of course much else. I followed their reasoning. North Vietnam was seen as the point of a lance firmly grasped by two other comrades in arms, the Soviet Union and its militant ally, the People's Republic of China.

A recent visit to China reminds me, however, that during the years of the greatest intensity of American involvement in the Vietnam War, resisting what we viewed as the coordinated expansion of three communist nations along the eastern rim of Asia, those very nations were practically at war with one another, and one of them was at the point of internal collapse.

This latter, of course, was China. In his masterful study, *Vietnam: A History*, Stanley Karnow writes: "Though American officials repeatedly portrayed Mao Zedong as the guiding spirit behind the Communist aggression in Vietnam, Mao actually took a cautious approach to the war." He was preparing to launch his Great Proletarian Cultural Revolution, what Karnow calls "his devastating purge of the Chinese Communist party," and needed his army to help him carry out the political campaign. A large war to the south would only weaken him at home. Further, the Chinese communists were by now thoroughly estranged from the Russian communists, and the military threat on Mao's northern and western borders was growing. (In 1966, the Soviets brought tactical nuclear weapons to support their growing deployments on the 4,150-mile border.) In *Dangerous Relations: The Soviet Nation in World Politics, 1970–1982*, Adam Ulam records that "as early as February 1964 Politburo member Mikhail Suslov, speaking before the Central Committee, attacked the Chinese leaders and warned that 'they would not refuse to improve relations with the United States, but as yet do not see favorable circumstances for such an endeavor.' "

According to Karnow, the Vietnamese later claimed that Mao "wanted to use them as proxies in a war that would . . . leave them too exhausted to resist Chinese domination."

It is 1964. Three communist nations are already well advanced in venomous assessments of treachery by one another. But somehow the United States sees instead a human wave of ecstatic red soldiery waving ancient rifles on their united way south. It was as if we were looking at one of those giant billboards you could see in Canton, and, as with the palace at Panmunjom, we did not realize that no matter how tall and how long, it was not even four meters deep.

For reality was so different. The communist powers were absorbed with internal divisions within the communist world and preoccupied with efforts to manipulate one another. No American in the 1960s could fail to be impressed by the manic menace of Chinese pronouncements concerning the United States. But it now appears that it was the Soviets the Chinese were actually trying to influence! Thus Adam Ulam: "China's virulent anti-Americanism before the 1970s had been largely designed to bar any reconciliation between the USSR and the U.S."

It would appear that the Chinese opening to the United States came primarily from fear that the Brezhnev Doctrine would lead to a Soviet invasion. To this day, visitors are shown about the fantastic underground cities in Beijing where the population was to go when the nuclear exchange began. Limited hostilities did indeed break out in March 1969, described in the *Selected Works of Deng Xiaoping* as the "Zhenbao Island counterattack in self-defense . . . made by Chinese frontier guards."

In the meantime the Cultural Revolution had commenced. Pronouncements apart, it first appeared to the West in the form of flotillas of bodies, bound hand and foot, floating down the Pearl River into the South China Sea at Hong Kong. Not an everyday event: But somehow something we could not interpret.

Simon Leys, in *Chinese Shadows*, describes the Red Guards as an "anarcho-revolutionary movement." Destruction reigned. Intellectuals were the primary target. Again the *Selected Works* of Chairman Deng: "During the 'Cultural Revolution,' the Gang of Four slandered the intellectuals as the 'stinking Number Nine'— the ninth category after landlords, rich peasants, counterrevolutionaries, bad elements, Rightists, renegades, enemy agents, and 'capitalist roaders.' " Universities were closed, high schools were closed. Faculties and party officials—Deng Xiaoping—were sent en masse to the countryside to plant rice and slop pigs, with (again the *Selected Works*) "disastrous consequences." Evidently millions died. (A few years ago, having remarked to Alexander Solzhenitsyn that few would have expected that the great literature of the 1960s would come out of Russia, I asked where he thought it would appear next. "In China," he replied, "in the 1990s." Which is to say, when those who survived the 1960s begin to write of their experiences.)

There were successive stages. First the monster rallies in Tian'anmen Square in Beijing: a million youth brandishing the Little Red Book. Next the sanctioned slogan, "Rebellion is Justified." Then, in the words of Joan L. Cohen and Jerome Alan Cohen in *China Today*, an "unprecedented assault" by Red Guard groups with the assistance of Lin Biao's army units on "Party organization at every level." A reign of terror in the cities. On New Year's Day 1967, Mao urged the nation to a "general attack" on "monsters and demons anywhere in society." The Cohens write: "By the summer of 1967, China seemed to have reverted to the civil war and chaos that had debilitated her during the century prior to Communist rule." Next the army under Lin Biao took over, and at Mao's orders turned on the youthful revolutionaries they had set loose in the first place. Then, evidently, Mao murdered Lin Biao, his named successor, and contrived a story of his attempted coup as a running dog of the Soviet revisionists.

And so it went: to the point, I would suspect, of simple exhaustion. I visited Beijing in 1975, about the last year of the convulsion, and as I wrote at the time, found nothing but "Stalinist art and Meiji manufacture." Although the break with the Vietnamese and the Soviets was complete by this time, it was not until 1979 that a shooting war would commence. I cite the *Selected Works* one last time: "The counterattack in self-defense on Vietnam was undertaken . . . to defend China's borders against the Vietnamese aggressors." As is well known, the Chinese forces were soundly licked.

I will refer only briefly to an event of almost equal significance. By 1965 Indonesia, the fifth most populous country in the world, with the largest communist party in a noncommunist nation, had broken with the United States, and its President Sukarno had got to proclaiming that a Beijing-Jakarta axis would marshal the "emerging forces" of the new Afro-Asian nations. The *Encyclopedia Americana* states plainly that "during most of 1965 Indonesia seemed destined to become a Communist country." Thereafter the united Soviet-Chinese-Vietnamese forces driving down the eastern perimeter of the continent would join forces with a massive new communist country, one pointing westerly and north towards India, such that the encirclement of the Eurasian land mass would proceed apace. This was not to be. An abortive communist coup in September in 1965 led in turn to the overthrow of Sukarno, and the total destruction of the PKI, the Indonesian Communist party. Upwards of 500,000 persons were massacred. Not an everyday event either, and one surely that required notice, like those corpses floating down the Pearl River. But little seeming notice was taken.

How could it have happened that, in thinking about this part of the world, these developments were not central to our calculations? From first to last, our foreign policy proceeded from something very like delusion. We saw unity where there was division, strength where there was weakness. Why did the evidence escape us?

There are those who, not without provocation, will ascribe America's blindness to rapturous accounts of carefully programmed visits by assorted academic and literary folk. This is a long-observed phenomenon. In *The Mill on the Floss*, written 125 years ago, George Eliot writes: "People who live at a distance are naturally less faulty than those immediately under our own eyes; and it seems superfluous, when we consider the remote geographical position of the Ethiopians, and how very little the Greeks had to do with them, to inquire further why Homer calls them 'blameless.' "

Of course there are more depressing judgments that can be made about the effect this phenomenon has had on the reputation of successive totalitarian regimes during this century. It *is* powerful, but I believe it is also, usually, temporary. Moreover, the half-life of the original rapture seems to me to be declining. The reports of prodigies of production, of poetry readings, of child-care facilities taper off fairly fast now. When was the last time any youth showed up in Cuba to help with the sugarcane harvest? I would concede the current enthusiasm of the "sandalistas," as Western journalists have come to call their compatriots in Managua, two years at most. In any event, such propagandists have had, or so I think, but little influence. Unsentimental people make American foreign policy. My concern is the degree to which they, we, are insensitive as well as unsentimental. Insensitive, that is, to political and social nuance of the sort a liberal education is designed to impart.

Even a casual reading of Orwell would have alerted the policy maker of 1966/76 to the type of totalitarian behavior on display in Mao's China. Recall, from *1984*, Emmanuel Goldstein's explanation in *The Theory and Practice of Oligarchical Collectivism* that party members are expected to live "in a continuous frenzy of hatred of foreign enemies and internal traitors." Or for that matter, a mild acquaintance with the early history of the Soviet Union—especially the "war scare" of 1927, which Stalin contrived as a cover for the collectivization of agriculture—would have offered a suggestive parallel. Which is to say no more than that foreign policy in an era of totalitarian states must take into account the possibilities of internal convulsion and chaos that simply do not exist in the democracies.

This is but another instance of President Kennedy's proposition that, above all, democratic government "requires knowledge." It requires a knowledge of texts, a perception of nuance, the art of association—to a degree I think we have not ever before required, simply because our adversaries are in all ways so distant and in some ways so new.

In the course of the Cultural Revolution, Madame Mao suppressed all opera in China. Leaving, in Ley's words, "this artistic, subtle, opera-mad people . . . to the strict regime of . . . six feeble Punch and Judy shows, where the only 'revolutionary' daring is to maneuver on stage, to the languorous saxophonic Khachatu-rian-like music, platoons of the People's Liberation Army com-plete with banners and wooden rifles." Statesmen needed to take note. I believe, although I could scarcely claim certainty, that the vulgarization of art in totalitarian regimes marks a decline in societal energy; the reemergence of art often marks a sign of revolt. No matter: *This is the world of politics also.* Until such concerns more deeply penetrate our political sensibilities, I fear we will miss much that is going on in the world.

Fair enough, analysts will say. But supposing the magnitude of these events and their implications had been fully appreciated at the time, *ought* we to have behaved differently? *Would* we have behaved differently? I reply, most emphatically, yes, while allowing that a whole range of different responses might have been chosen. At one extreme, we might simply have withdrawn from the mainland, leaving Vietnam to Hanoi and to border war with the Chinese and the Cambodians. (Would this have been any less honorable than the policy we arrived at eventually, in which we asked of Hanoi only a "decent interval" between the time of our departure and their final takeover?) At the opposite extreme, betting that the Chinese would not intervene, we might have taken the war directly to the enemy in the North. We might have seized Hanoi, as we could have done. Instead we sank into the protracted, low-level warfare that Orwell foresaw on a global scale, but which he quite understood could only be sustained by rigidly totalitarian regimes.

I think of Dean Acheson, an exemplary secretary of state, perhaps our greatest, and the way he had of making the obvious obvious. Here is a passage from his celebrated address at the National Press Club in Washington in January 1950, when the nation was still reeling from the implications of the communist triumph in China. He saw Chinese more than he saw Red, and gave to his address the title: "Relations of the People of the United States and the Peoples of Asia," with the subtitle, "We Can Only Help Where We Are Wanted." Here is the key passage.

I should like to suggest . . . that the Soviet Union's taking the four northern provinces of China is the single most significant, most important fact, in the relation of any foreign power with Asia.

What does that mean for us? It means something very, very significant. It means that nothing that we do and nothing that we say must be allowed to obscure the reality of this fact. All the efforts of propaganda will not be able to obscure it. The only thing that can obscure it is the folly of ill-conceived adventures on our part which easily could do so and I urge all who are thinking about these foolish adventures to remember that we must not seize the unenviable positions which the Russians have carved out for themselves. We must not undertake to deflect from the Russians to ourselves the righteous anger and the wrath and the hatred of the Chinese people which must develop. It would be folly to deflect it to ourselves. We must take the position we have always taken that anyone who violates the integrity of China is the enemy of China and is acting contrary to our own interest. That, I suggest to you, . . . is the first and the greatest rule in regard to the formulation of American policy toward Asia.

This is a classic perception of diplomacy: In the main, nations have different interests, or think they do, and rarely combine in a costly common enterprise. Still more rarely do they sacrifice themselves for others. Statesmanship is the craft of encouraging division and distraction among adversaries, especially by a nation such as the United States, which has no great designs on the existing international order. In particular, the statesman will be wary of accepting at face value the claims of adversaries that they have even so combined their forces and are on the way to invincibility. Had we thought no further, we might have avoided a lot of trouble in Southeast Asia.

Let me offer a suggestion as to why this proved so difficult:

more to the point, why it didn't happen. There is a rule, of sorts, that organizations in conflict become like one another. We associate it with the observation of the turn-of-the-century German sociologist Georg Simmel, who commented that the Persians finally figured out it was best to have Greeks fight Greeks. Somewhere in the course of the Cold War, the United States decided it was best to have ideologists fight ideologists.

I have argued, obviously, that this came after Acheson. A man of great intellect, he had, even so, a limited fascination with intellectuals. He was all his life busy with things of the world, in real time, real life settings. Dulles, if not so agile, was, even so, not all that different.

The change came with the 1960s. The surest mark was the appearance of academics in foreign policy positions: previously rare, soon to be routine. It was no longer enough to be anticommunist. It was necessary to understand dialectical materialism.

We had previously gone through bouts of, well, a vulgar anticommunism. Politicians, some of them demagogues, none of them especially or even faintly learned, preached the dangers of a monolithic and expansionist world communism. Curiously, in the age of Stalin they weren't that wrong. Although generally despised by American foreign policy elites, Simmel's law began to show itself. Elites, challenged, began to emulate their challengers, and to assert that they knew even *better* the dangers of communism, having read the *Collected Works*.

Something like that. An early result was Vietnam: in William Pfaff's phrase, "liberalism's war." Lyndon B. Johnson inherited it, and was suspicious of it, but couldn't persuade himself that he knew more about the subject than people whose good fortune it was to know more about it than the likes of him. A senior official of the Johnson administration said to me recently, defensively perhaps, but I think fairly, that by the time Mr. Johnson came to office, his predecessors had created such a myth of invincible communism that Johnson and his advisors could not break out of the conception, no matter how many corpses floated down the Pearl River.

Failure in Vietnam, or so it appears to me (and if it matters, it appeared so at the time), curiously strengthened this disposition. It was a limited failure; but the conclusions drawn from it were hardly such. First came a period of detente that had to it an edge of accommodation, almost deference, to the still presumptive leader of world communism.

By the 1970s, the most startling of facts had emerged. The Soviet system could not feed its own people. And yet this seems to me to have had little effect on our thinking. In 1976, Murray Fesbach and Stephen Rapany compiled an astonishing report for the Joint Economic Committee showing that life expectancy for males in the Soviet Union was *declining*. Few understood.

And now we are in the 1980s, when all or much is said to have changed. We are said to have awakened from complacency. Halfway through the decade, we have seen a sustained arms build-up—which dates from the middle of the 1970s—beginning to produce almost a profusion of new weapons systems. (Of which, for my money, the cruise missiles are by far the most innovative and formidable in their military implications.)

Does this bring any surcease? Ease? Evidently not. In September 1985, Mr. Reagan told a press conference: "The United States is still well behind the Soviet Union in literally every kind of offensive weapon, both conventional and in the strategic weapons." Senator Sam Nunn of Georgia, ranking Democrat on the Senate Committee on Armed Services, responded with a measure of incredulity, which only Southern manners managed to soften. "I think," he said in a television exchange, "the president needs to sit down with the joint chiefs and hear about our submarines, about our aircraft carriers, about our tactical air, about our cruise missiles, about our bombers and other advantages." In a different context, Stephen M. Walt of Princeton, writing in the *New Republic*, measures the various military weights of the NATO and Warsaw Pact nations, *and* the People's Republic of China (omitting those of the PRC is "something no Soviet strategist would ever do"). He concludes that "the balance against the USSR becomes almost overwhelming."

This is not to say there won't be a war, or that they can't win it, or destroy everything in attempting. It is surely not to say we have heard or seen the last of Marxist-Leninist successes. But History—there, I said it!—is not moving with them. Theirs is not the way things are going to turn out.*

Even so, we persist in a strangely Soviet-obsessed politics that, while rattling with symbolic belligerence—"evil empire"— is subdued if not actually submissive in the realm of deeds. I offer two examples, both in some sense personal.

At midnight on December 13, 1981, the Polish army and police raided the offices of the independent trade union Solidarity in Poland and arrested thousands of persons in their homes. The organization was crushed, clearly on Soviet orders. On December 15, I introduced and the Senate adopted by a vote of 95 to 0 a resolution calling on the administration "to develop a concerted and sustained response." It was my thought that we should create an international crisis: convene the Security Council, rally the Europeans, impose sanctions, bellow our rage. The administration did nothing—nothing—save to commence to pay American banks money owed by Poland, so that Polish loans would not go into default. Perhaps I exaggerate. Four years later, the president met for ten minutes with Jerzy Milewski, international representative of the now-outlawed Solidarity. In a press statement that followed, the president described Mr. Milewski as a "thoughtful observer" of the Polish situation, adding that "history proves that increased repression only aggravates current problems and sows the seeds of the future discontent." He called for "genuine dialogue between the [Polish] government and important elements of society, including free and independent trade unions." According to the meticulously reliable Lou Cannon of the *Washington Post*, a "White House official" explained that

---

* In October 1985, the Communist Party of the Soviet Union published in *Pravda* a Draft Party Program, the first since 1961. The tone was markedly subdued by contrast with that of its predecessor. In 1961, Khrushchev's party undertook "within the current 10 years [to exceed] the level of U.S. industrial output."

the quality of the statement reflected " 'the East-West climate' " as the president prepared to meet Mikhail S. Gorbachev.

He could expect to meet a remarkably well-informed Gorbachev. Since the publication in June 1975 of the *Report to the President by the Commission on CIA Activities Within the United States*, chaired by then Vice President Nelson Rockefeller (Ronald Reagan as a member), the Soviets have been conducting an increasingly massive interception of American telecommunications from their various embassy, consulate, and UN mission facilities on American soil. In October 1984, Walter G. Deeley, deputy director of the National Security Agency in charge of communication security, broke a long silence on what is viewed there as an increasingly grave security problem—and more: a problem of national integrity. The rights of Americans are being invaded as surely as if foreign troops were dropping from the skies. As Deeley told the *New York Times*:

> I want the country to be aware that if we don't protect our communications, it can do a great deal of damage to us. This is a problem that goes to the very fabric of our society. It is not just a worry of the national security agencies. . . .
> Anyone making a phone call to the West Coast or Boston from the Washington area . . . can presume the other guy is listening to it.

He continued:

> They are having us for breakfast. We are hemorrhaging. Your progeny may not enjoy the same rights we do today if we don't do something.

The *Wall Street Journal* rails against the outrage. William Safire speaks of laser beams directed to the north windows of the White House once the Soviets assume occupancy of their new Mount Alto site in Washington. And yet the administration will do nothing to stop this. The FBI speaks out: 30 to 35 percent of Soviet embassy personnel in Washington do nothing but intercept telephone conversations. As a "watch list" is developed on specific phone numbers, the possibility of blackmail, against which Rockefeller warned, grows ever more immediate—if it has not long since commenced. The recent conviction of Samuel Loring Morison for espionage would suggest that a very large portion of the senior officials of the United States government will find themselves at least potentially exposed not just to discomfiture but to ruin. I am referring to the normal Washington practice of officials passing on classified information to journalists. This happens most from the White House itself, in the sense, that is, of a secrets-per-sentence ratio or something such. But it is a widespread practice, a way we speak to one another here. Except in rare cases, it is never meant to do the nation harm, and does none. Even so, it is illegal, and soon the Soviets will have the goods on literally thousands of public officials, if they haven't already.

For eight years, I have been seeking legislation to put a stop to this. The technology is elementary. The politics is harder. It requires, in the first place, facing up to the Soviets, and in the second place, admitting to the American public that you have not done so previously. The Carter administration would have nothing to do with the legislation. Nor would its successor. When I managed to get the legislation adopted by the Senate, the Reagan administration killed it in conference.

At about this time, James Reston made up his mind about Mr. Reagan. He had given him almost five years as president, and now concluded that the president "is an escapist who prefers fantasy to reality." There is surely this quality: along with others far more admirable. But I write not of a person but a period and a disposition. This president seems notably influenced by persons whose disposition is to *angst*: the decline of the West, the rise of the SS-18.

As the new Republicans took office, Strobe Talbott wrote

that "principal among the new Administration's views was the belief that the United States was now No. 2 in its military competition with the USSR." The president can say this with a smile; not those who share this view from the vantage of serious inquiry, detailed knowledge, and, now, office.

Some part of this is a passing phenomenon. Mr. Reagan, with generosity and political foresight, brought into his administration a range of liberal Democrats who became estranged when their party turned on "liberalism's war." A more generous or insightful Jimmy Carter might have done this, but didn't. There are more than a few members of the Nixon administration returned to office still stirring with resentments of detente. All this is normal enough in a churning political system. Advisors come and go. The problem is that the economic policies of the present administration are going to make the nation look relatively weak in the 1990s.

Mr. Reagan has thought it possible to weaken American government without weakening American influence. It is not. This is an old disposition of his, and that it has not changed is significant. In 1975, preparing to challenge Gerald Ford for the Republican nomination, he stated that he had a plan to cut $90 billion from the budget without touching defense or Social Security. Ford replied with some asperity that this would mean cutting *half* the rest of government. Having served in Mr. Ford's cabinet, I can attest that Mr. Ford had no patience with, well, fantasy. But it was Mr. Reagan who was elected and then reelected in the 1980s, and such fantasy became policy. The result has been the massive budget deficits, which will ineluctably lead to military cutbacks, as the Defense Department is just now beginning to realize. In *these* circumstances, and with no little bitterness and suspicion as to how it all came about, the problem of overestimating and misreading our adversaries will persist, possibly worsen. The more then shall we have need of history and of steadiness.

My principal concern is with balance. The wise diplomatist,

like the successful general, will make every effort to avoid underestimating the strength of the adversary. That as much as anything is a frame of mind: audacity yes, if needed, but overconfidence never. The first principle of Sun Tzu, the Chinese strategist of the sixth century B.C., is "Know your Enemy." It is required reading for Marine Corps lieutenants, and ought to be for members of the national security staff! Far the most difficult and pressing task is to know the enemy's weaknesses. That is how battles are won. That is how eras are won.

The true diplomatist, like the true general, while aware of his adversary's strength, is primarily concerned to find his weakness. The weaknesses of the totalitarian world are twofold: First, it is as much or more rent by ethnic conflict as the world in general, with the added difficulty that Marxist-Leninist doctrine predicted the disappearance of ethnic conflict with the establishment of "socialist" regimes. Second, and more important, it is a political form of government that cannot successfully exploit modern technology. Leninist governments are based on the greatest control of information by the smallest number of persons. This could be adapted to the production of steel. It cannot adapt to technology based on the diffusion of information. A year ago in Washington, I asked an audience that I would describe as frenzy friendly: "How are you going to install home computers in a society that won't permit the publication of telephone directories?" My address was not a success, but I believe my question was fair, and I believe the answer is that you can't.

Managing the decline of these regimes will be a task requiring the utmost discipline *and* knowledge. For as they come to sense they are doomed, they must become ever more dangerous. Some, Walter Laqueur suggests, including China, might evolve "toward some modern version of bureaucratic autocracy." The Soviets won't; dare not. "In the name of God on high," as Mr. Gorbachev recently put it, let us watch *them* with hawklike alertness. But, it seems to me that true knowledge of the state of the world just now requires that we keep that Panmunjom palace in mind also,

and never for a moment neglect our own affairs, which in the
end will most determine the condition of freedom in the world.

West Point, New York
October 4, 1985

A Tale of Two Cities

This paper was given in 1985 at the opening dinner of the annual Conference on Setting Municipal Priorities, which began in the aftermath of New York City's near bankruptcy in 1975. A decade had passed. Finances had got better. The gap between "the two cities" had grown wider. I asked, was it not time to think back to the days when we thought about such things?

It is just twenty-five years now since Nathan Glazer and I finished work on *Beyond the Melting Pot: The Negroes, Puerto Ricans, Jews, Italians, and Irish of New York City.*

We said, in our opening, "This is a beginning book." We argued that ethnic identity, an attachment, far from being a holdover from the age of immigration, and by incorporation, of internal migration, was in fact continuing to play the role it had done for so very long in the nation's history. We ventured so far as to suggest it was beginning to take on aspects of a *postindustrial* social form, becoming "interest with effect" in Daniel Bell's felicitous summation. We were not all that certain what would come next, save that surely there would be many and better books on the subject.

Now of course our subject was larger than that of the City of New York: in all events, as far as Glazer was concerned. Something large was at stake. Put simply, if we were right, Marx was wrong. There would be no emergence of a united, militant international proletariat, destined to world hegemony. There would instead be an intensification of ethnic, racial, religious division and conflict. I leave it to others to judge. But events surely have evolved more in line with our predictions than with those of the classical Marxists.

Still, we were New Yorkers, and did deeply care about the city. Hence we were a bit surprised to find ourselves putting out a second edition in 1970. Nothing had come along to succeed us. I think it fair to say that this seems still to be the case, and after a quarter century the book is still in print.

Why? Because of its timelessness? Of course not. Because we were so right? To the contrary. I think the issues we dealt with have become so sensitive—and accordingly are avoided—for the simple reason that we were wrong about one absolutely essential particular. We expected the process of *incorporation* to continue. This is to say we expected the process of successful adaptation to go along, leaving successive groups retaining their identities whilst pretty much scattering across the political and social and economic landscape.

In our 1970 edition, we did qualify our early optimism to the extent of offering *two* models of incorporation. On the one hand, there was the "everybody up" mode. A group arrives in more or less uniform condition—some penniless, some well enough off already—and the next thing you know is that they are all on their way up together. I believe we are seeing a classic example in today's Koreans. Why have they seemingly taken over the produce outlets in many parts of the city? Simple. The capital costs of entering the fruit and vegetable business are for them what they were for the Italians in their day. Produce is bought and sold one day at a time. To buy a two-day supply of fresh lettuce is to invite bankruptcy. But if you can muster the price of the stock needed for a single day, and locate a storefront, you are in business. Your grandchildren will be engineers.

Our other model we called "up-and-down." Some groups arrive in the city and are fractured by it. Some rise, some *decline*.

Decline in the sense of their social competence. We took the nineteenth-century Irish as the prototype of this group: the Irish social worker and the Irish vagrant; the Church, if you like, and the saloon. (Not, mind, a respectable place, with a Ladies Entrance, but the gin-soaked cellar holes of the nineteenth century.) Even so, with time, it all worked out and ended happily enough.

Still, we never suspected that over a mere quarter century we would see an underclass emerge in New York City of a size that not only threatens the character of the city, but which seems also to defy any meliorative response.

We never thought we would become Two Cities.

We have.

The Two Cities are not an abstraction, they are a physical fact. New York is the richest city in the world today, and appropriately has the richest congressional district, the Fifteenth, the Silk Stocking District, on Manhattan's East Side. It also contains four of the nation's poorest congressional districts. One of these, the Sixteenth District, Harlem, directly adjoins the richest.

Another, the Eighteenth, is the South Bronx, reviving somewhat now, but reviving from a desolation, an Armageddonic collapse that I do not believe has its equal in the history of urbanization. Here, from an article by Adele Chatfield-Taylor that appeared in the July 1979 *Livable City*, a publication of the Municipal Arts Society, is an early account of the matter. Focusing on Charlotte Street, that soon-to-be Avenue of the Presidents, the report found that

by 1968, the place was beyond description. Wild dogs roamed the streets, tearing in and out of buildings and through the trash that covered the sidewalks and the streets. Persons scarcely recognizable as human were prey and predator to one another. Fires burned everywhere—in cans on the corners, in empty lots, in all kinds of buildings. Over the months, buildings could be seen to catch the disease and die.

(Recall that, in the 1930s, the Bronx was known as "the city without a slum," the one place in the whole of the nation where commercial housing was built during the Great Depression, a place where urban planners built parks with names such as Crotona, after the Greek city in southern Italy where Pythagoras was born.)

Now in the middle of all this, and not unconnected, came the great financial crisis, the near, or effective bankruptcy of the city in 1975. This is what concerns me today.

Until 1975, New York, with all its problems was, if anything, preoccupied with them. No effort seemed too great to deal with the obvious dysfunction that was affecting whole neighborhoods and populations. With the crisis, that stream of social energy all but dried up. Perhaps I exaggerate. Not, I think, a very great deal. In any event, surely, the development of the Two Cities proceeded. The Affluent City retreats to ever more concentrated and defended enclaves. (Would you believe me if I tell you that not long ago there was an effort afoot to acquire Governor's Island for luxury housing? What joy. A ferry to Wall Street. Perhaps a refurbished new wall. A helipad to the Hamptons, and a view of the Statue of Liberty, all in splendid and secure isolation. Who knows, even, a new Venice safe from the Visigoths or whoever it was who drove those ancient Italians into the marshes?)

The nation has taken notice. Part of the fatalism in social policy that we observed in Washington this past decade can, in my view, be ascribed to a mislearned lesson of the New York financial crisis. It was judged that those who sought to address urban problems of the kind we had in such display, well, ended up bankrupt or as near as makes no matter. From there it is no great distance to the judgment that problems arise from efforts to resolve them, a view pretty much in place in Washington just now.

The enduring value of Charles Brecher and Raymond D. Horton's work over this period has been the meticulous detail in which they have documented and helped guide the city's fiscal recovery, to the point where it can be said to have been substantially achieved. But in that process, we have seen a long hiatus in social policy. Arrangements in place before the fiscal crisis have been left pretty much undisturbed. Diminished but undisturbed. The problem is that those arrangements were not making any significant progress before, and have made even less since. The challenge of fiscal recovery, then, is the challenge of a rebirth of social policy.

It is not an unattractive thought for New York. A very great deal of American social policy of the first part of this century originated here, making its way to Washington sometimes directly, sometimes through Albany. (I noted just last month in the *New York Times* a letter from the son of the socialist Congressman Meyer London of the Lower East Side of Manhattan noting that in 1916 his father introduced a bill in Congress to establish "social insurance," meaning pretty much the panoply of old-age insurance, unemployment insurance, and the like that that stalwart Tammany Senator Robert F. Wagner introduced as the Social Security Act of 1935, just half a century ago.) We have had such success with so many of those measures—we have brought poverty among the elderly in the United States to the "vanishing point," as a White House statement recently put it. But then here we are with another provision of the same Social Security Act, the welfare provisions, which seem not at all to work, and in some ways work against those very persons they are designed to help.

Consider the problem of foster care.

Over the past five years, 45,000 children were discharged from the foster care system in New York City. There is plenty of evidence to suggest that we are simply sending these children out into the cold to fend for themselves. A 1981 study by the city's Human Resources Administration found that one-third of the young persons age eighteen to twenty-one who were discharged from foster care were back on welfare within fifteen months. Another study published last year by the Ittleson Foundation of the city's shelters found that as many as one-half of homeless/runaway youth in the city's shelters had previously been in foster care.

To respond to this problem, I offered an amendment in the Finance Committee to provide about $2,000 per year for special services for every older AFDC foster child about to be discharged from care. The administration opposed my plan. The official responsible for the foster care program told the Finance Committee that the administration felt we were currently spending all that was needed, to wit $120 per year per child.

This will pass. Government will once again become involved, and sooner or later we will pay for what we are not now doing.

Still I would offer the thought that there are huge areas of social policy of which it must be said that today either we don't know what to do or don't know how to do it. This is a true and worthy challenge. We need a rebirth of social policy as both a moral and an empirical exercise, free of the mindless millenialism of the past and the equally thoughtless meanness of the present.

Much is at stake. If matters take what seems to be their present course, by the end of the century, New York City will stand not just as an affront to the ideals of the American republic but as a refutation of their promise.

Are we to settle for that? I hope not. And so we have what? Fifteen years to get ourselves thinking and acting again.

For the first half of this century, the social thinkers and elected officials of New York City were the primary source of new social policy and social legislation in the whole of the nation. They were not isolated individuals. The Meyer Londons and Robert F. Wagners represented political dispositions with deep support within the polity. This is not so today; it has not been so for a decade or more. It could change.

Harriman, New York
November 8, 1985

1986

Letter to New York:
The $28-Billion Heist,
A Mystery

A Democratic secretary of the Treasury would have been impeached for using Social Security funds to pay the general obligations of government, the while concealing this from Congress.

Dear New Yorker:

It was an inside job and no doubt about it. $28,219,000,000 in bonds missing from the Social Security trust funds. They keep 'em in a big vault down deep under the Treasury Department building at 15th and Pennsylvania Avenue. There's an old Civil War tunnel that connects with the White House. And it could be that the president's so-called staff was in on the job; but them bozos are so big just now in their brand-new bulletproof limos with the $145,000-portable-telephone scramblers that keep the Russkies from knowing whom they're having dinner with (and maybe not just the Russkies, if you know what I mean), that they would rather be caught getting something straight in public than risk having it known that they ever went down on their hands and knees and crawled over to old Hamilton's place, even if it was for 28 of the Big Ones.

KAZZAM!!! *That's* why the T-men have been going all over

town for near five years now, tellin' everybody the Social Security trust funds were broke, busted, bankrupt, done. If nobody knew what a pile they had, nobody would know when they scooped it up! What was never there would never be missed when it was missing.

Well, this old gal called and wanted to know, would I take the case. Says she's a canny one, and knows there's something funny going on. Worried about her check; $468 per month, with a cost-of-living adjustment due on the third day of January in the year following a preceding year in which the Consumer Price Index attained a cumulative 3-point increase from the third quarter of the year previous to the third quarter of that annum just ended, as subject to change by the congressional reconciliation process.

Hold it, I got lost there. Just when I get going good on something they could make a movie out of, like Raymond Chandler used to do, I look up and there's the Capitol Dome (frowning), I look down and there's the *Economic Indicators* just in from the Joint Economic Committee (manufacturers' inventory–shipments ratio still flat). And besides, how can I pretend that I have not this moment received a three-page letter from an assistant secretary of the Treasury, explaining it all?

Still, let me assure you, it *was* a mystery. Along about Labor Day last year, word began to circulate here in Washington that the Treasury was cashing in Social Security bonds to pay the general expenses of government. The details are fairly complex (I will provide them to anyone who cares to write), but the essentials are simple enough. For three years running, Congress has allowed a fiscal crisis to come into being by refusing to raise the debt ceiling so the Treasury might borrow more money. In those circumstances, in 1983 and 1984 when the government received Social Security contributions—payroll deductions plus the employer share—the Treasury held them as cash and did not use them to purchase interest-paying Treasury bonds which make up the various trust funds. To have done so would have technically increased the debt beyond the debt ceiling. Then in 1985, the Treasury went further. Bonds held in the trust funds were actually cashed in to obtain money to pay the bills.

In this sense, government accounts are no different from yours or mine. If you don't have enough money in the bank to cover checks you have written, you had better cash in some of your savings bonds, or the checks will bounce.

In August 1985, the Social Security and Disability trust funds held $37 billion in Treasury bonds. By November, this was down to $9 billion. If you want to be lurid, money held in trust literally for widows and orphans was used to pay for—what?—B-1 bombers. Nothing like this has ever happened in the fifty-year history of Social Security.

The problem is they didn't tell us. By "us" I mean the committees of Congress which have what we call "oversight" responsibility, and the two *public* trustees of the trust funds—one Democrat, one Republican—created in the Social Security Amendments of 1983 to represent the public interest against the interest of a particular administration. I am the ranking Democrat on the Subcommittee on Social Security (of the Senate Finance Committee) and finally on November 7 got a Treasury official to testify and answer questions as to what was going on. It was hell's own time getting him to admit to the facts that by then we knew as well as did he. (Or it may be that he did not know, which was why he was sent to us. No matter.) We now have a formal opinion from the comptroller general that the secretary's actions were "in violation of the Social Security Act," but adding that "we cannot say that the secretary acted unreasonably given the extraordinary situation in which he was operating."

In legislation this fall, reducing the budget deficit, I included a provision directing the Treasury to make the Social Security trust funds whole, both principal and interest, and today's letter from the assistant treasury secretary informs me that henceforth, "as a matter of policy, the secretary has directed that both Congress and the trustees be kept informed on significant matters affecting the Trust Funds." Just to make certain, a number of us have filed a suit in court, as extra insurance.

So the trust funds are well, and there is the good news that while the government may go broke, Social Security is in surplus and will remain so into the next century. (An argument we made back in 1981 when just the opposite was being asserted with such great confidence.)

But what is this business of the *government* going broke? What is the "extraordinary situation" which we are told by the comptroller general forced the secretary of the Treasury to do what he did? Let me say that he *had* to do it. For the United States to default would have been a world disaster. But what has brought us to the brink of disaster?

This *is* a mystery. How has it come about that this decent and prosperous and otherwise well-governed nation of ours has in five years nearly ruined its public finances, such that a real fiscal crisis is going to be with us for the rest of this decade, maybe the rest of this century? With no guarantee of a "soft landing." None.

Sound like a vicious cycle to you? Right. But how did it happen?

I have been looking at a speech I gave in September 1981 to the Business Council of New York State, and for what it's worth, it seems to me it was all pretty clear at the outset. I told my business friends that a new idea had made its appearance in Washington:

> the idea that the revenue system of the federal government was not an institution of any great importance, that the most extraordinary things could be done to it with relative impunity.

It was the so-called supply-side economists whose idea it was to get money into circulation by a huge tax cut and to forget about the deficit that would follow. It didn't matter; or if it did, it would take care of itself. Or something.

Grant them this: They were open about their theories and

their plans, almost too eager to debate them. You can't say as much for another group of newcomers who found in the doctrine "deficits don't matter" the opportunity to dismantle what they regarded as a bloated and ruinously wasteful federal government. They would use the deficits to force cuts in the budget. I know I have said this before, and people have been skeptical. As a matter of fact, I have recently taken a poll of New Yorkers, and virtually *no one* believes it. Even so, last spring no less a person than Friedrich von Hayek, a friend of the president and a Nobel Prize–winning Austrian economist, confirmed that this was precisely the view in the White House, where it had been explained to him that "it is impossible to persuade Congress that expenditures must be reduced, unless one creates deficits so large that absolutely everyone becomes convinced that no more money can be spent."

There is a character in one of Disraeli's novels who is described as a man "distinguished for ignorance, as he had but one idea and that was wrong." In 1981, Washington was filled with just such folk. Deficits do matter because after a point, debt, if borrowed abroad, matters. Ask Brazil. Even internal debt matters to the extent it redistributes income. Almost half the revenue of the personal income tax is now required to pay interest to people who own government bonds: a transfer of wealth from labor to capital unlike anything we've ever seen. All that borrowing also raises interest rates, which hurt the auto, housing, and other industries that depend on borrowed money—and those who work in them.

Just as important—and I know that people are skeptical about this—the federal government just isn't all that big. (Often wasteful, yes. But not that big for the work we do in the world.) There was a great increase in government in postwar America, but *the increase was in state and local government*. The number of federal employees today is about what it was when President Nixon took office. For the most part, what the federal government does, it either has to do, or people really want it to do.

I believe President Reagan sees this. In five years in office, he has never *once* sent us a balanced budget. In the remaining years of his term, he never will.

In the meantime, the Senate has come up with a scheme, the Gramm–Rudman–Hollings bill, that in effect will balance the budget for us. Don't ask me how. I am one of the twenty-four Senators who voted against it, saying among other things that, if followed, it will lead to the dismantling of the president's defense program and the failure of his hopes for the Geneva arms control talks. As for the others, I can only confirm Flora Lewis's observation that "in private, people who voted for it denounced it as a monstrosity." I doubt if it is even constitutional.

The only way to balance the budget without damaging the nation is to increase revenues. I said this in 1981, and I say it again in 1986. What do you think? Will you write me? There comes a time when a mystery needs to be solved.

Mind, there is now no choice but to make budget cuts as well. Once I get a look at the president's budget, I will write some proposals of my own, starting with the so-called farm program which is making the great Teapot Dome scandal of the 1920s look like a tea party.

And Happy New Year! It will be a doozie down here!

Washington, D.C.
January 4, 1986

And wasn't it!

Political AIDS:
On the Immune System
of the American Parties

In the spring of 1986, an era was ending. David A. Stock-
man's memoirs had now appeared, demystifying, if that old New
York term may be used, the essential Reagan event, which is to
say the dismantling of the fisc. On the Democratic side we had
begun to awake to a vicious internal assault from the followers
of Lyndon LaRouche. The new age of ideology was coming apart.
But the question remained: Why were our political parties so
insensitive to such assault? In the Marnold Lecture at New York
University, I raised this question.

Over the years, I have written a fair amount about the relationship between politics and the study of politics. This has
come naturally enough, for my life has alternated between these
two pursuits: or if you like, these two sanctuaries. It is not the
case that I went from academe to politics: just the opposite. And
I have more than once slipped over the border into the political
realm to escape some particular *peripeteia* within the province
of learning. Personal experience aside, however, this seems to
me a necessary, almost urgent subject in this century when political life has been so much influenced by esoteric and even
concealed ideological movements.

Ideology is not the best term for what I wish to describe. In
common usage it is taken to mean opinion, perhaps strongly held

opinion, but little more. It is, of course, something different: a kind of secular religion. As a largely apolitical society, the United States has not generated much by way of ideology, although various institutions—the labor movement comes first to mind—have had to ward off assault from assorted Marxist movements. But in the main, our political parties have been left untroubled. This, however, has changed, leading to the question: How well are their immune systems working? Not very well, it would seem.

First the Democrats.

I have written recently of the extraordinary danger which the ideas of Lyndon H. LaRouche, Jr. seem to me to pose for the Democratic party. The primary victories of LaRouche candidates for lieutenant governor and secretary of state of Illinois in 1986 are well known, as is the fact that this neo-fascist, Jew-baiting, conspiratorial faction has made its way virtually unopposed into the Democratic party in congressional campaigns across the country. It is not well enough known, however, that this latest phase in the LaRouche movement began here in New York City in 1981 when a LaRouche candidate entered the Democratic primary contest for mayor; was not challenged, instead was afforded all the honors and dignities attendant upon a legitimate aspirant to the party's nomination; thereby attaining a previously unimaginable legitimacy. (In fairness, the LaRouche candidate was challenged by another "insurgent," on grounds of nonadherence to the principles of the Democratic party. But a state judge ruled that while such a charge could be sustained, it would have to come from the party leadership. Which did not happen.)

John LoCicero, a principal political strategist in the 1981 campaign, has been quoted as saying, "we didn't challenge anyone's signatures because it's not part of the democratic process." This is an honorable statement but calamitously wrong. In the name of this principle, anti-Semitism was welcomed into the Democratic party. (For those who have difficulty reading small print, the LaRouche newspaper *New Solidarity* provided sufficiently illuminating headlines. Thus from the edition of July 17, 1978:

> The Anti-Defamation League—
> Joint Distribution Committee:
> British Zionist Gestapo

The LaRouchites had by this time adopted *Pravda*'s charge that Zionists and the Nazis had collaborated in World War II. A photograph in this same issue shows Jews being herded from the Warsaw ghetto. The caption states: "Zionist lobby leaders supported Hitler's extermination camp system because it was cleansing Europe of non-Zionist Jews." LaRouche is routinely and wrongly described as Rightist. This line is pure Moscow communist.)

Ignorance can be no excuse here. Those who play a responsible role in the politics of our greatest city incur the responsibility to know what they are doing. In this event, however, the level of political literacy within the New York Democratic party was such that no one understood who these people were. In a quite literal sense, they spoke a political language which the political classes of the city simply did not understand. It was not *that* esoteric. A garbled Trotskyite version of a post-Stalinist world conspiracy with overlays of plain anti-Semitism, which was (and is) sometimes leftist and sometimes rightist. If you consider the difficulties our cryptanalysts are having just now breaking whatever new code the Libyans are using, deciphering LaRouchite literature of the early 1920s was high-school work. Even so, it was beyond the capacity of the political classes of New York, and they were let in.

The plain fact is that if the LaRouchites ever secure a position, however much a minority position, within the Democratic party, they could bring ruin to the oldest political party in the world. This is a genuine danger. In a recent letter to the *New York Times*, Carl Oglesby, a sometime national officer of the

Students for a Democratic Society, protests reports that identify LaRouche's then National Caucus of Labor Committees as a 1960s spinoff of that organization. Oglesby correctly states that the NCLC "emerged, rather, from the Progressive Labor Party, an organization fiercely opposed to SDS and a principal factor in the destruction of SDS in 1969." He concludes:

> Lyndon LaRouche is a parasite formerly of radical and currently of liberal organizations. His pattern of objectives has always been reactionary, whatever the rhetoric used to obscure the fact. It is wholly in character for him and his followers to pretend today to be Democrats, just as they pretended in the 1960s to be SDS'ers.

After the 1981 breakthrough, it was perhaps inevitable that LaRouche would seek to widen his salient. In 1982, I was running for reelection to the Senate. I had no opposition within the party as such, and all was peaceable until, all of a sudden, a LaRouchite candidate announced, and commenced to collect signatures in order to get on the ballot independently.

I don't wish to give offense, but neither would I wish to be misunderstood. I knew who the LaRouchites were, and so did the key members of my campaign. We could decipher their language, even if imperfectly. We had mostly broken their codes.

We were not about to give LaRouche a free ride. We fought him from day one. We spent every penny we had in our campaign chest. We even found the resources to deal with a group of high-minded New Yorkers who demanded to know whether my campaign manager Tim Russert had not engaged in unfair campaign practices when he called the LaRouche movement "anti-Semitic." (Something a New York supreme court judge had already ruled fair comment.)

I expect that this seemed quixotic behavior to the political classes. They are rarely comfortable with ideological battle—which is not a dishonor so much as a disability. Let it be noted that the electorate understood. Or understood something. I carried fifty of the sixty-two counties of New York State, and lost another by six votes. No Democratic candidate in our history had ever carried more than twenty, and only four had carried more than ten. We had declared that ideas matter to us, and I think voters responded that ideas matter to them as well.

And now to the Republican party!

Fairly early on in the administration of President Reagan, I began to charge that the unprecedented, triple-digit deficits that began in his second year in office had been consciously and deliberately brought about.

This was not, at first, a successful argument. Some independent support appeared, notably a 1985 interview with Friedrich von Hayek in the Viennese journal *Profil*. Asked about our deficits, von Hayek regretted them, but added:

> . . . one of Reagan's advisors told me why the President has permitted that to happen, which makes the matter partly excusable: Reagan thinks it is impossible to persuade Congress that expenditures must be reduced, unless one creates deficits so large that absolutely everyone becomes convinced that no more money can be spent.

But basically the argument was counterintuitive. To double the national debt in five years was a disaster. Who would deliberately bring about a disaster? Nonsense.

Agreed. But that was not the argument. The disaster was not deliberate: the deficits were. Which is to say that the deficits were meant to spur action, which however did not occur, thereby resulting in disaster. A nice distinction but not, I should have thought, impenetrably subtle.

We now have David Stockman's memoirs *The Triumph of Politics: Why the Reagan Revolution Failed*. I believe it fair to say that the argument is now shown to have been correct. Let me summarize the crucial events.

The story, as Alistair Cooke might say, to date:

Young David Stockman has become a close-in advisor to the Reagan election campaign of 1980 and will soon be named director-designate of the Office of Management and Budget. He is part of a foursome, the others being Representative Jack Kemp, the economist Arthur Laffer, and businessman Lewis Lehrman. They are advocates of what has come to be known as "supply-side" economics, a school that was reacting to the "demand side" and government-oriented emphasis of post-Keynesian economics. (The economics, let us say, of now Secretary of State George P. Shultz, who as director of OMB under President Nixon cheerfully and carefully constructed a "full-employment budget." This is to say a budget with a presumptively stimulative deficit equal to the shortfall of revenues from their "full-employment" level.) This was all wrong to the supply siders, who wanted to stimulate the economy through private rather than public spending, and to that end advocated large tax cuts.

These were heady young intellectuals. They could scarcely contain their energy or enthusiasm. Stockman writes that the history of their revolution, as he calls it, would be found scribbled on napkins, as they probed and challenged and stimulated each other over lunches and dinners.

As our story resumes, however, trouble has appeared within the group. Dr. Laffer's celebrated curve purports to demonstrate that tax cuts would generate so much additional revenue—through the stimulated private economy—that no reduction in government spending would be necessary to retain, or achieve, budget balance. Young David Stockman, however, wants to reduce spending: He is against big government *on principle*. "The capitalist idea of wealth creation," he writes, "stood at odds with the welfare-state notion of distribution." Fiscal debauchery—the inflation of the moment—was at odds with sound money, indeed the gold standard, for which the group had written a somewhat disguised endorsement into the 1980 Republican platform. In late August and September of 1980, Stockman begins to realize that he is on to something considerable.

I discovered that our two Napkins added up to a much more radical economic program than I had previously understood. If you implemented the Gold Standard Napkin and stopped inflation, Professor Laffer's Tax Cut Napkin didn't work. You would get more real economic growth but no gain in federal revenues. Consequently, only sweeping domestic spending cuts could balance the budget—an action that I believed was desirable but which the other supply siders had denied would be necessary.

At its 1980 convention, the Republican party had endorsed both a 30-percent tax cut and a radical reduction in business taxes to be brought about by collapsing depreciation schedules into three categories of ten, five, and three years. Stockman continues:

I discovered that to balance the budget we would need huge spending cuts too—more than $100 billion per year. The fabled revenue feedback of the Laffer curve had thus slid into the grave of fiscal mythology forty days after the supply-side banner had been hoisted up at the GOP convention.

These dramatic changes in both my comprehension of budget estimating and the true fiscal math of the supply-side program occurred almost overnight. That should have been cause for second thoughts and reassessment of the whole proposition.

But it didn't happen that way.

At the time, the prospect of needing well over $100 billion in domestic spending cuts to keep the Republican budget in equilibrium appeared more as an opportunity than as a roadblock. Once Governor Reagan got an electoral mandate for Kemp–Roth and 10–5–3, then we would have the Second Republic's craven politicians pinned to the wall. They would have to dismantle its bloated, wasteful, and unjust spending enterprises—or risk national ruin.

The idea of a real fiscal revolution, a frontal attack on

the welfare state, was beginning to seem more and more plausible.

It would not be easy work. Revolutions rarely are. Election night over, Stockman went home for four hours sleep. "Tomorrow, the revolution would begin." Mind, however,

> The supply-side economic policy revolution could add up only if deep dents were kicked in the side of the welfare state. This meant remaining in the political trenches year after year until the middle of the decade. The work of shrinking back the spending boundaries of the state had to proceed in tandem with the automatic fall of its revenue claim on the national economy, as the multiyear tax cuts achieved full maturity.

Enter, alas, the politicians.

> The Cabinet was not disposed to that kind of patient attack on spending. . . . The President never had the foggiest notion.

Stockman now states that not to have anticipated such a response was a failing on his part. But at the time, he saw it entirely as a failure on the part of the politicans. In his zeal, and it shines through his memoir, he could not imagine that they would not do what he had made it necessary for them to do.

> The success of the Reagan Revolution depended upon the willingness of the politicians to turn against their own handiwork—the bloated budget of the American welfare state. Why would they do this? Because they had to! In the final analysis, I had made fiscal necessity the mother of political invention.

The rest is now history. I will spare myself as well as the reader the details. It is to a prior event that I would draw attention.
Capitalism had become an ideology.

Aaron Wildavsky recently remarked that in years past, capitalism was merely a practice; something you did. Indeed, it was for the most part only socialists of various persuasions who called it capitalism, in a decidedly pejorative sense. It is important to be careful here; easy to be misunderstood. By ideology I intend the general sense of an intense belief system, a secular religion, that we associate with Karl Mannheim's early description. Stockman's vocabulary is replete with terms that we associate with ideology. He describes his migration from the student Left—SDS and suchlike—to the Republican Right in terms which are legitimately intellectual but also, at times, clearly at that point where a measured judgment as to the preponderance of evidence crosses over into the zone of radical conviction. He cites authors of meticulous clarity and caution with that element of fervor we associate with zealotry and even intolerance. In Washington, following divinity school, he "plunged into economics" and "emerged a disciple of F. A. von Hayek, the preeminent Austrian exponent of free market economics." Theodore Lowi's seminal work *The End of Liberalism* persuaded him that a virtuous First American Republic of government that built canals, lighthouses, and declared wars had been succeeded by a corrupt Second American Republic where the stern demands of citizenship succumbed to the false promises of the welfare state. Stockman is an absorbing figure to a student of ideology not least because of his near addiction. He goes on as if the Reaganites had appointed him a kind of party theorist responsible for doctrinal conformity. Writing of a budget plan he had worked up with then Representative Gramm of Texas, he notes:

> Both Gramm and I believed that the organs of international aid and so-called Third World development—the UN, the multilateral banks, and the U.S. Agency for International Development—were infested with socialist error.

He would have no part of the Moral Majority: "My soft-core Marxism had annealed into libertarianism. I didn't believe in economic regulation and I didn't believe in moral regulation." Yet on the same page he writes of his dream that "a Kemp campaign would give us a pulpit from which to broadcast the supply-side religion." He gives this chapter the title "The Coming of the New Order." Not perhaps the happiest reference given the history of ideological politics in the twentieth century. But then neither is his analogy to the zeal with which he took up the simple proposition of Mr. Wanniski, formerly of the editorial page of the *Wall Street Journal*.

> Over and over again he kept repeating it. It was his mantra: 'Overturning an existing order starts with one person and an idea. An idea persuades a second person, then a third, then a fourth. . . .' I'd studied Lenin's trip from Zurich to Russia in the boxcar, so I knew that Wanniski wasn't talking historical rot. Chain reactions occur in politics; the Soviet precedent, of course, was not exactly inspiring.

A sometime teacher is disposed at this point to exclaim: "Stop right there! Just exactly what do we mean by 'not exactly'?" But the most bizarre, if wholly unintended example of going too far, concerns Irving Kristol. Kristol is perhaps the preeminent conservative intellectual of our age. I say "perhaps" out of respect rather than reserve. As a devoted friend of more than a quarter century, I must insist that there is always a "perhaps" preceding any proposition set forth by Irving Kristol, as for example in his collection of immensely influential essays *Two Cheers for Capitalism*, with its echo of E. M. Forster's evocation of the virtues of democracy. Two. Not three. Kristol more effectively than any single thinker of this time took the socialist critique of capitalism, which he himself once espoused, and turned it on its head, as Marx declared he had done of Hegel. Behold, capitalism was not a source of oppression but of freedom, individual and collective. Recall that the traditional socialist charge against capitalism is that it undermined or thwarted democracy. But also other things; things not always agreeable. Hence *two* cheers; no more. And how does Stockman describe his first meeting with this eminently self-effacing Henry M. Luce Professor at New York University? "To me, Kristol was a secular incarnation of the Lord Himself."

I suggest that we are in the presence here of a fairly familiar phenomenon. Serious social thinkers (in this context I should of course mention Milton Friedman's *Capitalism and Freedom*) come along with fresh insights. There is more—or less—to a set of existing arrangements than has been realized. In this particular case, the association between capitalism and democracy began to be noted. It is not surprising that many of these intellectuals were at one point influenced by Marxist models, or at least worked in intellectual settings where Marxist ideas were much in vogue, specifically the idea that social systems are an epiphenomenon of economic systems. All good and useful stuff. But then a younger generation comes along which elevates thought into belief. Not only are the ideas of their mentors true, they are the *Only Truth*. Given by the Lord Himself. What began as skepticism concerning received doctrine transmutes into fierce conviction. Again, we have seen all this, indeed too much of it, in the twentieth century.

This is not to disparage David Stockman's idealism. Contrary to so much that passes for conservatism in this period, he is not an apologist for privileged access to public benefit. Just the opposite. His rage concerning the Second Republic is directed more to those who gorge at such public troughs as the Export-Import Bank, than to those who live on food stamps. It is not welfare mothers who upset him nearly as much as the offspring of plant managers whose tuition loans are subsidized by assembly-line workers.

The irony, of course, is that having pretty much vanquished and discredited the redistributionist impulses of—what? say, 1960s liberalism—the regime Stockman helped bring to power has been characterized by unbridled pillaging on the part of those Old Devil Interests. (Of late, owing to the protracted fiscal crisis, this has come through the tax code rather than budget outlays, but is all the better concealed that way.)

There are other things to be said. I think especially important the remark attributed to Herbert Stein that once Republican legislators found you could have a three-digit deficit and the heavens didn't fall—that day—there was no restraining them. Thus the week after enacting Gramm–Rudman, the Senate passed a $52-billion agricultural bill. Already we learn that federal courts cannot pay jurors; but no matter, agribusiness is munching away with great if disguised satisfaction.

What Stockman discovered, of course, is that after a first round of budget cuts, directed mostly to the poor and the nominally needy, Congress came up against the fact that the electorate wanted pretty much the government it was getting. While the interests, securely in power, wanted more. No New Order emerged. To the contrary, something like a latter-day version of Mark Twain's Great Barbecue commenced.

In some sectors, spending, free of Stein's restraint, went hog wild. Stockman watched his dream vanish, and slowly his faith began to weaken as well. He became less a radical, more a true conservative, even if an embittered one. Laffer and Wanniski, he ruefully notes, "weren't very good-natured about my eventual apostasy."

It was left for George Will to get it just right.

Only ideological spectacles kept Stockman from reaching age 34 unaware of the fact that the modern state is not an accident, or a conspiracy foisted on the nation—the Americans really do want mild social democracy, sacrificing some capitalist efficiency in the interest of equity and security.

Well, we have seen socialist ideals betrayed. Now, I suppose, we see capitalist ideals betrayed. Stockman's own verdict is harsh enough.

I joined the Reagan Revolution as a radical ideologue. I learned the traumatic lesson that no such revolution was possible. I end up giving two cheers for the politicians. But only that.

The fact is, politicians are a menace. They never stop inventing illicit enterprises of government that bleed the national economy. Their social uplift and pork barrel is wasteful; it reduces our collective welfare and wealth. The politicians never look ahead or around. Two years and one Congressional District is the scope of their horizon.

There is only one thing worse, and that is ideological hubris. It is the assumption that the world can be made better by being remade overnight. It is the false belief that in a capitalist democracy we can peer deep into the veil of the future and chain the ship of state to an exacting blueprint. It can't be done. It shouldn't have been tried.

Certainly someone whose idea of imagery is chaining the ship of state to a blueprint should be watched closely. But my point is different and has not, I think, been made with sufficient force even by observers who clearly grasp what happened. Thus Lou Cannon, whose grasp of the Reagan administration is unequaled, says in a column entitled "An Elitist's Troubling Memoir":

> David Stockman's account of his days as President Reagan's budget director should be required reading for all ideologues who conspire by legal means to subvert, undermine, or take over a democratic government.

Fair enough. But surely those who *most* need to read the book are your everyday campaign manager and chief of staff who need the ability to spot subversives when they first appear. If the putative grownups of American politics have not learned to spot a radical ideologue when they encounter one, they have no business in the business, be they Democrat or Republican. Stockman concludes that the Reagan administration's refusal to accept the need for new revenues when the need became obvious "was a willful act of ignorance and grotesque irresponsibility." He concludes: "In the entire twentieth-century history of the nation there has been nothing to rival it." Neither, in the entire history of the twentieth century, I would add, has there been a political class in Washington so incapable of recognizing a radical ideology when it was verily in the grips of one. Stockman is judged to have behaved *badly*, but not *differently*. He told untruths to Congress; he speaks unkindly of colleagues and disrespectfully of the president. That it was his *ideas* that mattered is a seemingly inaccessible thought.

The twentieth century has not been especially forgiving of such incapacity.

New York University, New York
April 21, 1986

A Return to
Social Policy

By the summer of 1986, Democratic spirits were reviving. These remarks were prepared for the newly formed Democratic Leadership Council. They are not optimistic.

Governor Robb has asked me to present, and I quote from his letter, "the historical perspective on social policy" and to do so in fourteen minutes.

Which was good advice, given our attention span on such matters. But this occasion is, even so, different from so many others of recent years. After almost two decades, we see in our panels this morning a return of social scientists to our counsels, which may indeed herald a return to social policy.

Which can only be a good thing for Democrats. At this moment, we are in perhaps the worst shape nationally as we've been in since the immediate aftermath of the Civil War.

The parallel is not perfect. The Copperhead Democrats of the Civil War never repented. The veterans and inheritors of the New Deal and the Great Society do little else.

There is a singular aspect of our recent malaise (!) with respect to social policy. We don't deserve it, but we think we do.

It has become a belief bordering on prejudice that the social ills of the present are the consequence of misguided Democratic social policies of the past two generations. None hold to this

289

belief more guiltily, if furtively, than Democrats themselves, or at least some Democrats. Consider the issue of welfare dependency. There is scarcely a Democratic forum in the nation in which it is not proclaimed as a matter of revealed truth that the social welfare policies of the New Deal and the Great Society are the root causes of this cluster of problems.

The origins of this view are many. I think, for example, of Edward C. Banfield's *The Unheavenly City*, a reasoned exposition of the limits of certain types of government intervention, elements of which appeared toward the end of the 1960s. Much mutated, the message is now proclaimed by that peculiar genus which has been described as "Flower Child Turned Social Darwinist." One of the many unanticipated consequences of that "slum of a decade," to use Dick Hofstadter's term.*

The evidence, in the main, is otherwise. David T. Ellwood and Lawrence H. Summers put it succinctly in the current issue of the *Public Interest*.

> Given the resources devoted to fighting poverty, the policies have done as well as we could have hoped.

But evidence has little influence in the early stages of debating new propositions, and that is where we are just now, as I will come to shortly.

First let us go briefly through that history of social policy.

Political scientists, following T. H. Marshall, divide aspects of citizenship into three clusters of rights and corresponding obligations: Civil, Political, and Social. In Western societies, these have been enhanced in a recognizable progression. To oversimplify, but to explain: first the right to a trial by jury; then the right to vote; next the right to, well, schooling. And, informally

---

* Alan Brinkley notes that a corresponding doctrine of the limits of growth—The Club of Rome—sprang up on the political left at about the same time. Some decade. In any event, both schools seem to be reaching limits of their own.

for a century and a half or so, and by statute for half a century, the right to a subsistence living.

Up until just about now, the United States has based most of its policies in each of these areas on European models. I will not disparage our own embellishments and singular generosity, but the individual legal rights of our Common Law are clearly British in origin, the political rights set forth in the Constitution are British and French in origin, whilst the legislative social rights which we associate with the New Deal are mostly British and German in origin. (Public schools being the possible exception.)

Early in the twentieth century, American social reformers began pressing for the adoption here of social policies already in place in Europe. Bismarck had introduced social security, Churchill unemployment insurance. The models were explicit, and in just about a six-month period in 1935, they were enacted here, in the Social Security Act of that year.

The only major changes since have been health insurance (a British import) for the aged and indigent enacted in 1965, together with various provisions for the disabled adopted in that and the previous decade. Again the models were in the main European, as were those of smaller ventures such as public housing.

Now to a large point. The issues of social policy the United States faces today have no European counterpart nor any European model of a viable solution. They are American problems, and we Americans are going to have to think them through by ourselves.

In many if not most of our major cities, we are facing something very like social regression. Or does that term libel the past? Perhaps our condition is postmodern. Whatever, it is defined by extraordinary levels of self-destructive behavior, interpersonal violence, and social-class separation intensive in some groups, extensive in others. I think *postmodern* may be the more accurate term. (Victorian Britain had its share of "urban" problems, and some responses, such as the temperance movement and the YMCA—later the Boy Scouts—soon appeared here. But our present problems of social control seem new to me.) In any event, it makes for a combination of misery and madness in the modern city.

I spent a part of my youth in a neighborhood not ten blocks from here known then as "Hell's Kitchen."* By today's reckoning it was a kind of peaceable kingdom. The violence of New York City today simply has no equivalent in the past, and shows no sign of diminishing in the future.

Further, we have become the first society in history in which children are the worst-off group in the populace. Not just a few children: by eighteen, perhaps half. Not long ago, in a searing commencement address at Keuka College, Judy Woodruff gave a single instance which will suffice:

> We are, in fact, the only major western nation, other than South Africa, without a national child care policy.

We have no social policy for this situation, and few social programs. The only thing we can be said to know is that the social problems which trouble us and baffle us at this time are exceedingly unlikely to cure themselves. A huge social effort will be required: something akin to social mobilization. Whatever else this will be, it will first of all be hand work. And second of all it will require the support of government. But that should be obvious. What is equally obvious is that we are grievously short of specific ideas.

This was nothing new. In the mid-1960s, even as a moment of great opportunity for social initiatives arose, there also appeared a considerable body of research arguing that we should not exaggerate what we knew or what would come of what we undertook. In the main, this research was rejected, and those who stood up for it were, well, knocked down.

This is called shooting the messenger. Twenty years later,

---

* Our meeting took place at the Sheraton Centre on Seventh Avenue near 52nd Street.

much the same thing happened, albeit more gently. Anyone who spoke up to say the Reagan administration was deliberately disabling the finances of the federal government was simply ignored by those who should have been paying attention.

Let me then summarize the outcome:

As of 1985, the operating revenues of the federal government have declined to 12.9 percent of GNP. This compares with 18.0 percent in 1965. (Operating revenues are distinct from the income of the Social Security tax, which, of course, become dedicated funds.)

Of 12.9 percent in operating revenues available in this fiscal year, 6.3 percent go to defense, and 3.4 percent to interest.

This leaves 3.2 percent of GNP for *all* the other activities of the federal government, from space shuttles to subway cars.

The deficits will not go away. We face a protracted fiscal crisis for the next two or three presidencies. Probably until the next century. We have sold out this generation of children, and have not even begun to think of the next. The only amends we can make is to *begin* to think.

In addition to the strategic coup which has so disabled us, we face an equally perplexing long-range economic decline. The great growth of productivity of the postwar United States has simply ceased. Hourly wages today are what they were in 1968. Median family income today is what it was in 1970. There cannot have been this long a period of economic stagnation—from the point of view of individuals and families—in the past three centuries.

This argues for both an active social policy and militates against one. It militates against in two senses: There is no money in the federal fisc, but just as important, the social space, if I may use that term, which one could feel in an economically booming decade such as that of the 1960s, is just not here in the flat 1980s. Or so I believe.

Even so, the one sure thing is to learn to use our heads again. By all means let us go on about self-reliance, gumption, and go-gettingness. Nothing the matter with any of the above. But if that is all there is to be by way of social policy, no one needs Democrats. And if that is all the social policy there is to be, Democrats shall have deserved their eclipse.

New York, New York
June 23, 1986

Government and Social Research: Reflections on an Uneasy Relationship

---

If there is a lesson to be learned from the Reagan years, it concerns the perils of an inadequate social science. To be sure, the president himself had no secret formula for changing the world, but he gave power to people who did. This paper was prepared for a conference at the Woodrow Wilson International Center for Scholars. The Stockman quote is from an interview with Peter Manso in OMNI of September 1986.

In the administration of John F. Kennedy, I was appointed to a newly created position, assistant secretary of labor for the Department of Policy Planning and Research. Outwardly this might have appeared as little more than a kind of "grade inflation" by which the long-established work of the department as a collector and collator of economic data was given a more honorific rank in the hierarchy of the federal establishment. As it happens, this was not at all the case.

True, I was given a nominal suzerainty over the Bureau of Labor Statistics, which in time acknowledged this by giving me the monthly unemployment rate some thirty or forty seconds before it reached the White House. But it was intended that my work be something quite different and quite new. Michael Lacy has noted how careful Carroll Wright, the first commissioner of labor statistics, was to assert that the bureau was not in the business of solving social or industrial problems but merely of providing information. This was in the 1880s. The 1960s had quite a different approach. My job and that of the policy planning staff which was shortly assembled was precisely *to* solve social and industrial problems and any others that came to hand. Similar policy planning staffs were springing up all over Washington in that brash season. The War on Poverty was but one of our great collective efforts.

In the spring of 1965, during my last months in the office, I composed an article entitled "The Professionalization of Reform," which appeared in the first issue of the *Public Interest*. Citing the vision of Wesley C. Mitchell, who founded the National Bureau of Economic Research two generations earlier, I suggested the time had indeed come when a convergence of theoretical models and statistical measurements made possible solutions to all manner of difficulty. Political problems would remain, of course. Good Keynesians, we had learned to cut taxes when doctrine decreed. (We had just done so.) But we had not yet shown our ability to raise taxes when required. (As indeed we would not do in the years immediately ahead.) Still I concluded:

The prospect that the more primitive social issues of American politics are at last to be resolved need only mean that we may now turn to issues more demanding of human ingenuity than that of how to put an end to poverty in the richest nation in the world. Many such issues might be in the area of foreign affairs, where the enormity of difficulty and the proximity of disaster is sufficient to keep the citizens and political parties of the nation fully occupied. And there is also the problem of perfecting, to the highest degree possible, the *quality* of our lives and of our civilization. We may not be accustomed to giving political priority to such questions. But no one can say they will be boring or trivial!

The innocence, a gentler way of saying the ignorance, of this observation is mildly interesting, but what is striking is how readily such assumptions had settled in the federal establishment. This came just a decade after the various assessments of the state of the social sciences at mid-century, lamenting what Peter Odegard described as "the monumental accumulation of data and the meager crop of significant concepts." Edward Shils put it that "social research in the present century has been characterized by an extraordinary scattering of attention over a great variety of uncoordinated problems which were investigated at a very concrete level." Precious little, in Leonard Cottrell's phrase, being in any sense "additive."

In my youth in New York, one heard the story of the Irish lady, babe in arms, ragamuffins in tow, leaving church on Sunday morning where a newly ordained pastor had been preaching on the joys of family life. "I wish," she was overheard to say, "I knew as little about the subject as that young man!" And I can imagine American scholars today wondering how on earth someone could have come to believe all that business about policy planning in the face of the testimony of Odegard and his colleagues.

The simple if unsatisfactory answer is that everyone did. The idea of policy planning had taken hold, and it was assumed that social investigation had reached the point where it could be a reliable, or at very least useful, guide to social policy.

Political economy was the queen of these battles. Edwin G. Nourse would comment in 1969 that the $11-billion tax cut of 1964 was "a more daring and more professionally designed experiment with a total economy than we had ever experienced before." The experimental mode went beyond the application of theory to inquiries modeled on laboratory science. As, for example, the "New Jersey Graduated Work Incentive Experiment, A Social Experiment in Negative Taxation Sponsored by the Office of Economic Opportunity." Name your issue; somewhere in Washington, some agency was conducting an experiment to develop or to demonstrate a policy. Typically, there was tension between the economists, who saw everything coming right if the GNP just kept growing, and offices such as ours in the Department of Labor, which saw social dysfunction as emerging quite independently of economic growth. I refer to our various studies of young males rejected by Selective Service, and of minority families.

I have the impression that it is generally supposed that this sort of behavior, nonsensical or otherwise, went out of style in Washington in the 1980s. I wish then to offer the thought that, to the contrary, *it has never been more in style.* The curve extrapolates nicely indeed from the 1960s.

I have mentioned the Kennedy tax cut and the Kennedy antipoverty program, both, as it happens, put into place under his successor President Johnson.

What has been the record in this regard of the present administration?

As for taxes, it came to office more or less committed to a large tax cut based on "supply-side" economic theory. Quickly enacted, the measure was designed to reduce revenues some $280 billion over three years: an order of magnitude greater than Kennedy's experiment. The advocates of the bill regularly referred to the Kennedy precedent by way of evidence, and by way of advocacy there was as much scholarly writing and learned disputation. That the party in office had changed meant little if any change in what had become an *executive style.*

As we know, the supply-side tax cut did not produce the economic stimulus anticipated.

In his memoir *The Triumph of Politics: Why the Reagan Revolution Failed,* Mr. David Stockman recounts how in late August and early September of 1980, which is to say well before the election of that year, his calculations led him to realize that a huge deficit would be the result from such a tax cut. But this led him further to the view that it should go forward anyway, as it would inevitably force the dismantling of the bloated welfare state, or words to that effect. More recently he has said that he could not "claim" sole responsibility for the events that followed:

> I was the person who pulled it all together, the guy who provided the intellectual rationalization and fleshed out the details of the blueprint. I thought that if we implemented the plan, the whole social order and economic system would be better off. But the plan was simply too sweeping, too radical. Whatever its theoretical merits, it had the unintended effect of unleashing forces in the legislative process that produced some very unbalanced and unsustainable results, namely, a huge tax cut coupled with very little change in spending which resulted in a radically unbalanced fiscal policy.

Having in his memoir described the program as "radical, imprudent, and arrogant," in this interview he allows that at the time, he was "an ideologue . . . [with] grand views of how you govern society."

As to problems of poverty, Mr. Sidney Blumenthal in his recent book *The Rise of the Counter-Establishment*, describes the extraordinary influence of a number of young social scientists on the new administration. They had reduced, in his words, the complex statistics of the matter to "an astonishingly simple thesis—poverty programs cause poverty."

This too has its parallel with the 1960s. The political economists have great schemes for universal prosperity, whilst social scientists ponder the situation of an "underclass" seemingly unresponsive to general movements in the economy. Thus in the midst of general well-being, the Bureau of the Census reports that in 1985 some 23 percent of children age three and under in the United States are living in households with incomes below the poverty line.

The discouraging thing is that for all this dither there is not much to show by way of results. The well-being of the median man and woman in this country got stuck at just about the time these assorted enterprises commenced to ensure continued progress. Median family income has been flat for seventeen years; surely the longest such period in the history of European settlement. Average weekly earnings today in constant dollars are lower than they were in 1962.

There is a certain irony in the data I have just cited. The availability of such data was the setting in which the large theories of recent decades have arisen, and the very same data attest to their seeming failure. But is that not important in and of itself? Yes, say I.

The uses of social research as measurement are indispensable to government today. We cannot think of fiscal policy save in terms that Simon Kuznets bequeathed us. But to go from there to large, untested, unproven theory, to accept uncritically a set of propositions about the political process which Madison would have judged so patently wrong as to be deliberately seditious, is something else altogether. I would even defend the 1960s. We may have written some silly articles, but on the whole, in domestic matters we did fewer silly things and perhaps more sensible ones.

If this is so, how are we to account for it? One explanation is that the hubris of scientific social policy was not so far advanced in the 1960s as it was two decades later. Another possibility is that we were better social scientists. A larger possibility is that we are seeing at work in both "liberal" Democratic and "conservative" Republican administrations the demon that Michael Oakeshott has identified as Rationalism—the great heresy of modern times.

Washington, D.C.
September 10, 1986

The "New Science of Politics" and the Old Art of Governing

This, the Britannica Lecture, given at the Smithsonian Institution in September 1986, must serve as a kind of summation. The defining failure of the Reagan era was that of political economy. Could this, at some deep level, be an institutional failure?

Anyone who has studied American government or taken some part in its affairs will often have asked: "How goes the science of the thing?"

As we approach the bicentennial of the Constitution, which is not to say our Independence, but our form of government, leafing through *The Federalist Papers*, pondering the unexampled endurance of the Constitutional arrangements put in place in those years, we are reminded of the role the "new science of politics," as the founders liked to call it, played in devising those arrangements.

It appears to me that the significance of this bicentennial is predicated on the extent to which the perception is widened that the government of the United States was not fashioned out of "self-evident truths," but rather was the work of scholar-statesmen who had studied hard, learned much, and believed they had come upon some principles—uniformities—in human behavior which made possible the reintroduction of republican government nearly two millennia after Caesar had ended the experiment.

We may doubt that the bicentennial discussion will attain to anything like the level of discourse two centuries ago. We are short on Madisons and Hamiltons and Jays. But it *is* possible to hope that we may acquire a more general understanding of what it was those men were discoursing *about*. Else all will be lost to fireworks and faith healing.

The argument was whether government could be founded on scientific principles; those who said it could be, won.

At the risk of reproach from persons more learned than I, let me state in summary the intellectual dilemma of that time. The victors in the Revolution could agree that no one wanted another monarchy in line with the long melancholy succession since Caesar. Yet given what Madison termed "the fugitive and turbulent existence of . . . ancient republics," who could dare to suggest that a modern republic could hope for anything better?

Madison could. And why? Because study had produced new knowledge, which could now be put to use. To cite Martin Diamond:

> This great new claim rested upon a new and aggressively more 'realistic' idea of human nature. Ancient and medieval thought and practice were said to have failed disastrously by clinging to illusions regarding how men *ought* to be. Instead, the new science would take man as he actually *is*, would accept as primary in his nature the self-interestedness and passion displayed by all men everywhere and, precisely on that basis, would work out decent political solutions.

This was a declaration of intellectual independence equal in audacity to anything done in 1776. Until then, with but a few exceptions, the whole of political thought turned on ways to inculcate virtue in a small class that would govern. But, wrote Madison, "if men were angels, no government would be necessary." Alas, we would have to work with the material at hand.

Not pretty, but something far more important: predictable. Thus, men could be relied upon to be selfish; nay, rapacious. Very well: "Ambition must be made to counteract ambition." Whereupon we derive the central principle of the Constitution, the various devices which in Madison's formulation, offset "by opposite and rival interests, the defect of better motives."

This is a near-mechanistic view of government, and we must assume it was influenced by the science of the time, which consisted principally of laws of motion. (Indeed, Franklin has a nice statement in which he joins the ancient and modern in comfortable proximity. Recommending a text expounding Newtonian mechanics, he writes: "Next to the knowledge of duty, this kind of knowledge is certainly the most useful. . . .")

As for the "opposite and rival interests" that would drive this government machine, we are all familiar with the proposition of the *The Federalist Papers*, No. 10, that "the most common and durable source of factions has been the verious [sic] and unequal distribution of property." A rough approximation of experience, one would say. But note: This is the *last* such source which Madison identifies. The second was "attachment to different leaders," what Weber in time would term the charismatic principle in politics. But *first* came:

> A zeal for different opinions concerning religion, concerning government, and many other points, as well of speculation as of practice.

Madison writes of these "causes of faction" as being "sown in the nature of man; and we see them everywhere brought into different degrees of activity, according to the different circumstances of civil society." Hence we ought not to ascribe any hierarchy to his principles (nor indeed take anything too literally in the patristic writings). Yet it may be noted that his first principle of faction is "passion"; only by degrees does he get to real estate.

The founders made a great deal of their practicality, but perhaps, from the point of view of posterity, did not sufficiently call attention to their belief that they proceeded on what they saw as a science of politics.

Among the elites of the nineteenth century, science steadily displaced religion as the locus of ultimate belief; theology gave way to physics in the universities and suchlike settings. We can speculate that the competition of political ideas might have gone better had the American system been more widely perceived as having proclaimed itself to be scientific, in the applied sense of the term. Alas, that laurel was borne off by Marx and Engels, whose wholly theoretical schema won the designation of "scientific socialism," and the fascination of three, perhaps four, generations of Europeans and others, including not a few Americans. It was a fascination which in time would convulse continents and transform civilizations.

Pitiful stuff, for the most part. It proved nothing. It forecast nothing. It failed especially to anticipate the most ominous form of "faction" in our century, which is to say ethnic conflict.

The general central *organizing* prediction of the *Communist Manifesto* was that there would emerge a worldwide proletarian class independent "of all nationality." Workers of the World. In the words of the *Manifesto*, modern capitalism would strip the worker

> of every trace of national character. Law, morality, religion, are to him so many bourgeois prejudices, behind which lurk in ambush just as many bourgeois interests.

In the 1950s, Nathan Glazer and I began to study the ethnic groups of New York City, noting not just their survival from the age of immigration, but indeed their emergence as a new political form. Ours has been a relatively mild experience of ethnicity; even so, it contrasted with the "liberal expectancy," to use Milton Gordon's term, that such identities would disappear altogether. More important, it contrasted utterly with the Marxist prediction, especially regarding the relation of white and black workers. In the 1970s, a seminar at the American Academy of Arts and Sciences pursued the ethnic base of conflict in severely divided societies around the world. We found the Marxist model of conflict useless. Scholars, especially Donald Horowitz, continue to add powerful specifics and generalizations. American scholarship has now falsified the central organizing principle of the Marxist forecast of the future. (Just as there has been no collapse of profits, immiserization of the masses, withering away of the socialist state, and so on.)

Of course, it has been events, not study, that have falsified Marx. Car bombs if you like. But it is something that scholarship had broken out of a set of presumptions that obscured reality.

I pose this question: If events are seen to have falsified Marx, why are they not also seen to have confirmed Madison? Why is Marxism not seen as just a variant on the prescientific notion of leadership by the chosen, with (as Glazer suggests) the Workers assuming the virtuous role of the Guardians? Why do we not discern on every hand the usefulness and nice shadings of Madison's tripartite model of conflict? In Beirut, Colombo, Johannesburg, Belfast, the purest sort of emotional, religious, racial, clannish "passion." In Teheran, the cult of the leader, as previously in Moscow and Beijing, Rome and Berlin? (In Mao's time, I have seen in Tian'anmen Square in Beijing effigies of hirsute Marx and Engels, stern Stalin and Mao reaching halfway to the heavens.) And in the legislatures of the United States, of Australia, of Canada, of the EEC, the primordial demands of economic interest groups on the national treasure?

I pose the question for two reasons. The first is immediate and specific. It appears to me that as the United States settles into a protracted and ominously expensive armed standoff with the Soviet Union, here and there enlivened with surrogate conflicts, or one-party interventions, we seem to have forgotten what the conflict is all about. The conflict, in William Pfaff's nice phrase, is about "the Soviet leaders' claim that theirs is not so much a nation as a step forward in history." This claim is false. It has been falsified.*

It appears to me that as time passes and the period in which the Marxist analysis first appeared becomes more remote, the *content* of that analysis becomes ever more fuzzy to American and, I suppose, Western leadership. (Try expounding Lenin's theory of imperialism in a Senate debate over selling subsidized wheat to the Soviet Union.) Far from being clear-eyed Madisonians, fully cognizant of the nonsense that followed, more and more we seem lost in the swirl of present events, and our great confrontation approaches the condition of "Dover Beach." In the main, our leaders don't know their jobs. They are both under-informed and overpreoccupied.

Note, for example, a 1986 editorial in *Science* by David A. Hamburg, raising the issue of the convergence of ethnicity with technical developments in weapons and other modes of destruction:

> The world is now, as it has been for a long time, awash in a sea of ethnocentrism, prejudice, and violent conflict. The worldwide historical record is full of hateful and destructive indulgences based on religious, racial, and other distinctions—holy wars of one sort or another. What is new is the destructive power of our weaponry: nuclear, enhanced conventional, chemical, and biological. Moreover, the worldwide spread of technical capability, the miniaturization of weapons, the widely broadcast justifications for violence, and the upsurge of fanatical behavior are occurring in ways that can readily provide the stuff of very deadly conflicts. To be

---

* I am grateful to Milton J. Esman for the observation that while there has been a virtual collapse of Marxism as an ideological force in world affairs, there remains an important exception. He writes: "Ironically, as the working class and young people have abandoned it, Marxist thought has achieved unprecedented respectability among academic social scientists. While Leninism is rejected as a deformation of Marxist thought and practice, the Marxist critique of capitalism remains one of the most influential paradigms in the contemporary social sciences." (Personal correspondence, December 24, 1986.)

blunt, we have a rapidly growing capacity to make life everywhere absolutely miserable and disastrous.

It doesn't much help to ascribe such trouble to the Soviets. Far
better to see it as something *The Federalist Papers* would put
under the heading of things not to be avoided, but somehow to
be moderated.

These are the second grounds on which I raise the question
of our continued appreciation of the intellectual constructs on
which our nation was founded. The framers of the American
Constitution put in place a system of government which they
believed could work. Not would; *could*. It was not to be assumed
that the affairs of men normally go well; far less, that some great
transcendence was under way that would once and for all put an
end to misfortune and strife. The "science of politics" indicated
no such thing.

It may be useful at this point to ask just what was the nature
of the "science" which the founders aimed to apply. It does not
appear to me that this presents any great difficulty. They sought
in an unsentimental way to observe such regularities as presented
themselves from experience. They turned frequently to the
"prophetic past," Chesterton's phrase which Daniel Bell (1964)
used to describe his own work (which would result in *The Coming of the Post-Industrial Society* [1973]) in seeking "to identify
the structural trends and structural possibilities in the society,"
such that plausible future outcomes can be envisioned without
exactly being forecast. This seems modest stuff until one con-
siders the outcome of some other modes of prediction!

It is the nature of such an approach to the "science of politics" that it has to be kept up to date. Ideas change; technologies
change; new trends, new possibilities appear; older ones recede.

Thus, in the past two centuries, there has been a great transformation in the problematic aspects of government, especially
the national government (with which I deal here). An eighteenth-
century government could do a great deal *to* you; not much *for*
you. Keep off the Indians, that sort of thing; but that's about all

the good things that would come of it. For the rest, it was a matter of securing the Blessings of Liberty by preventing government from doing bad things.

In the intervening centuries, and notably this one, there has been a great reversal. There is not much positive bad done by Western governments to individuals or communities any longer. This is not because human nature has changed or the inherent nature of sovereignty has changed. It is simply that in our case, to be specific, the restraints and prohibitions written into the Constitution have shaped the American polity such that by any historical and most contemporary standards it has no great disposition to abuse the power of government, and in the main does not.

However, a great increase in wealth and changed standards of social provision have led to seemingly ever increasing demands *on* government, such that the perceived danger nowadays is not that it should become too powerful, but that it has become too big.

My purpose is to ask whether we are approaching this newer question with anything like the clarity and method with which the founders approached the older one. My answer is no.

I detect a measure of dissembling, if not contradiction, in our well-known aversion to Big Government. (Years ago, passing through the lovely upstate village of Canadaigua, New York, de Tocqueville noted: ". . . it was by promising to weaken it [the federal government] that one won the right to control it.") It was clear enough that individuals and groups had considerable tolerance for government outlays that benefited *them*, such that a steady general growth in the size of government was the "logical" outcome of the political bargaining process.

But until recently the depth of this attachment to government had not been tested. What was needed was an experiment. This commenced with the election of President Reagan.

Previous presidents had assuredly preached the virtues of smaller government. Franklin D. Roosevelt in 1932 pledged to balance Mr. Hoover's extravagant budget. But this was a kind of civic religion, avowed but not constraining.

Now came a president who genuinely believed that the growth of government was truly threatening both to the society *and* to the economy, and that radical action was necessary to save the Republic. Not since 1932 was an inaugural address framed in terms of such immediate crisis calling for drastic measures.

These United States are confronted with an economic affliction of great proportions. We suffer from the longest and one of the worst sustained inflations in our national history. It distorts our economic decisions, penalizes thrift, and crushes the struggling young and the fixed-income elderly alike. It threatens to shatter the lives of millions of our people.

Idle industries have cast workers into unemployment, human misery, and personal indignity. Those who do work are denied a fair return for their labor by a tax system which penalizes successful achievement and keeps us from maintaining full productivity.

But great as our tax burden is, it has not kept pace with public spending. For decades we have piled deficit upon deficit, mortgaging our future and our children's future for the temporary convenience of the present. To continue this long trend is to guarantee tremendous social, cultural, political, and economic upheavals.

In this present crisis, government is not the solution to our problem; government is the problem.

It is my intention to curb the size and influence of the Federal establishment and to demand recognition of the distinction between the powers granted to the Federal Government and those reserved to the States or to the people. All of us need to be reminded that the Federal Government did not create the States; the States created the Federal Government.

This was much more than the boilerplate of a traditional conservative administration come to office. To the contrary, the new president was surrounded by new men with radically revisionist views of economics and government. For this group of new conservatives, capitalism had evolved during the postwar decades into an encompassing ideology. (I use the term as Edward Shils would do: a set of beliefs about social norms which it is necessary to realize in action without exception. Bolshevik Marxism was an ideology; so was National Socialism. The new ideology of capitalism—in no way brutal, much less totalitarian—was, even so, capable of recklessness in pursuit of an ordained ideal.)

Capitalism was seen to ensure not only a high level of production but a high level of civilization as well. The latter being the most important. No Cotton Mather ever preached against sin more fervently than these new men railed against subsidy, including subsidy to big business. No John Winthrop ever envisioned a city on a hill that excelled more in virtue than the free market of the new ideologues.

Later that inauguration day, the new president fulfilled a campaign pledge by signing a federal employee hiring freeze. He declared:

And beyond the symbolic value of this, which is my first official act, the freeze will eventually lead to a significant reduction in the size of the Federal work force.

Much writing will be necessary before the events that immediately preceded and followed this inaugural address can be reliably reconstructed, but the essential events, the most plausible explanation, and the early confessional record (oral and written) are by now in place. In sum: First, a strategy was devised to reduce the size of government by shrinking its financial base. Second, it quickly became apparent that revenues could be cut but that outlays were "sticky." Third, in differing degrees, key members of the administration either could not grasp this or could not admit it, such that a miscalculation as to the workings of the system brought it into the range of instability.

By midsummer of 1981, the administration had brought off an unprecedentedly large tax reduction, an intended $280 billion over three years. However, accompanying legislation provided only $131 billion in budget cuts over that same period, some $70 billion less than requested and less than one-half the prospective revenue loss. Thus, six months into office, the administration was moving decisively *away* from its pledge to balance the budget.

Now this sort of thing happens all the time in government. Honest mistakes are made; wishes don't come true. But generally speaking, the integrity of the process is preserved. Not this time. Ideology corrupted. Rather than give up its beliefs, the administration sacrificed its integrity. Laurence I. Barrett, in his 1983 study *Gambling with History, Reagan in the White House,* was the first to recount what by now seems indisputable. Well *before* the tax cut was passed, the economists and top officials of the Executive Office were of the view that a great deficit would result. Barrett writes that on August 3, 1981,

> his senior advisors . . . informed him [the president] in detail that Reaganomics was hitting the reefs. Some kind of major salvage operation would be necessary. He had . . . been told that OMB's *Mid-Session Review of the 1982 Budget,* published on July 15, was both obsolete and deceptive even before it went to the printer.

The size of government was not shrinking. The agencies were resisting. Barrett reports that the president was, even so, adamant. He gave orders: "We should just say to all the agencies, 'To the rear, march.' " Whereupon he asked about the hiring freeze he'd signed his first day in office. Was it still in effect? No, said Stockman. "Well," replied the president, "we're still basically lathered in fat where employment in the Federal government is concerned." Whereupon, again, according to Barrett, he suggested forced reductions.

Let us examine the record some six years out.

First to the size of government, which was the first issue the administration addressed.

At the beginning of fiscal year 1981, the total employment of the United States government (civilian employment in the executive, legislative, and judicial branches and in the postal service, and those on active military duty) was 4,966,000 persons. By the beginning of fiscal year 1986, it was 5,210,000. This was an *increase* of 244,000. The increase in the first five Reagan years for each category of worker was 143,000 civilian and 101,000 active duty military.

Federal expenditures? In fiscal year 1980, federal outlays totalled $590.9 billion. By fiscal year 1986, they were $979.9 billion, two-thirds again as much. In fiscal year 1980, federal debt was $914.3 billion; by fiscal year 1985, it had doubled to $1,827.5 billion and soon crossed the two trillion mark. Net interest on the debt had become the second largest item in the federal budget, after defense. (David A. Levy has called to my attention the extraordinary growth of real interest income during the 1980s, the nominal rate reaching 14.6 percent in 1984, a time of quite low inflation. Wage and salary income declined to 59 percent of personal income. A *rentier* society?)

The falling off of inflation was the one unquestioned success of the early Reagan years. On the other hand, owing in part to the huge capital inflows required to finance unprecedented deficits, the exchange rate of the dollar rose steeply from the time the administration took office until February 1985. This *can* be seen as a form of inflation, a rise in the price of our goods in *other* currencies. A result was a great falling off of American exports, and a corresponding increase in imports. In 1986, the United States became a net importer of food.

With one thing or another, by the mid-1980s, agriculture had declined into its worst economic condition since the 1930s. The predictable response of Congress was to appropriate money for the relief of constituents, but with two differences from the earlier period when Henry Agard Wallace had so scandalized the conservatives. For one thing, these rural constituents now numbered a very considerable number of millionaires. When millionaires get into financial difficulties, large sums are required to get them out. By mid-decade, it was routine to learn of individual farm price support payments in excess of a million dollars a year. In September 1986, a Senate committee refused to impose a $500,000 per farmer cap. The other difference was that *because of the deficits*, the money didn't seem to matter all that much.

In time, the attractions of this arrangement became evident to the president as well. In the summer of his sixth year in office, he was to be found in the Middle West telling farm audiences:

> No area of the budget, including defense, has grown as fast as our support of Agriculture.

David Hoffman, White House correspondent for the *Washington Post*, has provided a graphic account of this day at the Illinois State Fair.

> 'We're talking about a way of life,' Reagan said, 'a way of life nurtured and sustained by the soil—the oldest way of life that Americans know. And my friends, America has too much at stake in her farms—too much history, too much pride—not to help in hard times. I give you my promise— the nation will see the farmers through.'
>
> While Reagan held out the prospect of ultimately getting 'government out of farming so that our farmers can achieve complete economic independence,' what he did in Illinois last week was the opposite. He got the government a little deeper into farming at a time when agriculture is already expected to cost $30 billion this year—breaking all previous records. Reagan has turned this into a virtue, boasting that 'this year alone we'll spend more on farm support programs . . . than the total amount the last administration provided in all its four years.'

The flag-waving crowd loved it. Reagan was applauded 15 times in his 11-minute address.

The Reagan administration commitment to minimal government was notably specific in the area of international trade. Repeatedly the new president would declare that one in six of the nation's manufacturing jobs and one in four of our farm acres produced merchandise for overseas markets. The way to promote worldwide prosperity "is not to erect barriers, but to bring them down, not to decrease international trade, but to expand it." He would invoke the dread example of the Smoot–Hawley Tariff Act of 1930 and assert: "We are committed to free trade and believe free trade benefits all nations concerned."

But the administration's professed commitment to free markets and the presumed greater economic growth that accompanies them soon began to succumb to the pattern of calling for greater economic growth but opting for less, just as the administration, having proclaimed its commitment to smaller government, commenced to build a yet bigger one.

Here I must assert the limits of my knowledge. I do not know what government actions make for greater economic growth or lesser economic growth. Further, it is to be kept in mind that the American economy continues to grow in terms that would be the envy of earlier ages. (Assuming earlier ages paid much heed to such matters.)

Still, it is clear that the American economy grows at a lesser rate than other economies manage to do. Since 1960, the overall 2.7 percent per year increase in U.S. manufacturing productivity has been lower than that of nine European countries for which the Bureau of Labor Statistics has data (such as France at 5.5 percent and the United Kingdom at 3.6 percent, lower than Canada at 3.4 percent), and considerably less than the 8-percent increase in Japan. And it is also clear that, after a point, the new administration began to act in ways that *it* had said would impede economic growth.

Consider steel. From its 1953 peak of 726,000 workers, the

American industry had lost some 58 percent of its work force by 1985. Demands for protection grew during this period. The Carter administration engineered a limited cartel to share the American market with Japanese and European producers. Thus secured, the steel companies, in Hobart Rowen's view, went off to "use precious resources to buy retail shopping centers, S&Ls, or almost any other business instead of concentrating on their own." This, of course, fits the classic prediction of the effects of trade protection. The downward spiral continued. Employment in steel dropped 9.6 percent annually from 1979 to 1985. Whereupon the demand for more protection. *And* the Reagan administration complied. In the summer of 1986, Rowen reported:

> Now, despite the Reagan Administration's free-trade rhetoric, it has created a full-fledged cartel: The import share is supposed to be slashed to 18.5 percent of the market, with the pieces shared among a dozen foreign producers.
>
> But a funny thing happened to the protected steel industry as it attempted to cash in on an intended artificial scarcity. Consuming manufacturers, notably auto makers, discovered the virtues of plastic and other materials that reduce car weight, thus encouraging mileage efficiency. Today, the typical car uses hundreds of pounds less steel than one of equivalent size 10 years ago.

The administration's record is not one of capitulation, but of vacillation. One day it will stand its ground on textiles. The next day it will negotiate a quota agreement with Japan on the import of semiconductors. (Leading, predictably, to huge increases in the price Japanese manufacturers charged American customers, and a threat by United States electronics and computer industries to move production facilities offshore.) The pattern is seemingly now set: not that much different from that of predecessors, but with larger consequences.

Concomitantly, income in the United States somehow ceased growing. Per capita income rose some 25 percent from 1970 to

1985, and the proportion of the population employed rose to a record 60.1 percent, but somehow it didn't cumulate. In constant dollars, real average weekly earnings in 1985 were lower than in 1962 and well below their peak in 1973. In 1985, median family income at $27,735 was exactly $399 greater in constant 1985 dollars than in 1970. This 1985 level was well below the best Carter years, and lower still than the $29,172 peak in 1973 during the Nixon administration.

What an astounding distance traveled from that brave high noon of January 20 on the west front of the Capitol. On reading Stockman's book, David P. Calleo was moved to write:

> Few recent memoirs depict so vividly the incompetence of people in high places, or deflate so brutally expectations of rational governance.
>
> His [Stockman's] conclusion about the essential frivolity of the Reagan fiscal policy is difficult to fault. Economists can quibble over the size and significance of past Federal deficits. But it is hard to see deficits on the present scale as anything other than the breakdown of rational government. For Mr. Stockman, the 'Reagan revolution' was supposed to mean the restoration of free-market capitalism through a purging of the waste and boondoggling of the postwar welfare state. Instead, as he concedes, the Administration's neoconservative rhetoric has merely been a smokescreen for a policy that has, in fact, severely crippled the free market with an impossible load of debt.
>
> Moreover, while the Reaganites have heartily chanted the appropriate incantations, not one appears to have understood a rather fundamental conservative home truth: The free market—like other kinds of freedom—requires an orderly framework sustained by the state and a reasonable degree of self-discipline from its participants. Above all, for a market to work efficiently—that is, for individuals and firms to make rational market decisions—money must have a stable value. To create today's fiscal climate of colossal, wanton,

and unproductive indebtedness is to endow the American political economy with an almost irresistible propensity for inflation. Societies can live well enough with inflation, as governments control and manipulate to stave off disaster, but a free market cannot.

I would differ somewhat. I believe the administration wanted the outcomes it proclaimed. It failed to achieve them because it lacked an elemental grasp of the "science of politics" in our time. The men of the administration gambled—Barrett's term— without any comprehension of the odds and lost without any seeming understanding of what happened.

We have seen an administration pledged most fervently to reducing the size of government and increasing the rate of economic growth yet bringing about just the opposite. This is to say it acted in a manner that intensified the trends it most deplored. Moreover, it did so in tranquil circumstances both at home and abroad, such that nothing need have interfered with its fervently professed intentions.

Are there certain regularities which help account for this, such that if more widely understood we might moderate or even suppress this disposition? Supposing, of course, that that be our wish. In an interview in August 1986, Stockman offered the view that the American public mind is "totally schizoid" with respect to government. In his view:

There is a startling disconnection between Reagan the campaigner, the scourge of big government, and Reagan the chief executive officer of the American government. . . . In the second instance, he has proved to be very pragmatic. Constituencies are given their due, and if they demonstrate, he's willing to call it a day.

That's what he did on Social Security, on farm programs, even aid to education. Remember, we were going to abolish that Education Department monster. . . . Well, [it's] still intact with the biggest budget in history.

[Reagan] reflects the public mind which itself is totally schizoid. . . . He plays to the ambivalence of the American public. There's a big element of self-deception.

What is to be learned from this troubling experience? Thus George Will, writing as a "lapsed professor of political science":

From the practice to the theory of democratic governments as we now have it in the United States, it is my theory that we are in a momentous year [1986], perhaps the most momentous postwar year of politics in the United States. Because it is the year in which we need to come to grips with the mismatch that threatens not only the health of our economy but the stability of democratic institutions throughout the North Atlantic community. It is the mismatch between the readiness of national governments to spend money and the reluctance of the government to tax sufficiently to pay for their bills.

As for the readiness of national governments to spend money, there is no great mystery. It is in the nature of modern society to expand the range of desirable collective goods. With his own resources, Franklin could afford to purchase most of the essential scientific instruments of his age, and to keep them at home. We, by contrast, must own cloud chambers and space shuttles in common. And hospitals and hospices. We are not a mean people in such matters. But what do we encounter in the Reagan years? The demand for collective goods greatly exceed the supply of money to pay for them. Whereupon we borrowed a trillion dollars from the Japanese and gave a party.

There is, moreover, an imperative which accompanies the advancement of knowledge in modern society. What do we do, for example, when we know how to keep people alive but it costs money? Let them die? I have been long enough in government to have known a time when issues of health hardly intruded on the budget-making process. Antibiotics had arrived, but the cost of running hospitals went mainly to clean linen. Budget examiners never had to choose how many persons with kidney failure they would let live in the next fiscal year. Now they do. It is no discredit to society that it errs on the side of the patient. This will continue.

Further, it is arguably in the nature of a mature capitalism to encourage the consumption of private goods. This produces the return on all that previous saving. The career of Henry C. Simons, a leader of the "Chicago School," bears witness to the change in mores that a sensitive observer could detect. A fierce "libertarian," and no friend of the New Deal, in 1934 Simons produced a pamphlet, "A Positive Program For Laissez-Faire: Some Proposals for a Liberal Economic Policy." His four-point program began with "elimination of private monopoly in all its forms" and ended with "limitation upon the squandering of our resources on advertising and selling activities." Laissez-faire economics was deemed by a powerful intellect to be compatible with, indeed to require, a positive restraint in inducements to consume. But nothing could stop the dynamic of spending, including borrowing to spend, and that pattern has now reached government.

All this is sufficient to account for the present, protracted imbalance. Government in a general sense ought to be spending more as collective goods become more desirable and military goods, by any historical standard, more necessary, and as individuals want to spend more. Hence both the need for taxes and the resistance to them, an impasse that is temporarily resolved by borrowing; but since so much of present borrowing is from abroad, the question of long-range stability does arise. A Marxist outcome is not, after all, unthinkable. The system was expected to collapse under its ordained appetites. No one expected these appetites to turn to the exploitation of government, rather than the masses, but there is a rough analogy. This wants to be repeated. Paying government less (in taxes) than the value of the goods and services it provides is a form of exploitation by the social classes that benefit—in the main, middle- and upper-income groups.

Is this process ineluctable? The case could be made. Thus at mid-decade when deficits became seriously embarrassing, Congress decided to cut them back a bit, largely by cutting back military spending rather than forgoing other forms of consumption. The assertively pro-defense administration went along, even as it devised new modes of subsidizing voters in the farm belt. (Between fiscal years 1985 and 1986, budget authority for defense dropped for the first time since 1970–1971.)

Will ever greater government borrowing squeeze capital out of the private marketplace? Will we debauch the currency, or repudiate our debt, or settle on terms the Japanese dictate? These are questions increasingly asked in Washington with an also increasing awareness that no one is listening.

Still, the events of the 1980s, once their implications are understood, could just possibly bring on a reassessment of Madisonian principles. It is now clear that "opposite and rival interests" can prevent the formation of a tyrannical majority that would use government to trample the rights of minorities. This Madison undertook, and this he achieved. But it is also clear that in the changed circumstances of the present age, a majority coalition can be assembled to exploit government. If this cannot succeed in the long run, it gives the appearance of working fine for the moment. So much the worse then for Hamilton's admonition:

> Money is, with propriety, considered as the vital principle of the body politic; as that which sustains its life and motion and enables it to perform its most essential functions.

Which brings us back to virtue. It may be that I exaggerate the crisis of the 1980s, but I think not. I believe it is now revealed that the constitutional arrangements of 1787 are not necessarily

self-correcting, need not return to stability; that opposing appetites do not cancel each other out, that the "defect of better
motives" can be a defect indeed. A profound prudential error was
made in 1981. Persons in brief authority created a crisis which
they thought would greatly reduce the amount of government
spending, but which in fact greatly increased the amount of government borrowing. The "new science of politics" should have
told them that their conspiracy would not succeed. But something further ought to have deterred them. Those who are sworn
to uphold and defend the Constitution of the United States against
all enemies foreign and domestic do not engage in conspiracies
whilst exercising authority in the name of the president. Those
in such position do not withhold facts and misrepresent facts
whilst professing professionalism and candor. There was a failure,
as James Q. Wilson would put it, of character. In time, this failure
extended well beyond a small circle in the executive office of the
president.

And thus we return to the Declaration after all.

> And for the support of this Declaration, with a firm Reliance
> on the Protection of divine Providence, we mutually pledge
> to each other our Lives, our Fortunes, and our sacred Honor.

The "science of politics" can make the demands of virtue bear-
able but can never substitute for them. The 1980s produced not
a political crisis but an ethical one. At some level, official Washington has not wanted to know what happened. To do so would
lead, or so I think, to Will's assessment. And then what do you
do? If you are not seriously prepared to do something, it is perhaps
best not to know that you ought to. This is a form of cowardice
and a defect indeed of virtue.

It comes to this. The psychological realism of the founders
predicted much and served us well in a time of a small and distant
national government. It is not clear that this is still the case.
Something extra is required in an age when the costs of wholly

self-interested behavior can be so great because government is so large.

Washington D.C.
September 12, 1986

Toward the end of the year, Stockman published a postscript to his memoirs with the title "Exactly Who Shot John?" Anticipating no change in the remaining two years of the administration, his judgment was clear enough.

With the benefit of hindsight, [historians] will know the immense damage to the nation's balance sheet and living standard that resulted from these eight years of fiscal profligacy. By then, the secret of the Reagan era's fabulous free lunch will be beyond dispute. The records will show that within the span of a few short years the United States flung itself into massive hock with the rest of the world. And it occurred so swiftly that it was hardly even debated or remarked upon until it was too late.

All had begun with a "giant mishap of domestic economic governance in early 1981." Even so,

While the ultimate financial box score of the Reagan era is clear, historians are nevertheless destined to wrestle with a huge riddle. Why was this fiscal and financial mutation allowed to build and fester for seven years after it was evident that a stunning but correctable economic policy error had been made in the first six months of 1981?

His answer?

In the final analysis, only one conclusion is possible. The American economy and government have literally been taken hostage by the awesome stubbornness of the nation's fortieth President. That is how the history books will eventually explain the debt-spending spree of the 1980s.

I, of course, argue otherwise. More than one conclusion is possible. There was no "mishap" in the first six months of 1981. There was a conspiracy that both succeeded and failed. A correction could have followed. None did. This surely was a failure of politics, but it was equally a failure of ethical standards in high public office.

The result, according to Stockman?

[T]he politicians and policy makers of the 1990s will curse the legacy of Reaganomics as they struggle to scratch out the modest increases in American living standards that will be possible after huge amounts of current income are wired annually to creditors around the globe.

Epilogue

There is more, but you will have got the idea by now.

On election day, November 4, 1986, reports appeared in the American press that a weekly journal in Beirut had carried a story about American arms shipments to Iran. On November 13, the president held a news conference and said something like that had happened. The affair began to billow. The president seemed not to notice, leaving Washington on November 26 for Thanksgiving at his ranch in southern California. On Saturday, November 29, he gave his regular weekly radio broadcast. The stockmarket, he reported, had never been higher. There had never been more jobs. (Both things true.) When he had been in college, he reminisced, he was taught the economics of an Englishman named John Maynard Keynes who held that if you had a problem, government should throw borrowed money at it, but you can't spend yourself rich and you can't prime the pump without pumping the prime. (Not quite. The president graduated from Eureka College in 1932; the *General Theory* [of Employment, Interest, and Money] was published in 1936.) But wait. They didn't think it was necessary to get even small matters straight; which could only mean they didn't realize what happened.

I had been assigned to give the Democratic response. I went on thinking, My God, another presidency.

Fellow Americans, good afternoon.

I have been asked to deliver what has come to be known as the "Democratic response" to the president's weekly radio broadcast. And for certain, I am a Democrat. And yet I was also a member of the Cabinet of President Reagan's two immediate Republican predecessors. It is somewhat in that role that I would speak today. This is no occasion on which to respond to the president. This is a time to talk to him.

Mr. President, I listened to you at noon. I pray you are listening to me now. Your presidency, Sir, is tottering. It can be saved. But only you can save it, and only if you will talk to us, the Congress. Washington is awash with rumor, intrigue, treachery. Out there in the Santa Ynez Mountains you can't know how bad it is, for you have never been through anything like it. I have. I tell you it is deeply dangerous. Mind, we do not yet have a constitutional crisis. But it could come unless you act and act now.

Laws have been broken; that must be assumed. Men have betrayed your trust. Very well. Let it all come out, in the open, with greater than deliberate speed, immediately, regardless. You have made one excellent move. The FBI is on the case. They will carry out an investigation by the book. They will get the facts. Why not tell them this minute, and in public, to *get them all*?

But it can't stop at that. There is an institutional crisis between the executive branch and the legislative branch which has to be resolved. Staff can't do it for you. Staff can't do it for us. This is one of those moments when the most important fact to know about Washington is that there are only 537 persons in this capital who are elected by the people and sent here to govern. This is the moment of truth.

This issue is not that difficult.

For some years now, presidents have been coming to the Congress asking for additional staff resources under their personal direction. The National Security Council staff is an example, created in 1947 to assist you as presiding officer of the council. It is responsible to you and, in all truth, to no one else. It is there to help you.

Congress put it there. This is the essential fact. In doing so, we chose to trust the president to use that help wisely. It was unthinkable in 1947 and it is unthinkable today that the staff of the National Security Council would commence to act as a State Department and a Defense Department and a CIA all on its own, or in conjunction with secret agents in other agencies.

We gave you the staff to help you direct the other departments, not to evade or undermine them; not to roam about the world setting off wars, revolutions, panic, pandemonium. And most emphatically and fundamentally, Mr. President, not to break the laws which the Congress has enacted. For in the end, that undermines you, you who are responsible for executing the laws.

This nation does not need and does not want another destroyed presidency.

And so I plead, Mr. President: Clean house. Out with all the facts, out with all the malefactors. Come to the Hill and talk, elected official to elected official. We are your friends. We share this brief but sacred authority given us by friends. We want you to save your presidency, our presidency. And as you would say, thank you and God bless you.

This was on the front page of the *New York Times* the next morning. On NBC's "Meet the Press," Marvin Kalb asked how much time the president had. I answered "forty-eight hours." Forty-eight hours and forty minutes later, President Reagan appeared in the White House press room to introduce the attorney general, who thereupon announced he would seek the appointment of an independent counsel. In that act, or so I believe, Mr. Reagan saved his presidency. It was a fine and courageous act. But his administration? Fred Barnes, now with the *New Republic*, gave to his "White House Watch" column of December 22 the simple title: The End.

At about this time, a *Washington Post* report of the winter meeting of the Republican National Committee was headed:

GOP Leaders Compose a New Song
'88 Keyed to Compassion as Anti-Government
Tune Discarded

Retiring RNC general chairman Paul Laxalt of Nevada told the group: "President Reagan has been inaccurately portrayed as being purely antigovernment. . . . I would think Ronald Reagan has come to a better appreciation of the positives of government than he had before."

There remained the problem of respect. George Will would write of the "White House's fallen cowboys" that their "self-congratulatory exchanges reek of contempt for people who practice the patience demanded by democracy and who accept the procedural accommodations required by anything as orderly as government." Meg Greenfield would add that the men "involved in this pathetic, foolish, and costly conspiracy had one thing in common: a grand contempt for . . . government." Ed Yoder would write: "If you elect presidents with a contempt for government, you're all too likely to get contemptible government."

Haynes Johnson summed up. A "benumbed public" would have

one more disturbing disclosure to contemplate, or refuse to face, about an administration that operated as if above the law and exhibited contempt for constitutional checks and balances intended to thwart abuses of power.

There was some time left for the administration, and things that could be done. But, oh, the waste.

Index

Abrams, Floyd, 137–38
Academics, influence of, 16, 252
Acheson, Dean, 250–51, 252
Adoption, 106–8
Advisory Committee on
    Intergovernmental
    Relations, 212
Afghanistan, 55, 57, 82–83, 240
Agent Identities Protection Act,
    135–36
Agriculture, 312
  subsidies, 151–52, 157, 159,
    274, 312–14, 317, 320
Aid to Families with Dependent
    Children (AFDC), 94–95,
    96, 101–3, 155
Alexander, Lamar, 49
American Academy of Arts and
    Sciences, 305
American Bar Association, 93
American Dilemma (Myrdal), 101
American Enterprise Institute,
    157
American Newspaper Publishers'
    Association, address to,
    134–39
American Philosophical Society,
    141
Americans, The (Boorstin), 141

Americans, The (Lebergott), 227
Americans for Democratic
    Action, 4, 5
Andropov, Yuri, 81, 164
Annenkov, I. U., 56
Argentina, 57, 65, 70–71, 177,
    229
Associated Industries of New
    York, 29
Associated Press, 94
Association of State Governors,
    203
AT&T, 240
Atlantic Monthly, 61, 63n.
Australia, 57

Babbitt, Bruce, 49
Baker, Howard H., Jr., 10, 35, 130,
    196
Baker, James A., III, 131
Balanced budget, 31, 32, 274, 309,
    311
Balanced budget amendment, 19
Ball, Robert, 131
Banfield, Edward C., 290
Barnes, Fred, 3, 327–28
Barrett, Laurence I., 311, 317
Bell, Daniel, 12, 260, 307
Bell, Terrel H., 43–44

Beyond the Melting Pot (Glazer and Moynihan), 260–62
Bernanos, Georges, 186
Bismarck, Otto von, 291
Blumenthal, Sidney, 299
Boland amendments, 180
Boorstin, Daniel, 141, 142
Brady, Jim, 9
Brazil, 122
Breaking with Moscow (Shevchenko), 235–36
Brecher, Charles, 263–64
Brezhnev, Leonid, 81, 82, 85
Brinkley, Alan, 290n.
Britannica Lecture, 301–23
Brock, William E., 121
Brooks, Charles Wayland, 206
Brown, Bob, 26
Bryan, William Jennings, 41
Bryce, Lord James, 68
Buckley, William F., Jr., 42, 43
Budget, federal, 75–77, 312
    balanced, *see* Balanced budget
    cuts in, *see* Budget cuts
    for defense, *see* Defense budget
    deficits, *see* Budget deficit
    domestic, *see* Domestic budget
Budget cuts, 14, 15, 18–19, 20, 33, 109, 257, 274, 281, 282, 286, 311
Budget deficit, xviii–xix, 5, 14–15, 26, 33, 34, 73–77, 111, 151–60, 196–200, 217, 257, 293, 312, 316–17, 320–23
    foreign investment funding the, 227–28, 319, 320
    interest on debt, 152, 158, 160, 197, 198–99, 228, 312, 323
    1981, 152
    1982, 30, 32
    1983, 76, 151
    1984, 38, 38n.
    1989 projected, 152
    in previous administrations, 14–15, 152, 198, 280, 309, 316
    Reagan administration's strategy, xix, 151, 153, 154, 273, 279–82, 286, 287, 298–99
    Social Security and, 26–27, 158, 270–71
Bundy, McGeorge, 9, 189
Bureau of the Census, 95–96, 299
Burke, Edmund, 71
Burnham, David, 238, 239
Burns, Arthur F., 13
Bush, George, 10, 193
Business Council of New York State, address to, 29–35, 272
Busing, court's power to require, 88
Butz, Earl, 16
Byron, Robert, 176

Cabinet:
    Ford's, 16
    Johnson's, 193
    Kennedy's, 8–9, 295
    Reagan's, 9–10
    Truman's, 209
California, 200, 221
Calleo, David P., 316
Cambodia, 250
Campaign politics, 166–68
Canada, 228–29, 314
Cannon, Lou, 254–55, 287
Capital formation, 33, 39, 123, 159
    see also Investment; Savings
Capitalism, 283, 284–85, 286, 304, 310
Capitalism and Freedom (Friedman), 285
Capital of the United States, 202, 203
Carnegie Corporation, 105

Carter, Jimmy, and Carter
administration, xix, 14, 21,
31, 54, 100, 107, 143, 156,
157, 175, 208, 257
deregulation under, 37
education policy, 45–46
foreign policy of, 57
nuclear arms negotiations by,
82, 83
nuclear arms policy, 192
Soviet electronic surveillance
in U.S. and, 236, 237, 240,
256
steel industry and, 315
views of federal government,
73–74
Casey, William J., 169, 170,
174, 177, 178–79, 182,
185
Caterpillar Company, 57
Catherine the Great, 243
Catto, Henry, 34
CBS News poll, *The New York
Times/*, 163, 166
Census Bureau, *see* Bureau of the
Census
Central America, 155, 169,
172–73, 174, 179
see also individual countries
Central Intelligence Agency
(CIA), 169, 174, 178, 180,
181, 182, 234, 237–38
Chambers, Whittaker, 206
Chandler, Colby H., 231
Chatfield-Taylor, Adele, 262
Chesterton, G. K., 307
Children, 299
adoption and foster care for,
105–8
social programs for needy,
94–95, 96, 101–3, 104,
106–9, 155, 264–65, 292
Child Welfare and Adoption
Assistance Act, 106–8
Chile, 53

Chiles, Lawton, 145, 192, 195
China, People's Republic of, 229,
245, 246–47, 249–51, 253,
258
China Today (Cohen and Cohen),
247
Chinese Shadows (Leys), 246,
249–50
Christian Science Monitor,
162–65
Christmas, 51–52
Chrysler Corporation, 225, 226
Churchill, Winston, 291
CIA, *see* Central Intelligence
Agency
City College of New York, 100
Classified information,
nondisclosure agreement,
137–39
Cleveland, Grover, 51
Clymer, Adam, 166
Cohen, Jerome Alan, 247
Cohen, Joan L., 247
Colbert, Jean Baptiste, 120–21
Cold Dawn (Newhouse), 79
Coleman, James S., 47
Columbia University, 12, 188
*Coming of the Post-Industrial
Society, The* (Bell), 307
Commentary, 204
Commission on CIA Activities
Within the United States,
234–35
report of, 255
Commission on Critical Choices
for Americans, 14
Commission on the Role of Gold
in the Domestic and
International Monetary
Systems, 39n.
Communism in the United
States, 204–7
Communist Manifesto, 304
Compromise of 1790, 201–3,
208

Conable, Barber B., Jr., 130, 131
Conference on Setting Municipal Priorities, address at, 260–65
Congress, *see* U.S. Congress
Congressional Budget Office, 30, 32, 152, 157, 159, 197, 232
Constitution, U.S., 67, 168, 170–71, 202, 291, 308
    balanced budget amendment, 19
    electronic surveillance and rights under, 236, 237–38
    federalism and, 218, 219
    First Amendment, 136
    new science of politics and, 301–4, 307
    on powers of the courts, 88, 89, 90, 91
    see also Federalist Papers, The
Constitutional Convention, 68
Continental Congress, 45
Coolidge, Calvin, 124
Cottrell, Leonard, 297
Council of Economic Advisers, 13, 38, 142, 158
Council on Foreign Relations, 54, 171
Courts, 87–93
    restriction of jurisdiction of, 87–93
Covello, Leonard, 43
Crossman, R. H. S., 206
Cuba, 55

Dam, Kenneth W., 177
Danforth, John C., 153
Dangerous Place, A (Moynihan), 52
Dangerous Relations: The Soviet Nation in World Politics (Ulam), 245

Das Kapital (Marx), 56
Declaration of Independence, 67
Deeley, Walter G., 238, 255
Defense budget, 33–34, 74, 85, 153, 157, 159, 257, 320
Deficit, *see* Budget deficit; Trade deficit
de Gaulle, Charles, 70
Democratic Leadership Council, address to, 289–94
Democratic party, 6, 84, 85, 133, 155–56, 207, 208
    budget deficits and, 153, 158
    social policy of, 289–94
    threats to the, 276–79
Democratic Response to President Reagan's televised address (1981), xviii, 22–28
Democratic Response to President Reagan's weekly radio address (1986), xviii, 326–27
Deng Xiaoping, 246
Department of State Authorization Act, 239–40
Deregulation, 37
Deterrence, 145, 146–47, 148–49, 150, 188, 189, 193, 194, 195
de Tocqueville, Alexis, 308
Deutch, John, 195
Dewey, Thomas, 206, 207, 209, 210
Diamond, Martin, 302
Disraeli, Benjamin, 6, 273
Dole, Robert, 129, 130–31
Dollar, strength of the, 143, 228–31, 232, 312
Domenici, Pete V., 94
Domestic budget, 33, 217
Dungan, Ralph, 9
Durenberger, David, 185
Durkheim, Emile, 106

Earned Income Tax Credit, 101
Eastern Europe, 54–55, 187
Eastman Kodak Company,
    229–31
Economic Club of New York,
    address to, 12–17, 32
*Economic Consequences of Mr.
    Churchill* (Keynes), 40
Economics, 16–17
    as applied science, 12–13
Economist, 39
Economists, 16, 17, 20, 298
    see also names of individuals
Education:
    federal aid to, 42–50, 87,
        317–18
    tax credits, 47
"Education of David Stockman,
    The," 61, 63n.
Education Times, 48
Education Week, 44
Edwards, Tryon, 196, 200
Eisenberg, Theodore, 91–92
Eisenhower, Dwight D., 132, 152
Elazar, Daniel J., 219
Electronic surveillance, Soviet,
    233–41, 255–56
Elementary and Secondary
    Education Act of 1965, 48
Eliot, George, 248
Eliot, T. S., 83
"Elitist's Troubling Menace, An,"
    287
Ellwood, David T., 290
El Salvador, 169, 173
Emminger, Otmar, 13
End of Liberalism, The (Lowi),
    283
Engels, Friedrich, 304, 305
Equal Employment Opportunity
    Commission, 103
*Equality of Educational
    Opportunity,* 47
Esman, Milton J., 306n.

Ethiopia, 55
Eureka College, Reagan's address
    at, 78, 85
"Exactly Who Shot John?"
    322–23
Ex Parte McCardle, 89–90, 91
Export-Import Bank, 123
Exports, *see* Trade; Trade deficit

Falkland Islands, 65, 70–71
Families living in poverty, aid to,
    94–104
Family Assistance Plan (FAP),
    101, 104
Farley, James (Big Jim), 210
Farm subsidies, 151–52, 157, 159,
    274, 312–14, 317, 320
Federal Bureau of Investigation
    (FBI), 238, 256, 326
Federal funds rate, 25
Federalism, 218–24
Federalist Papers, The, 65–67, 72,
    301
Federal Legal Council, 93
Federal Reserve, 25, 25n., 110,
    111, 113, 143, 156, 159,
    160, 197
Feinstone Lecture, United States
    Military Academy, 242–59
Feldstein, Martin, 20–21, 119,
    120–21, 158, 159
Fesbach, Murray, 253
Final Reports (Rovere), 203, 208,
    209–10
Financial Times of London, 228
First Amendment, 136
First-strike policy, 145, 146, 148,
    149, 188–89
Flanner, Mollie, 202
Ford, Gerald, and Ford
    administration, xix, 14, 54,
    69, 234, 257
Foreign Affairs, 173–74
Foreign aid, 155

Foreign-exchange markets, 143, 228
Foreign Surveillance Prevention Act, 239
Foreign trade, *see* Trade
"Forging a Bipartisan American Foreign and Defense Policy," 171–72
Foster care, 106, 107, 108, 264–65
France, 119, 120–21, 291, 314
Franklin, Benjamin, 141, 303
Freedom of information, 134–39
Freedom of the press, 134, 137–39
"From Here to There: SALT to START," 83
Friedman, Milton, 285
Fuji, 229

Galbraith, John Kenneth, 17
Gambling with History, Reagan in the White House (Barrett), 311
Gardner, Richard N., 188, 189
Gardner, Theodore, 238
Gelb, Leslie, 81
General Agreement on Tariffs and Trade (GATT), 116, 117–23
General Motors, 225–26
General Services Administration, 9
Georgetown University, 171
Germany, 291
Gilder, George, 100–101
Gilpin, Robert, 40
Ginsberg, Benjamin, 166
Glazer, Nathan, 100, 260–62, 304, 305
God That Failed, The (Crossman), 206
Gold standard, 36, 39–41, 280, 281
Goldstein, Emmanuel, 249
Goldwater, Barry, 169, 170, 174,

175, 178–79, 180, 181, 182
Gorbachev, Mikhail, 255, 258
Gordon, Milton, 304
Government, 3, 6, 26
aversion to, 40, 308
cutting size of, 74–75, 154–55, 273, 281, 308–12, 314, 317
election rhetoric about, 73–74
founding fathers' ideas of, 66–67
Moynihan on, 6–7, 10, 14
public trust in, 165–66
science of politics and, 301–4, 307
social research and, 295–300
Stockman's strategy to dismantle "big," xix, 280–82, 286, 287, 298–99
Gramm, Philip, 283
Gramm-Rudman-Hollings bill, 274, 286
Great Britain:
economy of, 24, 314
Falklands and, 65
on gold standard, 40, 41
social policy of, 291
trade policy, 120
Great Society, 290
Green, Gordon, 96
Greenfield, Meg, 328
Greenspan, Alan, 130, 159
Grenada, invasion of, 176
Gridiron Address, xvii, 3–7, 10–11
Grieder, William, 61, 63n.
Gross national product (GNP), 13, 24, 37, 293, 298, 314

Hamburg, David A., 306–7
Hamilton, Alexander, 66, 201, 202, 203
Handgun law, 8
Hart, Gary, 145
Hartford, Huntington, 205
Harvard University, 47

Health insurance, 291
Helms, Jesse, 136
Helsinki Accords of 1975, 53–54
Hershey, Lewis B., 98
Hicks, Granville, 204, 205
Hiss, Alger, 206
Hoffman, David, 313
Hofstadter, Dick, 290
Honduras, 65, 177
Hoover, Herbert, 16, 117, 124, 309
Horowitz, David, 305
Horton, Raymond D., 263–64
Howard University, 100
Hull, Cordell, 120, 123–24, 231
Humphrey, Hubert H., 9, 47

ICBM, see Intercontinental ballistic missile
Imports, see Trade; Trade deficit
Income, see Personal income
Indonesia, 247–48
Inflation, 13, 21, 24, 25, 33, 110, 123, 155, 156, 160, 230, 312, 317
Institute of Social Science, University of Michigan, 165
Institutions, distrust of, 31
Intelligence Authorization Act, 173
Intelligence Oversight Act of 1980, 180–81, 182, 183, 184
Intercontinental ballistic missile (ICBM), 147, 148–49, 192, 194, 195
Interest rates, 25, 26, 29–30, 33, 113, 123, 157, 273, 312
real, 25, 111, 143, 156, 159
International Court of Justice at The Hague, 71, 172, 174, 177

"International Free Trade," 119–20
International law, 169–74, 179, 188
International Monetary Fund, 153, 155
International Roundtable, address to, 115–25
International Trade Commission, 122, 123
International Trade Organization (ITO), 117
Investment, 24, 39, 114, 159
interest rates and, 25, 112
see also Capital formation; Savings
Iran, shipment of arms to, 185, 325, 326–28
Iran-contra hearings, 180, 181

Jackson, Henry M. (Scoop), 240
Japan, 24, 40, 225, 226, 227, 229, 244, 314, 315
Ministry of International Trade and Industry, 119
Jay, John, 66, 68
Jefferson, Thomas, 201, 202, 203
Jobert, Michel, 120
Johnson, Haynes, 328
Johnson, Lyndon B., and Johnson administration, xix, 8, 52, 99, 100, 298
budget deficit under, 15
budgets of, 75–76
Kennedy conspiracy theories and, 9
nuclear weapons policy, 189
Vietnam War and, 244, 252
War on Poverty, 99, 296
Joint Chiefs of Staff, 149
Joint Economic Committee, 253
Jones, Jesse, 16
Judicial review, 88
Judicial system, see Courts; Supreme Court

Junior League of America, 105, 107

Kalb, Marvin, 327
Kaplan, Gilbert, 115
Karnow, Stanley, 245
Kasten, Robert W., Jr., 211, 213
Kemp, Jack, 31–32, 211, 213, 280, 284
Kemp-Roth tax bill, 31–32, 154, 281
Kennedy, John F., and Kennedy administration, xix, 24, 52, 75, 97, 152, 218, 224, 244, 249, 295, 298
  assassination of, 8–9, 10, 48, 205
  nuclear weapons policy, 189
  tariff policy, 116, 118
  tax cuts, 298
  Vietnam War and, 244
Keynes, John Maynard, 40, 198, 324
Khrushchev, Nikita, 254
Kissinger, Henry, 16
Kissinger Commission on Central America, 155
Korea, 242–43
Korean War, 207–8
Kristol, Irving, 12, 284–85
Kurland, Philip L., 135–36
Kuznets, Simon, 300

Lacy, Michael, 295
Laffer, Arthur, and Laffer curve, 19, 37, 39, 154, 280, 281, 286
Laird, Melvin, 193
La Prensa, 176
Laqueur, Walter, 258
La Rouche, Lyndon, 275, 276–79
Lash, Joseph, 207
Law of Sea Conference, 121
Laxalt, Paul, 192, 328

League of Cities, address to, 217–24
League of Nations, Covenant of, 170
Leahy, Patrick J., 185
Lebanon, 178–79, 194
Lebergott, Stanley, 227
Lehrman, Lewis, 280
Lenin, Vladimir, 56–57, 306
Letters to New York, 163–68
  on attempted assassination of Reagan, 8–11
  on budget deficit and Social Security funds, 269–74
  on foreign policy, 51–58
  on foreign trade, 225–32
  on Soviet electronic surveillance, 233–41
Levy, David A., 312
Lewis, Flora, 274
Leys, Simon, 246, 249–50
Limited Test Ban Treaty, 189
"Limits of Social Policy, The," 100
Lin Biao, 247
Lincoln, Abraham, 222
Livable City, 262
LoCicero, John, 276
London, Meyer, 264
London School of Economics, dinner of Fellows of, 13
Los Angeles Times, 130
Lowi, Theodore, 283
Loyalties (Moynihan), 171

McCarthy, Mary, 208
McFarlane, Robert, 170, 179–80
McGovern, George, 47
McMahon, John Jay, 181
McNamara, Robert, 9, 98, 99
Madison, James, 66, 201, 202, 301, 302, 303, 305, 320
Mann, Horace, 209
Manso, Peter, 295
Mao, Madame, 249

Mao Zedong, 245, 247, 305

Marbury v. Madison, 88

Marshall, Alfred, 6

Marshall, John, 88

Marshall, T. H., 290

Martin v. Hunter's Lessee, 91

Marx, Karl, 55–56, 304, 305

Marxism, 304–6, 306n.

Medicaid, 102, 103

Medicare, 159

Medina, Harold, 134

"Meet the Press," 327

Mexico, 112, 113, 122, 229

Middle of the Journey, The (Trilling), 206

Midgetman missile, 150, 194, 195

Milewski, Jerzy, 254

Millbrook School, address at, 42–50

Mill on the Floss (Eliot), 248

Mills, C. Wesley, 12

Minuteman III missiles, 192

Minuteman IV missiles, 145, 193

   MX missiles in silos for, 145, 147, 149, 150, 188–89, 192–96

Mitchell, Wesley C., 296

Molotov-Ribbentrop pact, 205

Money supply, 156

Moore, John Norton, 173–74

Moral Majority, 284

Morgan Stanley, 197

Morison, Samuel Loring, 256

Morrill, Justin Smith, 222

Mortgage interest rates, 25

Mosteller, Frederick, 47

Moynihan Report, 99

Municipal Arts Society, 262

Muskie, Edmund, 83

MX missiles, 85, 145–50, 188–89, 192–96

Myrdal, Alva, 105–6

Myrdal, Gunnar, 105

National Bureau of Economic Research, 12, 20, 296

National Caucus of Labor Committees, 278

National Commission on Deficit Reduction, 160

National Commission on Social Security Reform, 129, 130, 131, 158–59

National Security Act, 135

National Security Agency, 238

National Security Council, 326–27

National Security Decision Directive No. 145, 239

National Study of Social Services to Children and Their Families, 107

National Urban League, 103–4

Nation and Family (Myrdal), 105–6

NATO, *see* North Atlantic Treaty Organization

New Deal, 4, 290, 291, 319

   "Brain Trust," 16

Newhouse, John, 79

New Masses, 204, 205

New Republic, The, 3, 94, 95–104, 151–60, 253, 327–28

Newsday, 26, 145, 170–74

New Solidarity, 276–77

Newsweek, 27

New York City, 260–65, 292

   financial crisis, 263–64

   foster care in, 264–65

   national capital moved from, 202, 203, 209

   social policy in, 264, 265

   taxes, 212

   wealth and poverty in, 262–63

New Yorker, The, 202–3

New York State:

   effect of elimination of

New York State: (*cont.*)
  deductibility of state and
    local taxes on, 211–13
  federal grants to, 199, 200,
    212
New York State Association of
  Counties, 196
New York State Business
  Council, address to,
  xviii–xix
New York State Constitution,
  67–68
New York Times, The, 18, 76,
    121, 211–13, 221, 236–37,
    238, 255, 264, 277–78, 327
  /CBS News poll, 163, 166
New York Times Magazine, The,
    43
New York University, addresses
  at, 186–91, 275–88
Nicaragua, 55, 172–73
  contras, 65, 177
  mining of harbors of, 169–70,
    174, 177–82
  Sandanistas, *see* Sandanista
    regime
1981 speeches and articles, 2–58
1982 speeches and articles,
    59–125
1983 speeches and articles,
    127–59
1984 (Orwell), 163–64, 168
  see also Orwell, George
1984 speeches and articles,
    161–213
1985 speeches and articles,
    215–65
1986 speeches and articles,
    267–328
Nixon, Richard, and Nixon
  administration, xix, 101,
    132, 152, 207, 257, 280
  nuclear weapons policy, 189
Noel, Cleo, 235
Non-Proliferation Treaty, 189

North American Conference on
  Adoptable Children, 105
North Atlantic Treaty
  Organization (NATO), 70,
  253
North Vietnam, 245, 247, 248,
  250
Northwest Ordinance, 45
Norton, Eleanor Holmes, 103
Nourse, Edwin G., 297
Novak, Michael, 120
Novyi Zhurnal, 56–57
Nuclear weapons, 78–86, 164
  deterrence policy, 145, 146–47,
    148–49, 150, 188, 189, 193,
    194, 195
  ethnocentrism and, 306–7
  first-strike policy, 145, 146,
    148, 149, 188–89
  negotiations, 78, 81, 189
  U.S.–Soviet relations and,
    71–72, 186–89, 253,
    256–57
  see also Midgetman missile,
    Minuteman III and IV
    missiles, MX missile
Nunn, Sam, 253

Oakeshott, Michael, 300
Odegard, Peter, 297
Office of Management and
  Budget, 76, 280, 311
Oglesby, Carl, 277–78
OMNI, 295
O'Neill, Thomas P. "Tip," Jr.,
  130
"One Third of a Nation: A Report
  on Young Men Found
  Unqualified for Military
  Service," 98–99
OPEC, 40
Organization for Economic
  Cooperation and
  Development (OECD), 190

Organization of American States,
Charter of, 172–73
Orwell, George, 163–65, 249, 250
Oswald, Lee Harvey, 9

Packwood, Bob, 94, 136
Panama Canal treaties, 155
Panter-Downes, Mollie, 202
Patriot's Day Dinner address,
65–72
Peaceful Nuclear Explosions
Treaty of 1976, 189
Penner, Rudolph G., 157, 197,
232
Pérez de Cuéllar, Javier, 121
Personal income, 315–16
real, 33, 37, 300, 316
Petersen, Bill, 137
Pettigrew, Thomas F., 47
Pfaff, William, 252, 305–6
PL-5 missiles, 148
Poland, 254
Solidarity, *see* Solidarity
Polanyi, Michael, 80
Politics:
campaign, 166–68
science of, 301–4, 307, 317,
321
Polls, public opinion, 163,
165–68
Polygraph tests, 137
"Positive Program For Laissez-
Faire, A," 319
Potemkin villages, 243
Poverty, 94–104, 299
Aid to Families with
Dependent Children,
94–95, 96, 101–3, 155
foster care, 106, 107, 108,
264–65
Pravda, 206, 254n., 277
Prayer in public schools,
voluntary, 136
Presidency, 88
President's Commission on

Strategic Forces, 147,
149
Pretrial judicial proceedings,
public access to, 87
Price and wage controls, 13, 30
Private schools, aid to, 47–49
Productivity, 123
"Professionalization of Reform,
The," 12, 296
Profil, 279
Progressive Labor Party, 278
Public Interest, 12, 16, 290, 296
Public opinion polls, 163,
165–68
Pulling, Edward, 42, 43, 44–45

Radek, Karl, 56
Rapany, Stephen, 253
Ratner, Leonard G., 91
Reagan, Ronald, and Reagan
administration, xix, 4n.,
234
assassination attempt on, 3, 8,
9–11
budget cuts, *see* Budget cuts
budget deficit, *see* Budget
deficit
the courts and, 93–94
farm policy, *see* Agriculture
foreign policy, *see individual
countries and issues*
inaugural address, 309–10
1980 campaign platform, 74
nuclear weapons policy and, 78,
82, 145, 147, 148, 187,
192–95, 253, 256–57
reelection of, 133
Social Security policy, 18–20,
22, 26–28, 129, 132–33,
158–59, 317
Soviet electronic surveillance
and, 238–39, 240, 241,
256
tax cuts, *see* Taxes, cuts
tax reform, 218

Reagan, Ronald, and Reagan
   administration (*cont.*)
   trade policy, *see* Trade
   welfare and family policy,
      94–95
Regan, Donald, 39*n*.
Recession, 37, 110, 156
Reconstruction Finance
   Corporation, 16
Rensselaer Polytechnic Institute,
   address at, 140–44
*Report to the President by the
   Commission on CIA
   Activities Within the
   United States*, 255
Republican National Committee,
   20, 26
Republican party, 30, 85, 129, 207
   budget deficits and, 153
   as ideological, 17, 38
   threats to the, 279–88
Reston, James, 256
Revenue Act of 1981, xviii, 32
   criticism of, 23–26, 32–33,
      34–35, 38
Revenue sharing, 199
Revolutionary War, debts of the
   states incurred during, 202
Reykjavik summit, 78
Riegle, Donald W., Jr., 110, 113
Riesman, David, 46, 47
*Rise of the Counter-
   Establishment, The*
   (Blumenthal), 299
Rittenhouse, David, 141
Rockefeller, Nelson, 14, 233, 234,
   236, 241, 255
Rockefeller Foundation, 103, 104
Rodino, Peter, 93
Roosevelt, Franklin D., 5, 96–97,
   101, 104, 130, 205
   reduction of big government by,
      308–9
Roosevelt, Theodore, 173
Rovere, Richard, 201–10

Rowen, Hobart, 121, 315
Russert, Tim, 278

Safire, William, 260
St. John's University Law School
   commencement address,
      87–93
SALT, *see* Strategic Arms
   Limitation Talks; Strategic
   Arms Limitation Treaty
Sandanista regime, 169, 173, 176,
   177
Sarbanes, Paul S., 181
Sasser, James R., 110, 113
Saudi Arabia, gold standard and,
   36, 40, 41
Savings, 21, 24, 39
   see also Capital formation;
      Investment
Schlesinger, Arthur M., Jr.,
   209–10
Schlesinger, James R., 15, 16
Schumpeter, Joseph, 144
Science, 306–7
Science and technology, 140–43,
   164, 318–19
   political campaigns and,
      166–68
   U.S. competitive position, 142,
      143
   see also Science of politics
Science of politics, 301–4, 307,
   317, 321
Scowcroft, Brent, 194, 195
Secret Service, 9
Securities Industry Association,
   address to, 73–77
Selected Works of Deng Xiaoping,
   246, 247
Selective Service System, 98,
   298
Senate, *see* U.S. Senate
Shapiro, Robert J., 110
Sheet Metal Workers'

International Association,
address to, 110–14
Shevchenko, Arkady Nikolaevich,
235–36, 240
Shields, Mark, 74
Shils, Edward, 297, 310
Shriver, Sargent, 99
Shultz, George, 16, 177, 280
Silk, Leonard, 118
Simmel, Georg, 252
Simons, Henry C., 319
Smith, William French, 92–93,
137
Smithsonian Institution,
Britannica Lecture at,
301–23
Smoot-Hawley Tariff Act, 117,
231, 232, 314
Social policy of Democratic party,
289–94
Social research, government and,
295–300
Social Security, 257, 317
attempts to cut, 18–21, 22,
26–28, 158–59
missing funds from, 269–72
1983 reforms, 129–33, 159,
196, 271
Social Security Act, 20, 102, 103,
106, 108, 264, 291
Title IV, *see* Aid to Families
with Dependent Children
Solidarity, 52–53, 58, 69, 254
Solzhenitsyn, Alexander, 247
Somoza, Anastasio, 65
Sonnenfeldt, Helmut, 54
South Africa, gold standard and,
36, 41
Southern Economic Association,
159
Soviet Union, 53–58, 122,
186–91, 249, 253–55,
258
Chile and, 53
China and, 245, 246, 247, 251

Eastern Europe and, 54, 58, 69,
254
electronic surveillance in U.S.,
233–41, 255–56
gold standard and, 36, 41
leadership of, 81
Marxism and, 305–6
military adventurism, 55,
82–83
Nazis and, 205
Nicaragua and, 177
nuclear weapons and, 71–72,
145, 146–49, 186–89, 193,
245, 253, 256–57
negotiations with U.S., 78,
81–86, 189
Orwell's *1984* and, 163, 164
in Southeast Asia, 245
Spain, 121
SS-17, SS-18, and SS-19 missiles,
145, 147
SS-20 missiles, 187
SS-X-24 missiles, 148
Stalin, Joseph, 249, 305
START, *see* Strategic Arms
Reduction Talks; Strategy
Arms Reduction Treaty
State University of New York at
Binghamton, address at,
78–86
Steel industry, 110, 314–15
Stein, Herbert, 19
Steinbeck, John, 142
Stevenson, Adlai, 83
Stigler, George, 156
Stockman, David, 15n., 61–64,
153, 275, 279–88, 311, 316,
317–18
budget deficit strategy, xix, 151,
279–82, 287, 298–99
on fiscal policy, 12, 316
Gridiron Address, 3
at Harvard, 5–6, 62
postscript to memoirs of,
322–23

Stockman, David (*cont.*)
  Social Security and, 27, 131–32,
    133
  Triumph of Politics, The, 61,
    279–284, 287, 288, 298–99,
    316
Story, Joseph, 91
Strategic Arms Limitation Talks
  (SALT), 79, 193
Strategic Arms Limitation Treaty
  (SALT):
  I, 84, 189
  II, 79, 80, 82–84, 85, 189
Strategic Arms Reduction Talks
  (START), 78
Strategic Arms Reduction Treaty,
  (START), 84
Students for a Democratic Society
  (SDS), 278, 283
Sukarno, 248
Summers, Laurence H., 290
Sun Tzu, 258
Supplementary Security Income
  program, 101
Supply-side economics, 37,
  39–40, 272, 280–82, 284,
  298
Supreme Court:
  decisions of, 88, 89–90, 91
  jurisdiction of, 89–91, 136–37
Surrey, Stanley, 218
Suslov, Mikhail, 245

Taft, Robert A., 207
Talbott, Strobe, 256–57
Task Force on Manpower
  Conservation, 98–99
Task Force on Poverty, 99
Taxes, 22–26, 318
  "bracket creep," 21, 24, 155
  credits, 101
    for parents of private school
      students, 47–49
  cuts, 15, 19, 20–21, 23–26,
    31–35, 37–38, 74, 75,

  153–54, 155–56, 272, 280,
    281, 296, 298–99, 311
  need to modify, 35–36, 38
  elimination of deduction for
    state and local, 211–13,
    217, 220–24
  increases, 13, 196, 296
    need for, 151, 274, 288, 319
  property, 200
  for social programs, 13
  tax reform, 218
  windfall profits, 30
  see also Revenue Act of 1981
*Tax Reform for Fairness,
  Simplicity, and Economic
  Growth,* 218, 221
Technology, *see* Science and
  technology
Terrorism, 191
Texas, 212, 213
Thatcher, Margaret, 177
*Theory and Practice of
  Oligarchical Collectivism,
  The* (Goldstein), 249
This World, 219
Threshold Test Ban Treaty of
  1974, 189
Time, 238–39
Title I (federal aid to education
  program), 44
Trade, 115–25, 225–32, 314–15
  General Agreement on Tariffs
    and Trade (GATT), 116,
    117–23
  quotas, 116–17, 122, 315
  tariffs, 116, 117–18, 122, 231,
    232
  technology and foreign imports,
    142, 143
Trade deficit, 115, 124, 142, 226,
  228–29, 230, 231–32
Trident submarine, 187
Trilling, Lionel, 206–7
*Triumph of Politics, The: Why the
  Reagan Revolution Failed,*

(Stockman), 61,
279–84, 287, 288, 298–99,
316
Truman, Harry S, 83, 172, 206,
207, 209, 210, 238
Two Cheers for Capitalism
(Kristol), 284
Typhoon Class submarine, 187

Ulam, Adam, 245, 246
Unemployment, 13, 24, 97, 106,
112, 114
full employment, 160
minority male, 99
Unemployment insurance, 291
UNESCO, 164
Unheavenly City, The (Banfield),
290
United Nations, 83, 117, 118,
119, 241
Charter of, 70, 116, 118, 170,
171
Moynihan as U.S. ambassador
to, 233
United Press International, 36
U.S. Congress, 23, 84, 88, 117,
155, 173, 196–97, 202, 206,
326–27
House, *see* U.S. House of
Representatives
power to limit jurisdiction of
courts, 88, 89–92
Senate, *see* U.S. Senate
Social Security and, 27, 158–59,
196
U.S. Commerce Department, 123,
124–25
U.S. Defense Department, 75,
257
U.S. Department of Education,
43, 45, 95, 318
U.S. Department of Health,
Education and Welfare
(HEW), 46

U.S. Government, *see*
Government
U.S. House of Representatives,
84, 122, 201
Banking Committee, 197–98
Intelligence Committee,
175–76, 178
Judiciary Committee, 93
subcommittees, 137
Ways and Means Committee,
222, 226
U.S. Justice Department, 57, 58,
93, 123–24, 172
U.S. Labor Department, 97, 99,
295, 298
Bureau of Labor Statistics,
295–96, 314
United States Military Academy,
Feinstone Lecture at,
242–59
U.S. Senate, 80, 131, 136–37,
155, 201
Armed Services Committee, 85,
253
Finance Committee, 20, 21, 22,
24, 155, 226, 230–31, 265,
271
foreign policy function of,
69–72
Foreign Relations Committee,
84–85, 172, 239, 240
founding fathers' concept of,
67, 72
Judiciary Committee, 135
MX missiles and, 145, 147,
192–93, 195
SALT I and, 84
SALT II and, 82, 84
Select Committee on
Intelligence (SSCI), 135,
139, 169, 170, 174, 175–76,
177, 178, 180, 237
Moynihan resignation from,
170, 180, 182
Procedures Governing

U. S. Senate (*cont.*)
  Reporting to, on Covert Action,
    182–85
  Social Security system and, 18,
    19, 20, 196
  Subcommittee on Social
    Security, 107
U.S. Trade Representative, Office
  of, 123
U.S. Treasury Department, 112,
  113, 123
United Steel Workers, 110
University of Chicago Law
  School, 135–36
Ustinov, Dmitri Fedorovich,
  187

Van Rensselaer, Stephen, 141
Vessey, John W., Jr.,
  149–50
Vietnam: A History (Karnow),
  245
Vietnam War, 207–8, 244–45,
  250, 252–53
Volcker, Paul, 197–98
von Hayek, Friedrich, 273, 279,
  283

Wage and price controls, 13, 30
Wagner, Robert F., 264
Walesa, Lech, 53
Wallace, Henry, 206, 209, 312–13
Wall Street Journal, 121, 177,
  239, 255, 284
Walpole, Horace, 209
Walt, Stephen M., 253
Wanniski, Jude, 284, 286
War on Poverty, 99, 296
Warsaw Pact, 52
Warsaw Pact nations, 253

Washington, D.C., 202–10
  capital moved to, 202, 203
Washington Post, 28, 44, 74,
  97–98, 121, 129, 137, 155,
  254, 313, 328
Washington Star, 23
Washington Times, 179–80
Wealth and Poverty (Gilder),
  100–101
Weber, Max, 303
Weicker, Lowell P., Jr., 137
Welfare, 94–95, 96, 100–105,
  264, 265, 290
Welniak, Edward, 96
Western Europe, 57, 69–70, 291,
  314, 315
West Point, Feinstone Lecture at,
  242–59
White, Eric Wyndham, 117
Wildavsky, Aaron, 283
Will, George, 40, 61–62, 85, 133,
  217–18, 286, 318, 321,
  328
Wilson, James Q., 321
Windfall profits tax, 30
Wirtz, W. Willard, 98
Wolff, Alan, 143
Woodrow Wilson International
  Center for Scholars, address
  to conference at, 295–300
Woolsey, R. James, 195
World Bank, 24
World Court, *see* International
  Court of Justice at The
  Hague
Wright, Carroll, 295

Yamal pipeline, 57
Yoder, Edwin M., Jr., 328
Yorktown, battle of, 86